Web Design

Introductory Concepts and Techniques

Gary B. Shelly
Thomas J. Cashman
Linda A. Kosteba

COURSE
TECHNOLOGY

THOMSON LEARNING

SHELLY
CASHMAN
SERIES®

Australia • Canada • Denmark • Japan • Mexico • New Zealand • Philippines • Puerto Rico • Singapore
South Africa • Spain • United Kingdom • United States

COURSE TECHNOLOGY
THOMSON LEARNING

COPYRIGHT © 2002 Course Technology, a division of Thomson Learning.
Printed in the United States of America

Asia (excluding Japan)
Thomson Learning
60 Albert Street, #15-01
Albert Complex
Singapore 189969

Japan
Thomson Learning
Palaceside Building 5F
1-1-1 Hitotsubashi, Chiyoda-ku
Tokyo 100 0003 Japan

Australia/New Zealand
Nelson/Thomson Learning
102 Dodds Street
South Melbourne, Victoria 3205
Australia

Latin America
Thomson Learning
Seneca, 53
Colonia Polanco
11560 Mexico D.F. Mexico

South
Constantia Square
526 Sixteenth Road
P.O. Box 2459
Halfway House, 1685
South Africa

Canada
Nelson/Thomson Learning
1120 Birchmount Road
Scarborough, Ontario
Canada M1K 5G4

UK/Europe/Middle East
Thomson Learning
Berkshire House
168-173 High Holborn
n, WC1V 7AA United Kingdom

Spain
Thomson Learning
Calle Magallanes, 25
28015-MADRID
ESPANA

For more information, contact Course Technology, 25 Thomson Place, Boston, MA 02210.

Or visit our Internet site at www.course.com

PHOTO CREDITS: *Chapter 1, page 1.1* Keyboard, .com text, man on computer, Courtesy of PhotoDisc, Inc.; *Chapter 2, page 2.1* Keyboard, monitor, people on computer, Courtesy of PhotoDisc, Inc.; monitor, Courtesy of Image Club; *Chapter 3, page 3.1* log on text, monitor/hand, man on computer, Courtesy of PhotoDisc, Inc.; *Chapter 4, page 4.1* www.tin, lady on computer, Courtesy of PhotoDisc, Inc.; *Chapter 5, page 5.1* Keyboard, lady on computer, Courtesy of PhotoDisc, Inc.; *Chapter 6, page 6.1* Keyboard, code, girl on computer, Courtesy of PhotoDisc, Inc.; *Chapter 7, page 7.1* Computer with @ symbol, keyboard, lady on computer, Courtesy of PhotoDisc, Inc.; *Appendix, page A.1* ch.com image, Courtesy of PhotoDisc, Inc.

ISBN 0-7895-5960-9

1 2 3 4 5 6 7 8 9 10   BC   06 05 04 03 02

Web Design
Introductory Concepts and Techniques

Contents

Preface

In the Shelly Cashman Series® *Web Design: Introductory Concepts and Techniques* book, you will find an educationally sound and easy-to-follow pedagogy that artfully combines screen shots, pictures, drawings, and text with full color to produce a visually appealing and easy-to-understand presentation of Web design. This textbook conveys useful design concepts and techniques typically not addressed in Web authoring textbooks. It explains the connection between a detailed design plan, one that considers audience needs, Web site purpose, and various technical issues, and a successful Web site.

The book's seven chapters emphasize key written concepts and principles with numerous Web Design Tips boxed throughout the text. It also contains a variety of challenging written and hands-on activities at the conclusion of each chapter that test comprehension, build Web research skills and design awareness, and encourage critical thinking about current issues in Web design.

OBJECTIVES OF THIS TEXTBOOK

Web Design: Introductory Concepts and Techniques is intended for a one-unit introductory Web design course or in a course that teaches Web design techniques in a Web authoring course that also covers HTML or Microsoft FrontPage. The objectives of this book are to:

- Present a practical approach to Web design using a blend of traditional development with current technologies
- Define and describe in detail the six steps in developing a solid Web design plan: define the purpose, identify the audience, plan the content, plan the structure, plan the Web pages, and plan the navigation
- Present the material in a full-color, visually appealing and exciting, easy-to-read manner with a format that invites students to learn
- Provide students with a summary of Web Design Tips to which they can refer quickly and easily
- Give students an in-depth understanding of Web design concepts and techniques that are essential to planning, creating, testing, publishing, and maintaining Web sites
- Make use of the World Wide Web as a repository of the latest information in an ever-changing discipline
- Provide an ongoing case study and assignments that promote student participation in learning about Web design

DISTINGUISHING FEATURES

The distinguishing features of *Web Design: Introductory Concepts and Techniques* include the following:

A Blend of Traditional Development with Current Technologies

This book does not present a superfluous, theoretical view of Web design. Every effort has been made to use procedures, tools, and solutions that parallel those used by Web designers in today's business world.

Numerous realistic examples support all definitions, concepts, and techniques. The examples and case study are drawn from actual Web-related projects. Real-world examples such as these enable students to learn in the context of solving realistic problems, much like the ones they will encounter in industry. In this textbook, students learn what works and what they need to know on the job. In addition, numerous Web Design Tips are provided for many topics.

Visually Appealing

The design of this textbook purposely combines screen shots, pictures, drawings, and text into a full-color, visually appealing, and easy-to-read book. The many figures throughout the book clarify the narrative and reinforce important points. The pictures and drawings reflect the latest trends in Web design.

Introductory Presentation of Web Design

No previous Web design experience is assumed, and no prior programming experience is required. This book is written specifically for students with average ability, for whom continuity, simplicity, and practicality are characteristics we consider essential. Numerous insights based on the authors' many years of experience in teaching, consulting, and writing, are implicit throughout the book.

Web Design Tips

More than 100 Web Design Tips are boxed throughout the book. The function of the Web Design Tips is to emphasize important Web design concepts of which students should be aware as they design a Web site.

Web Info Feature

The Web Info boxes in the margins throughout the book encourage students to research further using the World Wide Web. The purpose of the Web Info annotations is to (1) offer students additional information on a topic of importance, (2) provide currency, and (3) underscore the importance of the World Wide Web as a basic information tool that can be used in course work, for a wide range of professional purposes, and for personal use.

ORGANIZATION OF THIS TEXTBOOK

Web Design: Introductory Concepts and Techniques provides basic instruction on how to design Web sites. The material is comprised of four sections: Section 1: Before You Begin; Section 2: Planning Your Web Site; Section 3 Creating Your Web Site; and Section 4: Publishing Your Web Site. The four sections include seven chapters and conclude with an appendix.

Chapter 1 – Web Design Basics In Chapter 1, students are introduced to the Internet, World Wide Web, Web sites, and Web pages. Topics include home pages; splash pages; Internet service providers; Web design browser-related issues; types of Web sites; methods for doing Web design research; tools for creating Web pages and Web sites; and Web design roles.

Chapter 2 – An Overview of Web Publishing In Chapter 2, students are introduced to the advantages of Web publishing, basic design principles, and writing techniques for the Web. Topics include timeliness; interactivity; reduced production costs; economical, rapid distribution; balance and proximity; contrast and focus; unity; and accurate, comprehensive, and concise writing.

Chapter 3 – Developing a Design Plan for a Web Site: Part 1 In Chapter 3, students are introduced to the initial four steps of the six steps for developing a solid design plan for a Web site: (1) define the purpose, (2) identify the audience, (3) plan the content, and (4) plan the structure. Topics include identifying a specific topic for a Web site; defining audience goals and needs; choosing content; and outlining a Web site.

Chapter 4 – Developing a Design Plan for a Web Site: Part 2 In Chapter 4, students are introduced to the remaining two steps for developing a design plan for a Web site: (5) plan the Web pages and (6) plan the navigation. Topics include organizing information; establishing a visual connection; layout and navigation elements; and navigation guidelines.

Chapter 5 – Typography and Graphics on the Web In Chapter 5, students are introduced to typography and graphics for the Web environment. Topics include typography principles, guidelines, and tips; Web graphics file formats and sources; and methods to optimize graphics for Web display.

Chapter 6 – Multimedia and Interactivity on the Web In Chapter 6, students are introduced to the basics of Web multimedia and interactivity and methods to add these elements to Web pages. Topics include guidelines and sources for utilizing multimedia; slide shows; animation; downloadable and streaming audio and video; and online forms and other interactive page elements.

Chapter 7 – Testing, Publishing, Marketing, and Maintaining a Web Site In Chapter 7, students are introduced to basic guidelines and methods to test, publish, market, and maintain a Web site successfully. Topics include acquiring server space, obtaining a domain name, and uploading a Web site; the steps to test a Web site; Web-based and traditional marketing and advertising; and the importance of regular maintenance and updating.

Appendix – Web Design Tips The Appendix that follows Chapter 7 lists the Web Design Tips developed throughout the book. It serves as a quick reference and includes the page numbers on which the Web Design Tip is presented in the book.

END-OF-CHAPTER STUDENT ACTIVITIES

A notable strength of the Shelly Cashman Series textbooks is the extensive student activities at the end of each chapter. Well-structured student activities can make the difference between students merely participating in a class and students retaining the information they learn. The activities in this book include the following:

- **Key Terms** This list of key terms found in the chapter together with the page numbers on which the terms are defined will aid students in mastering the chapter material.
- **Checkpoint** Four pencil-and-paper activities are designed to determine students' understanding of the material in the chapter. Included are matching, fill in the blanks, multiple-choice, and short-answer questions.
- **At Issue** Web design is not without its controversial issues. At the end of each chapter, two scenarios are presented that challenge students to examine critically their perspective of Web design and the technology surrounding it.
- **Hands On** To complete their introduction to Web design, these exercises require that students use the World Wide Web to obtain information about the concepts and techniques discussed in the chapter.
- **Section Case Study** The Case Study is an ongoing development process in Web design using the concepts, techniques, and Web Design Tips presented in each section. The Case Study requires students to apply their knowledge starting in Section 1 and continuing through Section 4 as they prepare, plan, create, and then publish their Web site.

SHELLY CASHMAN SERIES TEACHING TOOLS

The two basic ancillaries that accompany this textbook are Teaching Tools (ISBN 0-7895-5966-8) and MyCourse.com. These ancillaries are available to adopters through your Course Technology representative or by calling one of the following telephone numbers: Colleges and Universities, 1-800-648-7450; High Schools, 1-800-824-5179; Private Career Colleges, 1-800-477-3692; Canada, 1-800-268-2222; and Corporations and Government Agencies, 1-800-340-7450.

Teaching Tools

The Teaching Tools for this textbook include both teaching and testing aids. The contents of the Teaching Tools CD-ROM are listed below.

- **Instructor's Manual** The Instructor's Manual is made up of Microsoft Word files. The files include lecture notes, solutions to exercises, and a large test bank. The files allow you to modify the lecture notes or generate quizzes and exams from the test bank using your own word processing software. The Instructor's Manual includes the following for each chapter: chapter objectives; chapter overview; detailed lesson plans with page number references; teacher notes and activities; answers to the end-of-chapter exercises; a test bank of 110 questions for every chapter (25 multiple-choice, 50 true/false, and 35 fill-in-the-blank) with page number references; and transparency references. The transparencies are available through the Figures in the Book. The test bank questions are the same as in ExamView. Thus, you can print a copy of the chapter test bank and use the printout to select your questions in ExamView or Course Test Manager.

- **Figures in the Book** Illustrations for every screen and table in the textbook are available in electronic form. Use this ancillary to present a slide show in lecture or to print transparencies for use in lecture with an overhead projector. If you have a personal computer and LCD device, this ancillary can be an effective tool for presenting lectures.
- **ExamView** ExamView is a state-of-the-art test builder that is easy to use. ExamView enables you to create quickly printed tests, Internet tests, and computer (LAN-based) tests. You can enter your own test questions or use the test bank that accompanies ExamView. The test bank is the same as the one described in the Instructor's Manual section.
- **Course Syllabus** Any instructor who has been assigned a course at the last minute knows how difficult it is to come up with a course syllabus. For this reason, sample syllabi are included that can be customized easily to a course.
- **Interactive Labs** Eighteen completely updated, hands-on Interactive Labs that take students from ten to fifteen minutes each to step through help solidify and reinforce mouse and keyboard usage and computer concepts. Student assessment is available.

MyCourse.com

MyCourse.com offers instructors and students an opportunity to supplement classroom learning with additional course content. You can use MyCourse.com to expand on traditional learning by accessing and completing readings, tests, and other assignments through the customized, comprehensive Web site. For additional information, visit MyCourse.com and click the Help button.

ACKNOWLEDGMENTS

The Shelly Cashman Series would not be the leading computer education series without the contributions of outstanding publishing professionals. First, and foremost, among them is Becky Herrington, director of production and designer. She is the heart and soul of the Shelly Cashman Series, and it is only through her leadership, dedication, and tireless efforts that superior products are made possible.

Under Becky's direction, the following individuals made significant contributions to these books: Doug Cowley, production manager; Ginny Harvey, series specialist and contributing writer; Ken Russo, senior Web and graphic designer; Mike Bodnar, associate production manager; Mark Norton, Web designer; Hector Arvizu, interior design and layout; Meena Moest, product review manager; Bruce Greene, multimedia product manager; Michelle French and Christy Otten, graphic artists; Jeanne Black and Betty Hopkins, Quark experts; Ginny Harvey and Dave George, developmental editors; Lyn Markowicz, copyeditor; and Cristina Haley, proofreader/indexer.

We would like to thank Richard Keaveny, associate publisher; John Sisson, managing editor; Jim Quasney, series consulting editor; Erin Roberts, product manager; Erin Runyon, associate product manager; Francis Schurgot and Marc Ouellette, Web product managers; Rachel VanKirk, marketing manager; and Reed Cotter, editorial assistant. Thanks to Ed Sullivan, Jen Krogh, Shawn McCombs, Linda Rubio, Dr. Anthony Villegas, and Lorraine Bergkvist for reviewing the manuscript.

Gary B. Shelly
Thomas J. Cashman
Linda A. Kosteba

CHAPTER 1

Web Design Basics

OBJECTIVES

After completing this chapter you will be able to:

- Define the Internet and the World Wide Web

- Describe how data moves from one computer to another over the Internet

- Differentiate between a Web page and a Web site

- Describe a home page and a splash page

- Locate and access information on the World Wide Web

- Discuss the public switched telephone network and its effect on Web design

- Describe an Internet service provider

- Identify Web design browser-related issues

- Describe the different Web page viewing devices available

- Identify the different types of Web sites

- Discuss the impact of the Internet and Web

- Differentiate among the different types of Web sites

- Discuss methods for doing Web design research

- Describe the various tools for creating Web pages and Web sites

- Identify Web design roles

INTRODUCTION

Creating Web pages and Web sites that successfully communicate, educate, entertain, or conduct business requires the somewhat mysterious element of design. This book explains design and shows you how to use it as a tool to develop effective Web pages and Web sites for specific purposes and audiences. Chapter 1 begins the process by discussing various features of the Internet and the Web and techniques to navigate this environment productively. In addition to revealing methods for doing Web design research, the chapter discusses the various roles, responsibilities, and necessary skills essential to successful Web design.

THE INTERNET

WEB INFO

For more information about the Internet, visit the Web Design Chapter 1 Web Info page (scsite.com/web/ch1/webinfo.htm) and then click Internet.

The Internet is the most popular and fastest growing area in computing today. Using the Internet, you can do research, get a loan, shop for services and merchandise, job hunt, buy and sell stocks, display weather maps, obtain medical advice, watch movies, listen to high-quality music, and converse with people worldwide.

The **Internet** is a worldwide collection of networks (Figure 1-1), each of which is composed of a collection of smaller networks. A **network** is composed of several computers connected together to share resources and data. For example, on a college campus, the network in the student lab can be connected to the faculty computer network, which is connected to the administration network, and they all can connect to the Internet.

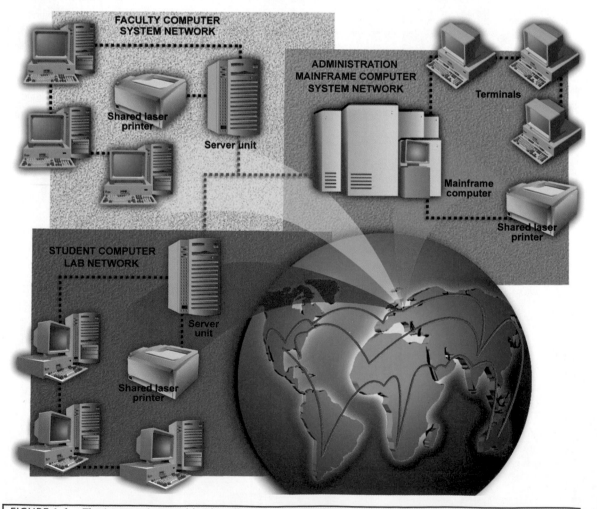

FIGURE 1-1 The Internet is a worldwide collection of networks.

Networks are connected with high-, medium-, and low-speed data lines that allow data to move from one computer to another (Figure 1-2). The Internet has high-speed data lines that connect major computer systems located around the world, which form the **Internet backbone.** Other, less powerful computers, such as those used by local Internet service providers often attach to the Internet backbone using medium-speed data lines. An Internet service provider (ISP) is a business that has permanent Internet connections and provides temporary connections to individuals and companies free or for a fee. Finally, the connection between your computer at home and your local Internet service provider, often called **the last mile,** employs low-speed data lines such as telephone lines. Today, cable increasingly is replacing telephone lines over the last mile, which significantly improves access to information on the Internet.

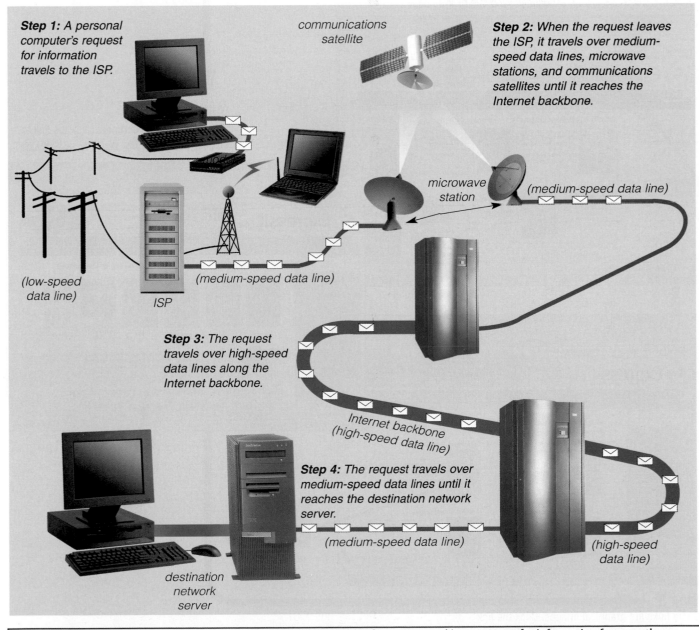

FIGURE 1-2   An example of a possible connection between a personal computer making a request for information from another computer connected via the Internet.

WEB INFO

For more information about the World Wide Web, visit the Web Design Chapter 1 Web Info page (scsite.com/web/ch1/webinfo.htm) and then click World Wide Web.

THE WORLD WIDE WEB

Computer systems have the capability of delivering information in a variety of ways, such as graphics, sound, video clips, animation, and, of course, regular text.

On the Web, you access such information using a hyperlink, or simply link (Figure 1-3), which is a special software pointer that points to the location of the computer on which the specific information is stored and to the information itself. A link can point to information on any computer connected to the Internet that is running the proper software. Thus, clicking a link on a computer in Los Angeles could display text and graphics located on a computer in New York.

Step 1:

Some links display a different color when you point to them. Click the link to display its associated Web site or Web page.

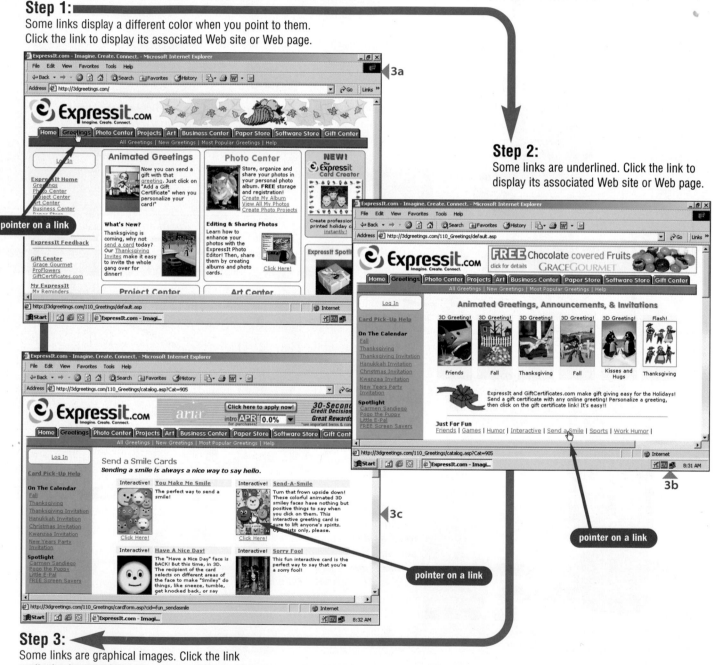

Step 2:

Some links are underlined. Click the link to display its associated Web site or Web page.

Step 3:

Some links are graphical images. Click the link to display its associated Web site or Web page.

FIGURE 1-3   A home page and secondary pages make up a Web site. As visitors click links, related Web pages and Web sites display.

The collection of links throughout the Internet creates an interconnected network called the **World Wide Web**, which also is referred to as the **Web**, or **WWW**. Each computer within the Web containing information that can be referenced with a link is called a **Web site**. Millions of Web sites around the world are accessible through the Internet.

Graphics, text, and other information available at a Web site are stored in a specifically formatted electronic document called a **Web page**. When you click a link to display a picture, read text, view a video, or listen to a song, you are viewing a Web page.

On the Web, a link can be a word, phrase, or image. You often can identify a link by its appearance. Text links usually are underlined or in a color different from the rest of the document. When you point to a graphical link, its appearance may remain the same or it may change its look in some way. As shown in Figure 1-3, the shape of the pointer on the screen changes to a small hand with a pointing index finger when you position it on a link, or point to the link.

To activate a link, you point to it and then press the mouse button, or click the link. This causes the item associated with the link to display on the screen. The link can point to an item on the same Web page, a different Web page at the same Web site, or a separate Web page at a different Web site in another city or country. In most cases, when you navigate using links, you are jumping from Web page to Web page. Some people refer to this activity of jumping from one Web page to another as **surfing the Web**. To remind you visually that you have visited a location or document, some browsers change the color of a text link after you click it.

A Web site, which is a collection of linked Web pages, typically starts with a home page. A **home page** provides information about the Web site's purpose and content (upper-left screen in Figure 1-3). Figure 1-3 shows how to navigate using links.

A splash page sometimes precedes a home page. A **splash page** is a lead-in page often containing multimedia. **Multimedia** is some combination of text, graphics, animation, audio, or video. Like a billboard, a splash page's primary intent is to grab visitors' attention and draw them into the Web site (Figure 1-4).

4a Splash page action

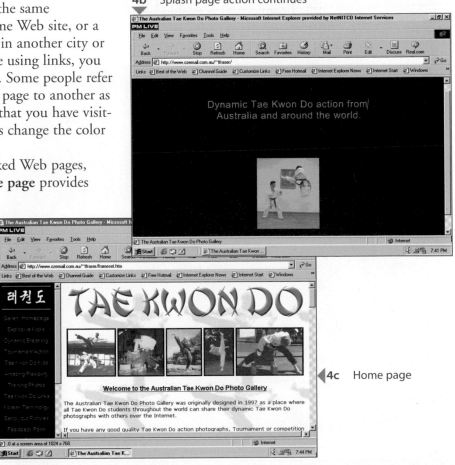

4b Splash page action continues

4c Home page

FIGURE 1-4 The Australian Tae Kwon Do splash page utilizes action-packed graphics and twirling letters to entice visitors into the home page.

ACCESSING INFORMATION ON THE WEB

The Web can seem both mysterious and intimidating. It is awesome that something virtual and so vast can be accessed and productively searched. Users access the Web using a variety of means. The more common connections to the Internet involve some use of telephone lines, but newer methods that include cable and wireless transmissions also are being used. The following sections describe connecting to the Web using the various connection methods and Internet service providers that make accessing and searching the World Wide Web possible.

Connecting to the Web

Users access Web sites through the public switched telephone network. The **public switched telephone network (PSTN)** is the worldwide telephone system that handles voice-oriented telephone calls (Figure 1-5). Nearly the entire telephone network today uses digital technology, with the exception of the final link from the local telephone company to a home, which usually is analog.

While initially it was built to handle voice communications, the telephone network also is an integral part of computer communications. Data, instructions, and information can be sent over the telephone network using dial-up lines or dedicated lines.

Dial-Up Lines

A **dial-up line** is a temporary connection that uses one or more analog telephone lines for communications. A dial-up connection is not permanent. Using a dial-up line to transmit data is similar to using the telephone to make a call. A modem at the sending end dials the telephone number of a modem at the receiving end. When the modem at the receiving end answers the call, a connection is established and data can be transmitted. When either modem hangs up, the communications end.

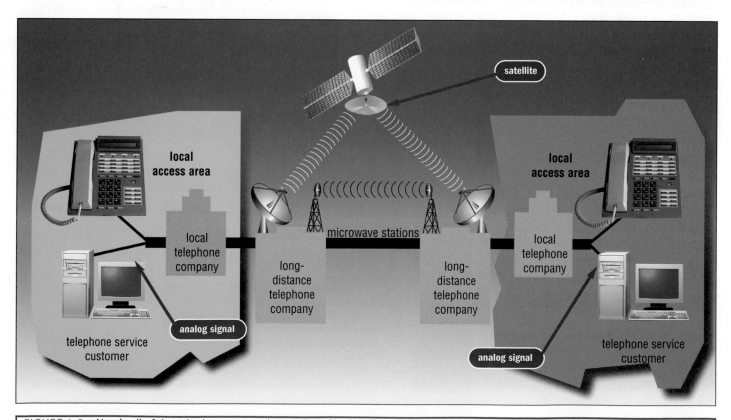

FIGURE 1-5   Nearly all of the telephone network uses digital technology, with the exception of the final link from the local telephone company to a home or office, which usually is analog.

One advantage of a dial-up line to connect computers is that it costs no more than making a regular telephone call. Another advantage is that computers at any two locations can establish a connection using modems and the telephone network. Mobile users, for example, often use dial-up lines to connect to their main office network so they can read e-mail messages, access the Internet, and upload files.

A disadvantage of dial-up lines is that you cannot control the quality of the connection because the telephone company's switching office randomly selects the line.

Dedicated Lines

A **dedicated line** is a connection that always is established between two communications devices (unlike a dial-up line in which the connection is reestablished each time it is used). The quality and consistency of the connection on a dedicated line is better than a dial-up line because dedicated lines provide a constant connection.

Businesses often use dedicated lines to connect geographically distant offices. Dedicated lines either can be analog or digital. Digital lines increasingly are connecting home and business users to networks around the globe because they transmit data and information at faster rates than analog lines.

A **transfer rate** is the speed at which a line carries data and information. The faster the transfer rate, the faster you can send and receive data and information. Transfer rates usually are expressed as **bits per second** (**bps**) — that is, the number of bits the line can transmit in one second. Transfer rates range from thousands of bits per second, called **kilobits per second** (**Kbps**), to millions of bits per second, called **megabits per second** (**Mbps**), to billions of bits per second, called **gigabits per second** (**Gbps**). The table in Figure 1-6 lists the transfer rates (speeds) and approximate monthly costs of various types of lines, as compared with dial-up lines.

Four popular types of digital dedicated lines are ISDN lines, digital subscriber lines, cable lines, and T-carrier lines.

ISDN Lines

For the small business and home user, an ISDN line provides faster transfer rates than dial-up telephone lines. **Integrated Services Digital Network** (**ISDN**) is a set of standards for digital transmission of data over standard copper telephone lines. With ISDN, the same telephone line that could carry only one computer signal, now can carry three or more signals at once, through the same line, using a technique called **multiplexing**.

WEB INFO

For more information about the Integrated Services Digital Network (ISDN), visit the Web Design Chapter 1 Web Info page (scsite.com/web/ch1/webinfo.htm) and then click ISDN.

SPEEDS OF VARIOUS CONNECTIONS TO THE INTERNET

Type of Line	Transfer Rates	Approximate Monthly Cost
Dial-up	Up to 56 Kbps	Local or long-distance rates
ISDN	Up to 128 Kbps	$10 to $40
ADSL	128 Kbps – 8.45 Mbps	$39 to $110
Cable TV (CATV)	128 Kbps – 2.5 Mbps	$30 to $70
T1	1.544 Mbps	$1,000 or more
T3	44 Mbps	$10,000 or more

FIGURE 1-6   The speeds of various lines that can be used to connect to the Internet.

DSL

DSL is another digital line alternative for the small business or home user. **DSL** (**digital subscriber line**) transmits at fast speeds on existing standard copper telephone wiring. Some of the DSL installations can provide a dial tone, so you can use the line for both voice and data.

ADSL (**asymmetric digital subscriber line**) is a type of DSL that supports faster transfer rates when receiving data (the downstream rate) than when sending data (the upstream rate). ADSL is ideal for Internet access because most users download more information from the Internet than they upload.

Cable Television Lines

Although **cable television** (**CATV**) **lines** are not a type of telephone line, they are a very popular type of dedicated line that allows the home user to connect to the Internet. Data can be transmitted very rapidly via a cable modem connected to a CATV line.

T-carrier Lines

A **T-carrier line** is any of several types of digital lines that carry multiple signals over a single communications line. Whereas a standard dial-up telephone line carries only one signal, digital T-carrier lines use multiplexing so that multiple signals can share the telephone line. T-carrier lines provide extremely fast data transfer rates. Only medium to large companies usually can afford the investment in T-carrier lines because these lines also are so expensive.

The most popular T-carrier line is the **T1 line**. Businesses often use T1 lines to connect to the Internet. Many service providers also use T1 lines to connect to the Internet backbone. A **T3 line** is equal in speed to twenty-eight T1 lines. T3 lines are quite expensive. Main users of T3 lines include large companies, telephone companies, and service providers connecting to the Internet backbone. The Internet backbone itself also uses T3 lines (Figure 1-2 on page 1.3).

Service Providers

An **Internet service provider** (**ISP**) is a business that has a permanent Internet connection and provides temporary connections to individuals and companies free or for a fee. The most common ISP fee arrangement is a fixed amount, usually about $10 to $20 per month for an individual account. For this amount, many ISPs offer unlimited Internet access. Others specify a set number of access hours per month. With these arrangements, you pay an additional amount for each hour you connect in excess of an allotted number of access hours.

If you use a telephone line to access the Internet, the telephone number you dial connects you to an access point on the Internet, called a **point of presence** (**POP**). When selecting a service provider, be sure it provides at least one local POP telephone number. Otherwise, you will pay long-distance telephone charges for the time you connect to the Internet.

Two types of ISPs are regional and national (Figure 1-7). A **regional ISP** usually provides access to the Internet through one or more telephone numbers local to a specific geographic area. A **national ISP** is a larger business that provides local telephone numbers in most major cities and towns nationwide. Some national ISPs also provide a toll-free telephone number. Due to their larger size, national ISPs usually offer more services and generally have a larger technical support staff than regional ISPs. Examples of national ISPs are AT&T, EarthLink, and WorldCom.

Like an ISP, an **online service provider** (**OSP**) supplies Internet access, but an OSP also has many members-only features that offer a variety of special content and services such as news, weather, legal information, financial data, hardware and software guides, games, and travel guides. For this reason, the fees for using an OSP sometimes are slightly higher than fees for an ISP. The two more popular OSPs are America Online (AOL) and The Microsoft Network (MSN).

WEB INFO

For more information about Internet service providers (ISPs), visit the Web Design Chapter 1 Web Info page (scsite.com/web/ch1/webinfo.htm) and then click ISP.

A **wireless service provider (WSP)** is a company that provides wireless Internet access to users with wireless modems or Web-enabled handheld computers or devices. Notebook computers can use wireless modems. Web-enabled devices include cellular telephones, two-way pagers, and hands-free (voice activated) Internet devices in automobiles. An antenna on the wireless modem or Web-enabled device typically sends signals through the airwaves to communicate with a WSP. Examples of WSPs include GoAmerica Communications, OmniSky, and SprintPCS.

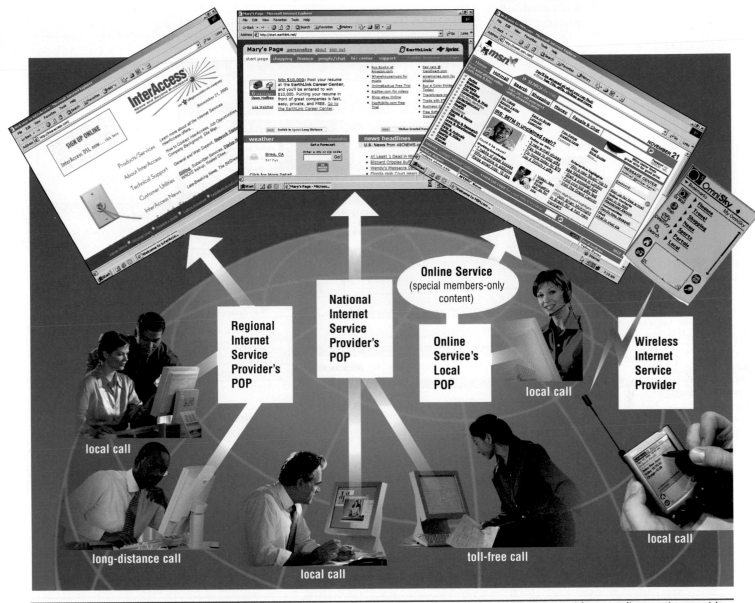

FIGURE 1-7   Common ways to access the Internet are through a regional or national Internet service provider, an online service provider, or a wireless service provider.

WEB INFO

For more information about popular Web browsers, visit the Web Design Chapter 1 Web Info page (scsite.com/web/ch1/webinfo.htm) and then click Browsers.

WEB BROWSERS

To view Web pages on a computer monitor, you need a **Web browser**, also called a **browser**, which is a specific software program that allows for the display of Web pages. Netscape Navigator and Microsoft Internet Explorer are today's most widely used browsers (Figure 1-8). Because a Web page may display differently depending on the browser, remember to test with different browsers as you develop your Web site. Keep in mind the following Web Design Tip:

Web Design Tip

As you develop a Web site, make sure you test the Web pages using different browsers.

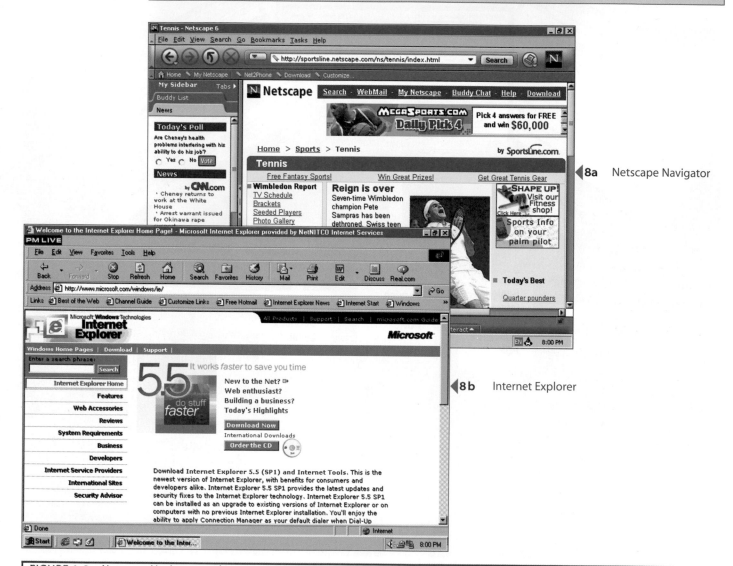

8a   Netscape Navigator

8b   Internet Explorer

FIGURE 1-8   Netscape Navigator and Internet Explorer are today's two most popular Web browsers.

One way to access a Web page is to enter its unique address, called the **Uniform Resource Locator (URL)** in the browser's address bar or location field. A URL begins with the **protocol**, which specifies the format to be used for transmitting data. Most often, that protocol will be **Hypertext Transfer Protocol (HTTP)**, which is the communications standard to transmit data on the Web. The **domain name**, which is the text version of a numeric address for each computer on the Internet, follows the protocol. The numeric address, commonly referred to as an **IP address**, seldom appears in a Web URL. A domain name or IP address entered properly each will take you to its respective Web page. Figure 1-9 distinguishes between domain names and IP addresses and illustrates common domain name abbreviations.

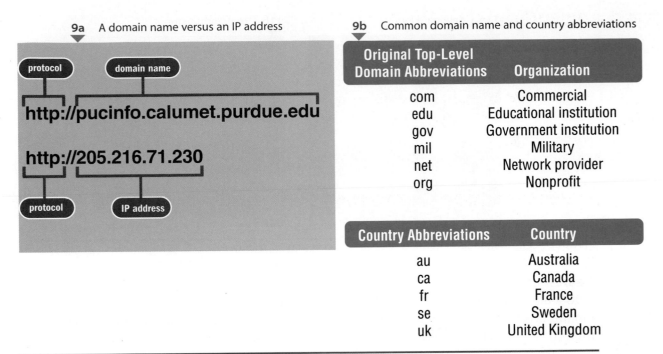

9a   A domain name versus an IP address

protocol   domain name

http://pucinfo.calumet.purdue.edu

http://205.216.71.230

protocol   IP address

9b   Common domain name and country abbreviations

Original Top-Level Domain Abbreviations	Organization
com	Commercial
edu	Educational institution
gov	Government institution
mil	Military
net	Network provider
org	Nonprofit

Country Abbreviations	Country
au	Australia
ca	Canada
fr	France
se	Sweden
uk	United Kingdom

FIGURE 1-9   The components of a Uniform Resource Locator (URL).

Alternative Web Page Viewing Devices

Besides viewing Web pages on a desktop computer monitor or a notebook computer, you can view Web pages using WebTV and handheld computers. Microsoft-owned **WebTV** incorporates Internet access into a television set, which serves as the monitor (Figure 1-10). WebTV owners can send e-mail, surf the Internet, and chat with other viewers without purchasing a computer or acquiring any computer skills. **Handheld computers** are wireless, portable computers designed to fit in a user's hand. Such computers often use pen input (Figure 1-11 on the next page). A **Personal Digital Assistant (PDA)**, a popular type of handheld computer, manages personal information and provides Internet access. As you design your Web pages, consider that some of your audience may be viewing your pages with WebTV or handheld computers. A language developed to create Web pages specifically for viewing with small, wireless devices is introduced later in this chapter.

FIGURE 1-10   Chat capability and interactive Web pages are recent additional features available to WebTV customers.

11a Keyboard input   11b Handwritten input

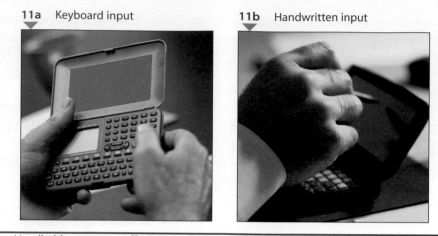

FIGURE 1-11   Handheld computers offer convenience and portability.

WEB INFO

For a list of search engines, visit the Web Design Chapter 1 Web Info page (scsite.com/web/ch1/webinfo.htm) and then click Search Engines.

Search Engines

To look for information on the Web, you could rely on printed directories, word of mouth, or simply surf interesting links. Such sources, however, soon may become outdated, time-consuming and unproductive. Web sites that offer search services are more current, time-saving, and productive alternatives. Search services use **search engines**, which are software programs that find Web sites and Web pages. To locate Web pages on particular topics, you enter a **keyword** or phrase in the search engine's text box and click the appropriate button (usually a button labeled either Search or Go) to initiate the search. The search engine then displays a list of Web pages that includes the keyword or phrase you entered. Frequently, via a Help or Tips link search services provide directions for searching. For example, you might be instructed to enter keywords only in uppercase letters or to use special words to limit a search.

Typically, search services also provide **directories**, which classify Web pages into such categories as arts and entertainment, jobs, health and fitness, travel, news, and media (Figure 1-12). If you click a directory's Business and Economy category, for example, subcategories such as Business Schools, Employment and Work, and Global Economy may display. To find the information you desire, click your way through the categories and subcategories.

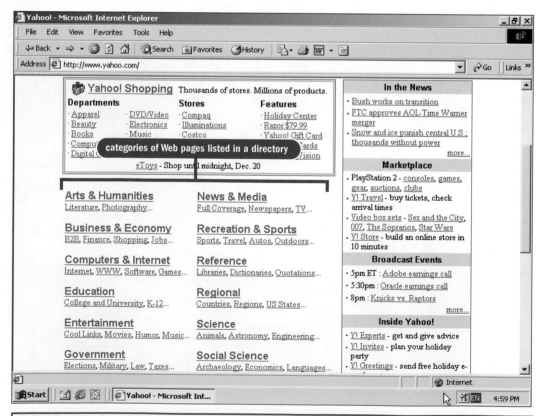

FIGURE 1-12   An example of a directory Web page.

Search services create their own Web site databases in different ways. People manually create the databases of some services. Others use **spiders** or **robots**, which are software products that search new Web pages, index, and return URLs and content information to other services' databases.

Several search engines use meta tags to build their indexes. With **meta tags**, which are special tags added to Web pages (Figure 1-13), you can add information such as keywords and descriptive data regarding your Web pages. Keep in mind the following Web Design Tip:

Web Design Tip

Include meta tags in Web pages to increase the possibility that they will be added to some search services' databases.

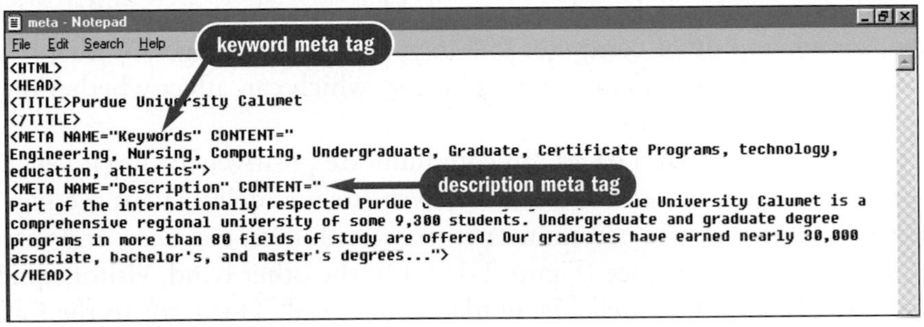

FIGURE 1-13   By including meta tags in Web page documents, you can increase the probability that your Web pages will appear in search engine indexes.

WEB INFO

For more information about portals, visit the Web Design Chapter 1 Web Info page (scsite.com/web/ch1/webinfo.htm) and then click Portals.

Portals

Portals are Web sites that offer not only search services but also e-mail, chat rooms, news and sports, maps, and more (Figure 1-14). Some of the more widely used portals include Excite, Lycos, AltaVista, and Yahoo!

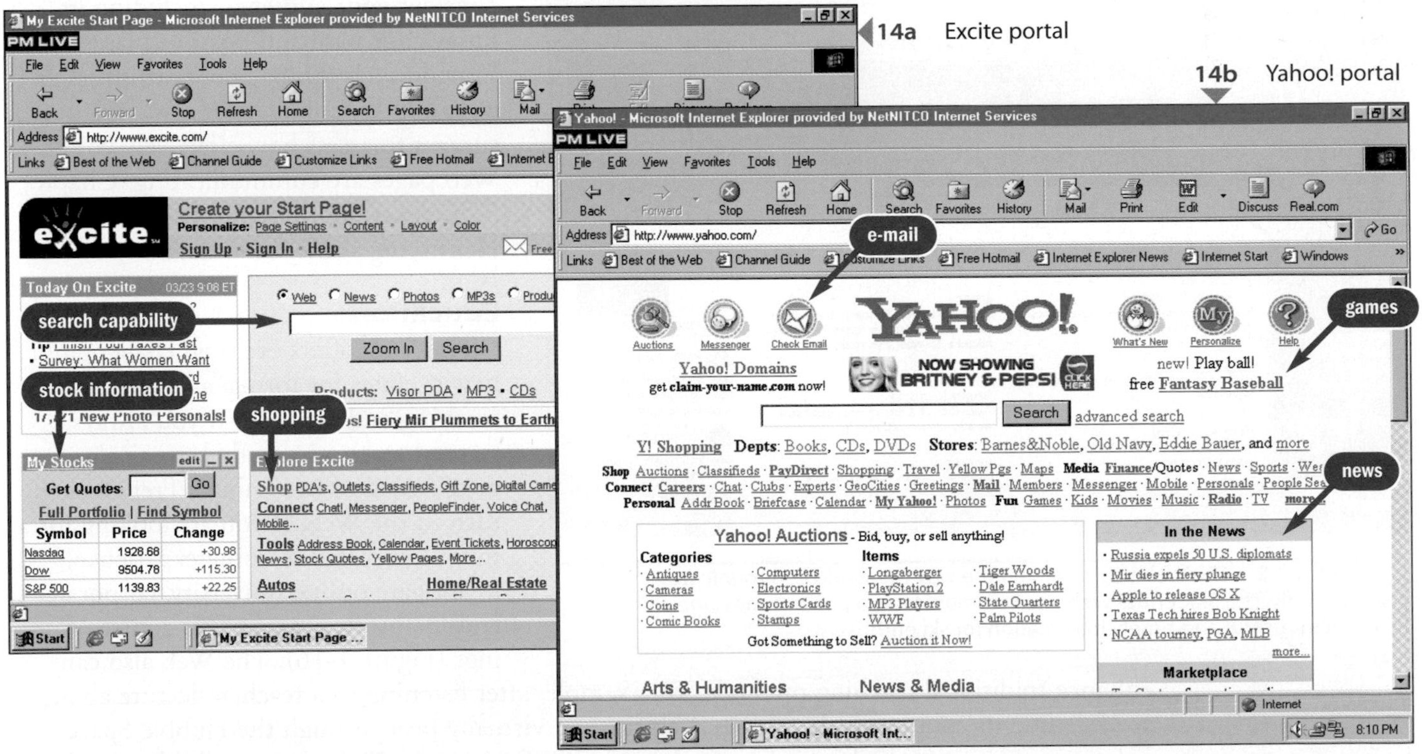

FIGURE 1-14   The more frequently used portal Web sites offer search services, e-mail, chat rooms, news, sports, maps, and more.

IMPACT OF THE INTERNET AND THE WEB

Today, friends, families, and business people exchange e-mail addresses as frequently as telephone numbers. A child will turn to the Web to research a book report, as will a scientist to publish research findings. Many people seeking home entertainment choose an interactive Web multimedia experience over TV or a rented video. Shoppers avoid crowds, parking problems, and long lines by shopping and banking online. The Internet and the Web have significantly impacted the way the world communicates, educates, entertains, and conducts business. These changes in human interaction have specific implications for designing Web pages and Web sites and are discussed in this section.

Communication

Businesses and individuals rely heavily on e-mail. Most e-mail programs allow you to attach graphic, video, sound, and other computer files to your e-mail messages. With e-mail you cannot see the sender's facial expression or body language, which can affect whether the message is communicated positively or negatively.

Similar to e-mail messages, Web pages can communicate positively or negatively. If you effectively design and selectively choose content, your Web site will deliver your message successfully and persuasively. If your Web site communicates trustworthiness, currency, and value, visitors will bookmark it for future reference (Figure 1-15). On the other hand, visitors quickly will pass over your Web site if it appears unreliable, outdated, or trivial. This leads to the following Web Design Tip:

> **Web Design Tip**
>
> Design your Web site so it communicates trustworthiness, currency, and value.

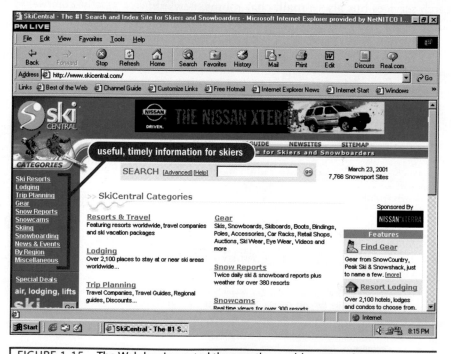

FIGURE 1-15 The Web has impacted the way the world communicates significantly. The SkiCentral Web site communicates a positive message with abundant useful and timely information for ski enthusiasts.

When planning your Web site, carefully define its purpose and the message you want to convey. Also, thoroughly consider your audience, including its knowledge base and possible biases. Provide such feedback opportunities as e-mail links, comment forms, and surveys to assess how effectively your Web pages are communicating. Chapter 3 discusses defining purpose and identifying audience in detail.

Education

The Web offers exciting, challenging new avenues for formal and informal teaching and learning. If you always wanted to know exactly how airplanes fly, or dreamed of becoming a French chef, turn to the Web. If you are looking for a more structured learning experience, investigate online university, corporate, and for-profit organization course offerings (Figure 1-16). The Web also can enhance traditional teaching methods. For example, after listening to a teacher's lecture about space, students could visit the NASA Web site and virtually peer through the Hubble Space Telescope to witness the birth of a star. Instructors often use the Web also to publish syllabi, grades, URLs to research, and more for their students.

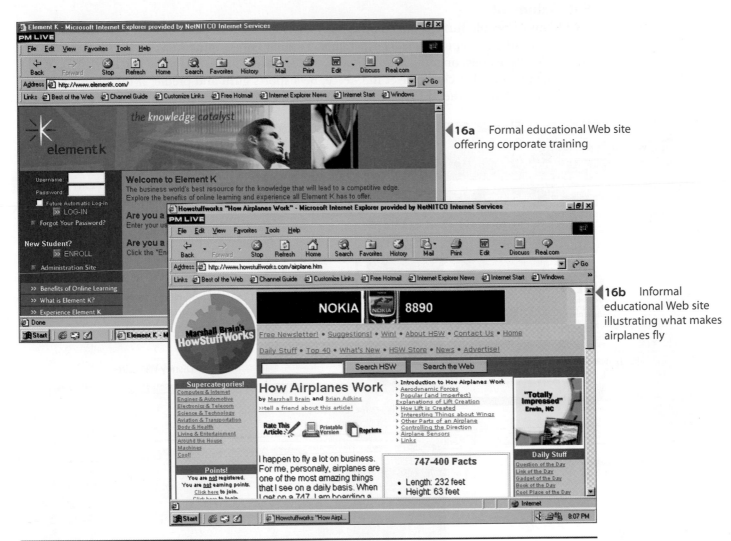

16a Formal educational Web site offering corporate training

16b Informal educational Web site illustrating what makes airplanes fly

FIGURE 1-16   The Web has influenced education in important ways.

If you are creating either a formal or informal educational Web site, ensure that the content is timely, accurate, and appealing. Keep up with current trends and statistics, and find out what experts in the field are saying. The following Web Design Tip summarizes the key points regarding a formal educational Web site design:

Web Design Tip

To develop a formal educational Web site, you must understand effective approaches to teaching and learning online and methods to overcome barriers to online learning, such as attention span and lack of discipline. You must include elements to successfully convey content, provide feedback, maintain records, and assess learning.

WEB INFO

For more information about how the Web has influenced education, visit the Web Design Chapter 1 Web Info page (scsite.com/web/ch1/webinfo.htm) and then click Educational Web Sites.

Entertainment

Millions of people turn to the Web daily for entertainment because of its unique capability of offering an interactive, multimedia experience. Popular entertainment Web sites offer music, videos, sports, games, ongoing Web episodes, sweepstakes, chats, and more (Figure 1-17). Will you match wits with a chess player in Greece; be a sports guru and predict if the Flyers will win tonight; help CROC the 3D crocodile rescue the Gobbos; or chat with your favorite celebrity online? Sophisticated entertainment Web sites often partner with other technologies. For example, MSNBC combines its Web site with its television component — you can read or watch a video about the show you missed, cast your vote about a topic raised on the show, and more.

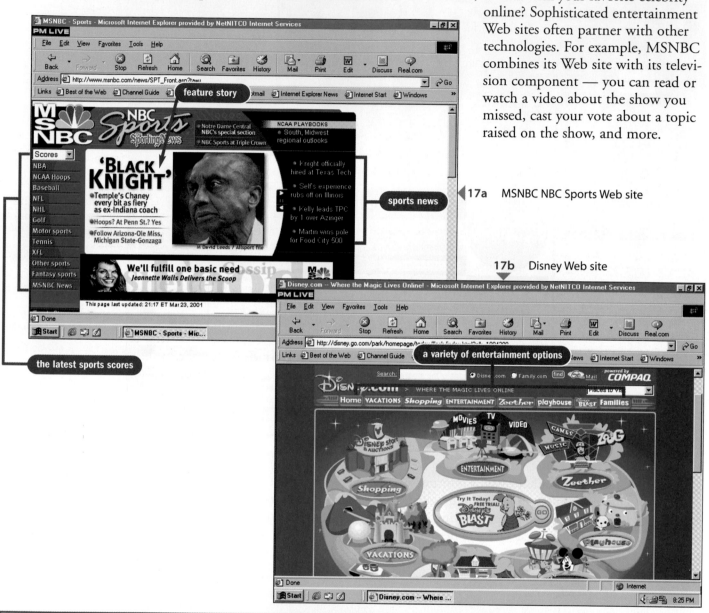

17a MSNBC NBC Sports Web site

17b Disney Web site

FIGURE 1-17 The Web affects how people are entertained, with fascinating choices among the multitude of offerings.

To include an entertainment element on your Web site, first identify what would appeal to your audience — a selection of Retro music, mind teasers, a Swing Dance video, or a chat room to discuss who was the best three-point shooter in NBA history, for example. Determine if you have the resources and skills necessary to develop the components yourself or if you need to outsource. The following Web Design Tip contains advice about incorporating entertainment into a Web site:

Web Design Tip

To develop an entertainment element on a Web site, identify what would appeal to your audience and what type of multimedia should be included.

Business

Conducting business online offers a range of possibilities. For example, via a Web site, you might find the perfect dog groomer for your dog, including the telephone number, location, services, and rates charged. On the other hand, within minutes, you could transfer funds to a 401K and buy your granddaughter's birthday present online. **Electronic commerce, or e-commerce,** is the conducting of business activities online, including shopping, investing, and any other venture that uses either electronic money or electronic data interchange. Initially, many doubted the future of e-commerce. Yet today, millions rely on e-commerce to buy an endless assortment of products and services and to conduct such financial transactions as investing, trading stocks, and transferring funds (Figure 1-18). Security, a critical component of e-commerce, is discussed in Chapter 2.

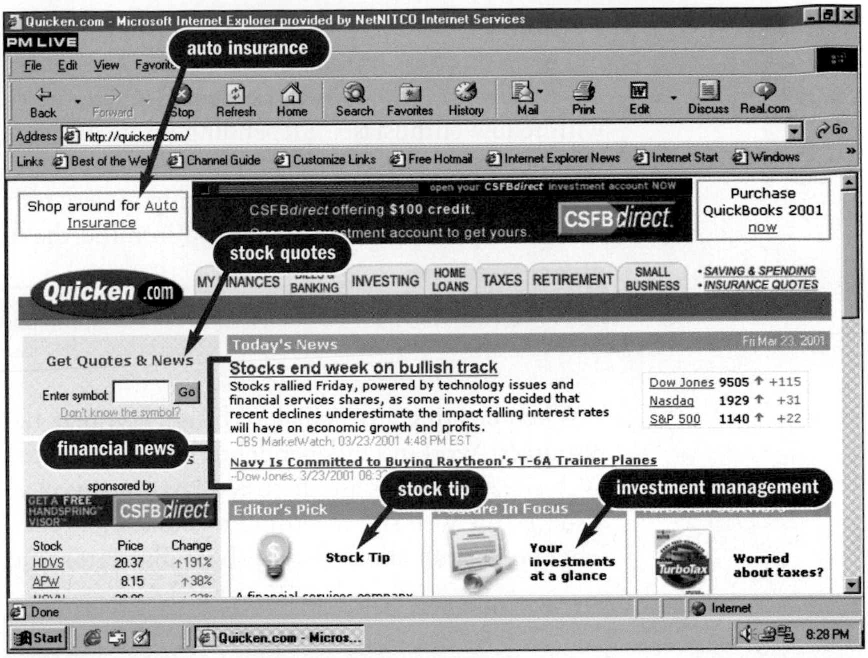

FIGURE 1-18　The Web has changed the way the world conducts business, called electronic commerce. Quicken.com is an example of a Web site that provides many financial services.

If you want to promote a product or service through your Web site, determine the features that make it desirable or necessary. Next, identify elements that will sell your product or service — perhaps color photos, an instructional video, or audio testimonials. Then, decide which interactive features to include for potential customers, such as e-mail links and comment and order forms. To develop an e-commerce Web site, you must understand the methods for building e-commerce capability into your Web pages, and the role and the support your ISP or OSP must supply to make e-commerce function on your Web site. This is summarized in the following two Web Design Tips:

Web Design Tip

To develop an e-commerce Web site, determine the features that would make the product or service desirable or necessary.

Web Design Tip

Gain an understanding of the methods for building e-commerce capability into Web pages, such as forms for customers to fill out. You also need to understand the role and support your OSP must supply to make e-commerce function on your Web site.

TYPES OF WEB SITES

The types of Web sites that dominate the Web can be categorized as personal, organization/ topical, and commercial. Type of Web site differs from purpose of Web site in that purpose is the factor that will determine the content you include. Defining purpose is discussed in detail in Chapter 3. An overview of personal, organization/topical, and commercial Web sites follows, along with the individual design challenges they present.

WEB INFO

For more information about the categories of Web sites found on the World Wide Web, visit the Web Design Chapter 1 Web Info page (scsite.com/web/ ch1/webinfo.htm) and then click Web Site Categories.

Personal

The Web offers unique opportunities for individuals. A **personal Web site**, allows you to advertise your employment credentials, meet new friends, or share a common interest or hobby with fellow enthusiasts. Depending on its purpose, you might include on your Web site your resume, biography, e-mail address, or a passionate description of Tae Bo or English roses.

One of the major issues confronting society today is the misuse of information that is readily available by electronic means. Keep in mind the following Web Design Tip:

Web Design Tip

Do not create Web pages that include personal information that can be misused.

When creating a personal Web site, you may have limited software, hardware, and other resources. Working independently means you must assume all the roles necessary to build the Web site. Web roles are discussed later in this chapter. Despite these challenges, you can publish a successful Web site to promote yourself and services you can offer, or simply tell the world what you are all about. Figure 1-19 illustrates a personal Web site.

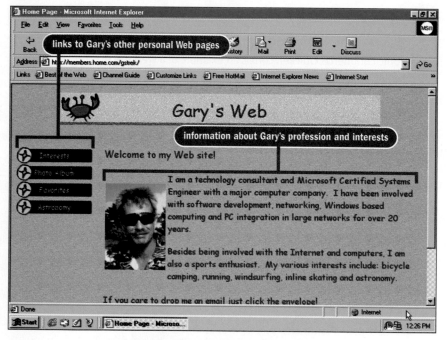

FIGURE 1-19 A personal Web site offers unique opportunities for individuals. Gary's Web site consists of information about Gary's profession and his interests, and includes photos and links to his other personal Web pages.

Organization/Topical

If you belong to the Advertising Photographers Association of North America, you might volunteer to create an **organization Web site** to promote member accomplishments or to encourage support and participation. Conversely, as a camera buff instead of an organization member, you might choose to design a **topical Web site** devoted to black and white photography, including tips for amateurs, photo galleries, and online resources.

If the Advertising Photographers Association of North America lacks funding, you may encounter the same challenges as an individual creating a personal Web site — specifically, limited resources, including people to share roles. A time constraint also may be added if the organization, for example, wants to coordinate introduction of the Web site with another event. Examples of organization and topical Web sites are shown in Figure 1-20.

Professional, nonprofit, international, social, volunteer, and various other types of organizations abound on the Web, as do Web sites devoted to diet and nutrition, health, entertainment, arts and humanities, sports, and many additional topics. What is lacking on some topical Web sites is correct content. Too many people who surf the Web believe that whatever is on a Web page is fact. Keep in mind the following Web Design Tip:

Web Design Tip

Only use content that has been professionally verified to create a Web page.

20a   Habitat for Humanity Web site

Web site encourages support for an organization

20b   Adventure Living Web site

Web site allows visitors to experience the thrill of skydiving

FIGURE 1-20   An organization Web site recognizes and promotes members in a group. The Habitat for Humanity Web site encourages backing and involvement, including sharing the personal experiences of those who have been helped by the organization. A topical Web site focuses on a specific theme. A visitor to the Adventure Living Web site can experience the thrill of skydiving.

Commercial

A small businessperson and the CEO of an international corporation share a common goal for their **commercial Web sites** — to promote and sell a product(s) or service(s). A corporate versus a small business Web site will be larger and more complex (Figure 1-21 on the next page), and may include sophisticated technologies such as e-commerce. A corporate Web site providing e-commerce opportunities and customer interactivity will achieve greater success than a competitor's Web site that simply puts its product catalog online. Financing the initial development and ongoing maintenance of a complex Web site and being competitive with rival companies, however, present major challenges. When creating a Web site to promote and sell products, obtain a list of features and related benefits from the marketing department. Keep in mind the following Web Design Tip:

Web Design Tip

When designing a Web page to promote and sell products, make sure you include the benefit associated with each feature you list.

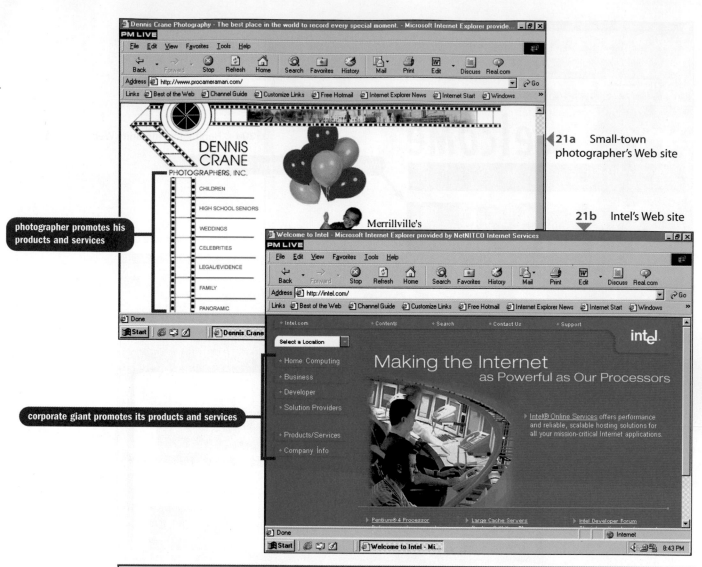

photographer promotes his products and services

21a Small-town photographer's Web site

21b Intel's Web site

corporate giant promotes its products and services

FIGURE 1-21   Commercial Web sites foster a company's business commodities. A small-town photographer and Intel share a common goal to promote and sell products and services.

In addition to a public Internet Web site, a large organization or corporation frequently creates an **intranet**, which is a private network for information management and sharing among only its members or employees. A corporate intranet might make available to its employees policies and procedures and access to databases. Although an intranet can present security issues, most employees consider it a highly useful tool.

WEB DESIGN RESEARCH

WEB INFO

For more information about how to do research on designing a Web site, visit the Web Design Chapter 1 Web Info page (scsite.com/web/ch1/webinfo.htm) and then click Web Design Research.

Before designing a Web site, you need to do research. The three major areas your research needs to address before you begin to plan and create are:

1. How to develop a Web site that stands out

2. How to identify your audience

3. Which new Web technologies you should incorporate

Methods for researching these three areas are discussed in this section. Planning and creating a Web site is discussed in detail in subsequent chapters.

Develop a Web Site That Stands Out

More than 100 million people globally are using the Internet. The number of Web sites also is growing at an astronomical rate. Your challenge is to develop a Web site that will stand out from the rest and gain the attention of users who already are suffering from information overload. Compare this situation to being invited to a black-tie formal party. What will you wear and say to make yourself noticed in a room full of people in formal wear engaged in repetitive light conversation? To gather ideas to make your Web site stand out:

- Explore other Web sites and identify those that impress you.
- Describe design elements that contributed to that positive impression.
- Identify the means by which information was presented to you — photos, text, video, sound.
- Describe what made the information easy to find.
- List the reasons you would want to return.

To make your Web site highly visible, also carefully design your promotional strategies. Strategies to successfully market your Web site are discussed in Chapter 7.

Identify Your Audience

Literally anyone in the world can visit your Web site. Although you welcome all visitors, you need to identify your audience. Perhaps you want to attract people who share a similar interest, might want to hire you, would support your organization or become members, or would buy your product or service.

To identify and learn more about your Web site's visitors, include in your Web site design e-mail links, surveys, and comment forms that can tell you:

- Are the visitors to your Web site members of your audience?
- How did they come to your Web site — surfing, by means of a search engine, as a result of your Web site promotion?
- Did they find what they were looking for on your Web site?
- Was there anything they did not like about your Web site?
- Will they visit your Web site again? Why or why not?

Methods to identify your audience are discussed in detail in Chapter 3. Identifying and knowing your audience's needs and goals will help you create a highly usable Web site. Usability creates a positive experience for visitors and encourages them to return.

Incorporate New Web Technologies

Every day, it seems, you hear about another hot Web development tool hitting the market, a new browser feature, or a wireless handheld device that will revolutionize the way the world accesses the Internet. As soon as these new technologies surface, some Web designers charge ahead so their Web sites can be some of the first to feature these latest advances. Without question, true advancements in Web technology should be implemented. To determine the merit of these new technologies as they appear, prompt several questions:

- What specifically can this technology do to further the purpose of my Web site?
- Will it appeal to my audience?
- What will it cost to put it into action?
- How soon will I see a return on investing in this new technology?
- What impact will adding this technology have on security and other Web site elements?

WEB INFO

For more information about the tools available for creating Web pages, visit the Web Design Chapter 1 Web Info page (scsite.com/web/ch1/ webinfo.htm) and then click Web Design Tools.

TOOLS FOR CREATING WEB PAGES

Various tools are available for creating Web pages. These tools differ as to the skills and knowledge required to use them and the results they produce. For example, you can create basic Web pages using any of the standard Office XP applications; Web authoring packages such as FrontPage and Dreamweaver; or Hypertext Markup Language (HTML). You can add dynamic content, animation, and interactivity with more advanced software programs. Keep in mind the following Web Design Tip:

> **Web Design Tip**
>
> Choose tools based on your skill and knowledge level, and the degree of sophistication and complexity desired for your Web site. Make sure you and your developers have a strong working knowledge of HTML.

Hypertext Markup Language (HTML)

Hypertext Markup Language (HTML) is not a programming language; rather, it is a formatting language used to create Web pages. HTML defines a Web page through **tags**, or **markups**, which are codes that specify how text, graphics, and other elements display and where links lead. You can create a Web page by inserting HTML tags, which appear within brackets (for example <B> to boldface words), into a text file using a basic text editor such as Windows Notepad. When you view a Web page with a browser, it reads and interprets the tags. Figure 1-22 illustrates a basic HTML document and the resulting Web page. The **World Wide Web Consortium (W3C)** sets the standards for both HTML and Hypertext Transfer Protocol (HTTP), the protocol for transferring Web pages on the World Wide Web. Currently, the W3C recommends the use of HTML Version 4.01 and support for the previous versions HTML 3.2 and 2.0. Refer to the W3C Web site for the latest recommendations (http://www.w3.org/).

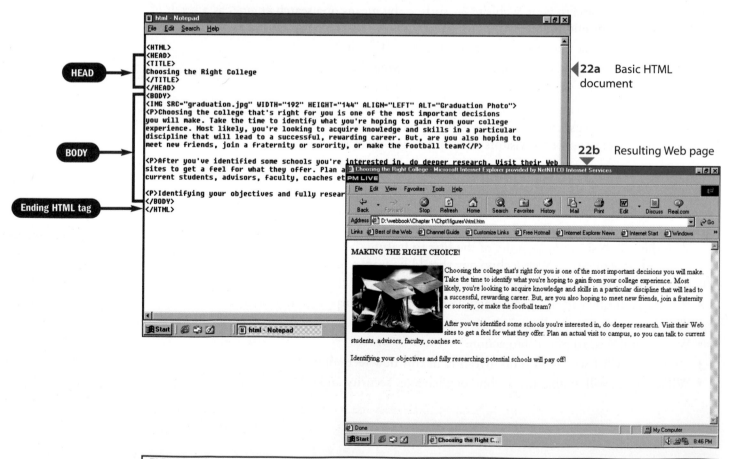

FIGURE 1-22   A Web page contains both text and HTML. By inserting the HTML tags into the text file, the Web page is created.

Scripts, Applets, Servlets, and ActiveX Controls

Scripts, Applets, Servlets, and ActiveX controls are **short programs** that your visitors' Web browsers run. These programs, when added to basic HTML documents, make your Web pages dynamic and interactive, with such features as multimedia, animation, forms that allow you and your visitors to communicate, and scrolling text. For an ActiveX control to run, it must be viewed with a browser that supports ActiveX technology, developed by Microsoft. Browser plug-ins can be downloaded to run ActiveX controls.

Scripts, applets, or servlets exchange data between a computer and a Web server utilizing the common gateway interface. The **common gateway interface (CGI)** is a specification that defines how information is transferred between a Web server and an outside source, such as a database. A **CGI program** manages the data exchange across the CGI. CGI programs perform different tasks and allow dynamic interaction, such as processing information submitted by a user via a form (Figure 1-23). These programs can be purchased, downloaded from the Web, or written as described in the following section.

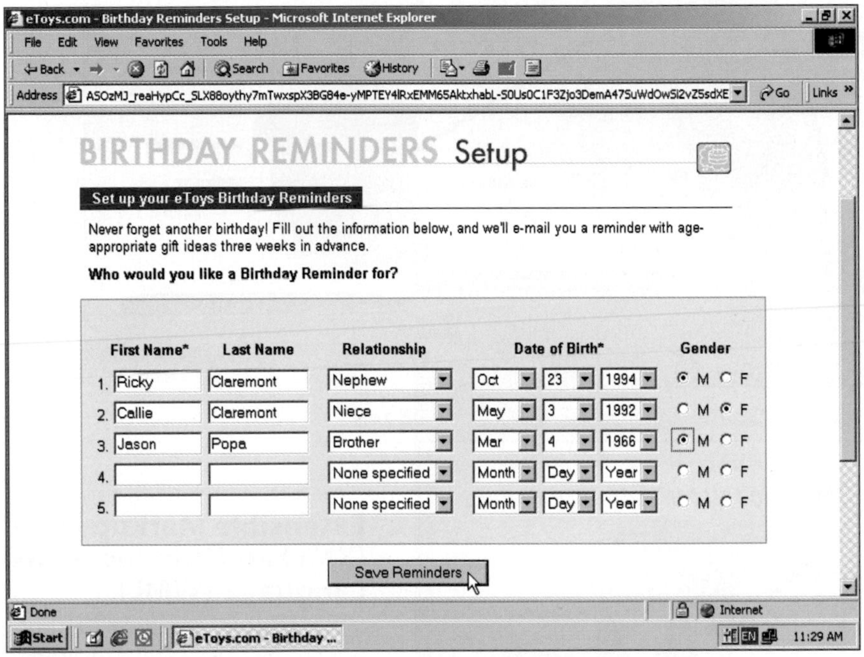

FIGURE 1-23   A processing form that utilizes a CGI program. If you submit the requested information, the Web site will send you birthday reminder messages.

JavaScript, VBScript, and Perl

JavaScript, VBScript, and Perl are popular **scripting languages** utilized to write CGI programs or scripts. The scripts, or instructions, can create customized, interactive Web pages.

Netscape Communications and Sun Microsystems developed JavaScript. By inserting **JavaScript** code into HTML documents, you can design dynamic, highly interactive Web sites with scrolling text, animations, and interactive quizzes and forms. Netscape Navigator 2.0 or later and Internet Explorer 3.0 or later will display Web pages with JavaScript. You can purchase ready-made JavaScripts on CDs or download them from specific Web sites.

In response to JavaScript, Microsoft developed **Visual Basic Scripting Edition (VBScript)**, a subset of the Visual Basic language. As with JavaScript, you can create dynamic, interactive Web pages by embedding VBScript in your HTML documents. Because Netscape does not support VBScript, use it only if you can be certain that your visitors will view your Web pages with Internet Explorer.

WEB INFO

For more information about scripting languages that can help you create customized, interactive Web pages, visit the Web Design Chapter 1 Web Info page (scsite.com/web/ch1/webinfo.htm) and then click Scripting Languages.

Practical Extraction and Reporting Language (**Perl**) is a third scripting language frequently utilized for creating CGI programs or scripts. Perl's popularity partly results from its strong capability of manipulating text. Larry Wall developed Perl at NASA's Jet Propulsion Laboratory.

Scripting languages and other technologies combined with HTML make **Dynamic HTML** (**DHTML**). DHTML creates more animated and interactive Web pages than possible with straight HTML (Figure 1-24).

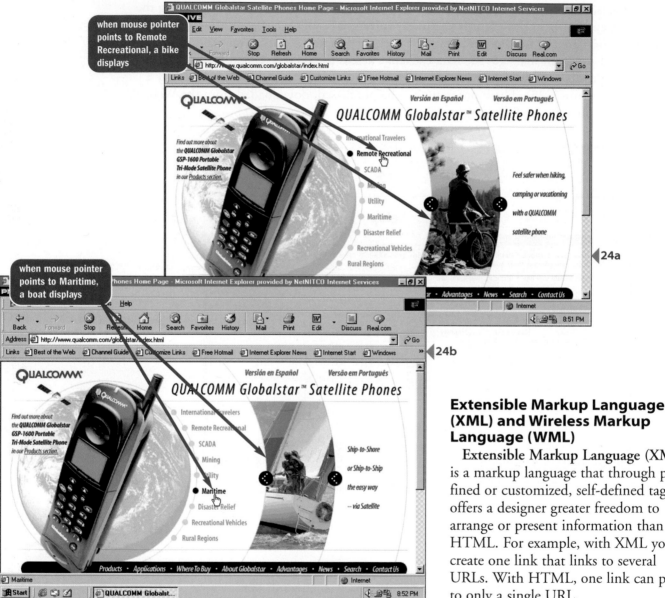

FIGURE 1-24   This Web page utilizes DHTML. The images and descriptions change as different links are pointed to.

Extensible Markup Language (XML) and Wireless Markup Language (WML)

Extensible Markup Language (XML) is a markup language that through predefined or customized, self-defined tags offers a designer greater freedom to arrange or present information than HTML. For example, with XML you can create one link that links to several URLs. With HTML, one link can point to only a single URL.

Like HTML, XML uses markups to define the content of a Web page. HTML defines content regarding how it looks or interacts. For example, HTML can define a text link, text color, or the size of an image. XML, on the other hand, defines content related to the information being described. For example, <SERIALNUM> could indicate that the information following is a serial number. This information could be utilized in various ways. XML facilitates the consistent sharing of information, especially within large groups. Expectations are that XML and HTML will be used together, for instance using XML markup within an HTML document.

Wireless Markup Language (WML) is a subset of XML. WML is used to design Web pages specifically for microbrowsers such as handheld computers, PDAs, cellular telephones, and pagers. WML allows for the display of the text portion of Web pages. WML uses Wireless Application Protocol (WAP) to allow Internet access by wireless devices. Almost all mobile telephone browsers globally support WML.

Web Authoring Packages

If you do not want to learn HTML to create your Web pages, consider Web authoring packages that automatically generate HTML code. Which package you should choose will depend on your skill level as a designer and the degree of sophistication and complexity you intend for your Web site. A discussion of various Web authoring packages follows.

If you are comfortable with other Microsoft products and plan to build a basic business Web site, **Microsoft FrontPage** is a great choice with its wizard and template assortments (Figure 1-25). You can manage your Web site easily with link verification, automatic graphic themes, and navigation updates. FrontPage supports DHTML and JavaScript. Handling form data and allowing search capability, however, require that specific FrontPage Server Extensions be installed on the server that hosts your Web site.

WEB INFO

For more information about Web authoring packages available for creating Web pages, visit the Web Design Chapter 1 Web Info page (scsite.com/web/ch1/webinfo.htm) and then click Web Authoring Packages.

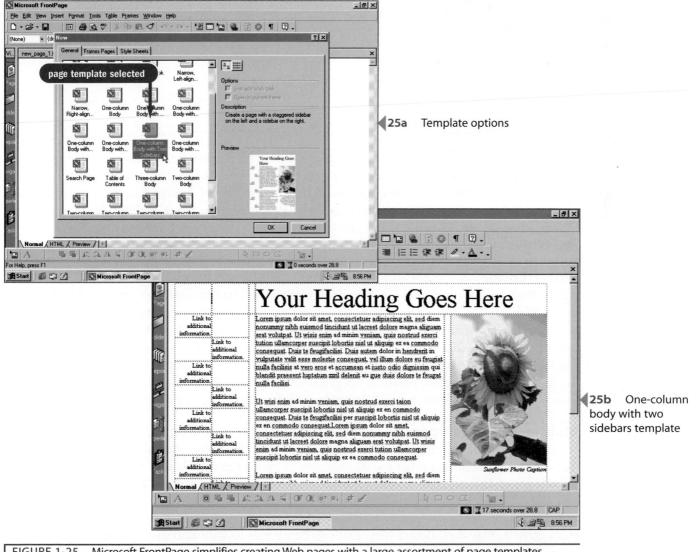

25a   Template options

25b   One-column body with two sidebars template

FIGURE 1-25   Microsoft FrontPage simplifies creating Web pages with a large assortment of page templates.

If you are an experienced designer, you will appreciate **Adobe Go Live** with its many extras, including a JavaScript editor and a QuickTime movie video editor. This package, which has no wizards or templates, is appropriate for developing more complex Web sites. Go Live comes with JavaScript and DHTML actions and Cascading Style Sheets. It also has the capability of creating master objects and HTML 4.0 forms and building tables visually.

If you are looking for a powerful Web authoring package to design complex, interactive, and animated Web sites, choose **Macromedia Dreamweaver**. If you couple this package with considerable design experience, you easily can add to your Web site animations and interactive elements created with Flash, another Macromedia product. Dreamweaver, which contains no predesigned templates or wizards, offers sophisticated Web site management capabilities and many other features for the experienced Web designer.

Macromedia Flash is an almost required tool if you are a seasoned Web designer. Choose Flash for generating quick loading graphics and sound, interactive movies, and basic Web forms, as well as creating Web pages and Web sites. You also can use this package for drawing and animating, and producing small, scalable graphics.

Microsoft Office Applications

Although Office XP programs efficiently generate basic HTML documents, they are not highly recommended for creating Web pages or Web sites, as are true Web authoring packages. On the positive side, with any program in the Office XP suite — Word, Excel, Access, and PowerPoint — you quickly and easily can create Web pages simply by clicking the Save as Web Page command on the File menu.

WEB INFO

For more information about careers in Web design, visit the Web Design Chapter 1 Web Info page (scsite.com/web/ch1/webinfo.htm) and then click Careers.

WEB DESIGN ROLES

Depending on circumstances, when creating a Web site, you may be working independently, with a partner, or with a group as part of a Web development team. In a partner or group situation, each participant's strengths should be identified so the appropriate role can be assigned. When working independently or in small company or organization situations, you may need to assume several or all of the following roles. The role depicts the responsibilities, not the specific position title that might be assigned.

Writer/Editor

As a **Web page writer/editor**, you create and revise the text that visitors read when they visit a Web site. To achieve your Web site's purpose, you must write specifically for the Web environment and a targeted Web audience. Text simply cut and pasted from a print publication into an HTML document will not deliver effectively the message you want to send. Writing for the Web environment and targeting an audience are detailed in Chapters 2 and 3, respectively. To fill a Web writer/editor position, an employer frequently looks for a highly creative applicant with a liberal arts background and demonstrated print and Internet writing experience.

Multimedia Developer

As a **multimedia developer**, you design and produce animation, digital video and audio, 2D and 3D models, and other media elements to include in a Web site. This role demands knowledge of and experience with sophisticated hardware and software, as well as art theory and graphic design principles. If you do not have the required developer skills, you can purchase multimedia elements, such as animations and video clips on CD-ROM or download them free from certain Web sites. Before downloading, be sure no hidden restrictions or fees apply.

Artist/Graphic Designer

As a **Web artist/graphic designer**, you create original art such as logos or stylized type, and frequently the overall design concept for a Web site, including the way it looks and feels. You also may prepare photographs and other graphic elements and redesign print publications for the Web environment. In the workforce, this highly creative role demands experience with high-end illustration and image editing software, such as Adobe Illustrator and Photoshop, as well as specialty hardware, such as scanners and digital cameras. Chapter 5 discusses graphics and type in detail.

Web Page Designer

As a **Web page designer**, your primary role is to convert text into HTML documents. Your responsibilities also may include graphic design and Web site setup and maintenance. To be a marketable Web page designer, you must communicate effectively, know HTML thoroughly, and have graphic design talent and some programming skills beyond HTML. This role requires a solid understanding of how Web pages and browsers interact.

Web Programmer

A **Web programmer** must be highly skilled in advanced programming languages, such as Practical Extraction and Report Language (Perl), Java, JavaScript, and Virtual Reality Modeling Language (VRML). These languages are used to create extremely interactive and dynamic Web pages, as well as handle form data. As corporate reliance on databases continues to expand, a Web programmer today additionally needs to know how to integrate databases successfully with the Internet and intranets.

Webmaster

A **Webmaster's** responsibilities vary dramatically, depending primarily on the staffing and other resources devoted to developing a Web site. If working independently, the Webmaster assumes all the roles. In an organizational or business setting, the Webmaster might oversee a Web development team comprised of a writer/editor, artist/graphic designer, multimedia developer, Web page designer, and Web programmer. A corporate Webmaster often assumes the responsibilities for both the Internet and an intranet. A Webmaster, therefore, must have a broad range of skills and knowledge, including familiarity with databases, HTML, and other programming languages, content development, creative design, marketing, and growth and maintenance of the hardware connecting computers and users.

CHAPTER SUMMARY

The Internet is the most popular and fastest growing area in computing today. The Internet is a worldwide collection of neworks each of which is composed of a collection of smaller networks.

The World Wide Web, the highly visual, dynamic, and interactive segment of the Internet, dramatically changed the communication, education, entertainment, and business practices of millions of people worldwide. To access a Web page, enter its unique address, called a Uniform Resource Locator (URL) in the browser's address bar or location field.

Alternatives to traditional computer-based access include set-top boxes, such as WebTV, and handheld computers. To locate information on the Web, search engines and online directories are popular choices.

Users access Web sites through the public switched telephone network (PTSN). Data, instructions, and information can be sent over the telephone network using dial-up lines or dedicated lines. Internet service providers and online service providers provide temporary Internet connections to individials or companies.

The types of Web sites on the WWW can be categorized as personal, organization/topical, or commercial. Depending on resources, developing a Web site may be assigned to a single person, two or three people, or a large Web development team. Although actual titles may vary and responsibilities overlap, the primary Web design roles include writer/editor, multimedia developer, artist/graphic designer, Web page designer, Web programmer, and Webmaster. Those responsible for designing a Web site may utilize basic HTML, Web authoring packages, Office applications, or advanced languages and technologies. Successful Web site creation requires developing a site that stands out, identifying the audience, and assessing new Web technologies before incorporating them.

KEY TERMS

Instructions: Use the following terms from this chapter as a study review.

Adobe Go Live (1.26)
asymmetrical digital subscriber line
    (ADSL) (1.8)
bits per second (bps) (1.7)
browser (1.10)
cable television (CATV) lines (1.8)
CGI program (1.23)
commercial Web sites (1.19
common gateway interface (CGI) (1.23)
dedicated line (1.7)
dial-up line (1.6)
digital subscriber line (DSL) (1.8)
directories (1.12)
domain name (1.10)
Dynamic HTML (DHTML) (1.24)
electronic commerce (e-commerce) (1.17)
Extensible Markup Language (XML) (1.24)
gigabits per second (Gbps) (1.7)
handheld computers (1.11)
home page (1.5)
hyperlink (1.4)
Hypertext Markup Language (HTML) (1.22)
Hypertext Transfer Protocol (HTTP) (1.10)
Integrated Services Digital Network
    (ISDN) (1.7)
Internet (1.2)
Internet backbone (1.3)
Internet service provider (ISP) (1.8)
intranet (1.20)
IP address (1.10)
JavaScript (1.23)
keyword (1.12)
kilobits per second (Kbps) (1.7)
link (1.4)
Macromedia Dreamweaver (1.26)
Macromedia Flash (1.26)
markups (1.22)
megabits per second (Mbps) (1.7)
meta tags (1.13)
Microsoft FrontPage (1.25)
multimedia (1.5)
multimedia developer (1.26)
multiplexing (1.7)

national ISP (1.8)
network (1.2)
online service provider (OSP) (1.8)
organization Web site (1.18)
Personal Digital Assistant (PDA) (1.11)
point of presence (POP) (1.8)
portals (1.13)
Practical Extraction and Reporting Language
    (Perl) (1.24)
protocol (1.10)
public switched telephone network
    (PSTN) (1.6)
regional ISP (1.8)
robots (1.13)
scripting languages (1.23)
search engines (1.12)
short programs (1.23)
spiders (1.13)
splash page (1.5)
surfing the Web (1.5)
T1 line (1.8)
T3 line (1.8)
T-carrier line (1.8)
tags (1.22)
the last mile (1.3)
topical Web site (1.(18)
transfer rate (1.7)
Uniform Resource Locator (URL) (1.10)
Visual Basic Scripting Edition (VBScript)
    (1.23)
Web artist/graphic designer (1.27)
Web browser (1.10)
Web page (1.5)
Web page designer (1.27)
Web page writer/editor (1.26)
Web programmer (1.27)
Web site (1.5)
Webmaster (1.27)
WebTV (1.11)
Wireless Markup Language (WML) (1.25
wireless service provider (WSP) (1.9)
World Wide Web (WWW or Web) (1.5)
World Wide Web Consortium (W3C) (1.22)

CHECKPOINT Matching

Instructions: Match each term with the best description.

_____ 1. Web page

_____ 2. hyperlink

_____ 3. browser

_____ 4. Web site

_____ 5. home page

_____ 6. HTML

_____ 7. Internet service provider (ISP)

_____ 8. online service provider (OSP)

_____ 9. Uniform Resource Locator (URL)

_____ 10. search engines

_____ 11. e-commerce

_____ 12. HTTP

a. The communications standard used to transmit data on the Web.

b. A format language used to create Web pages.

c. A business that supplies Internet access but also has many member-only features that offer a variety of special content and services.

d. A Web page's unique address.

e. The initial Web page of a Web site that provides information about the Web site's purpose and content.

f. The conducting of business activities online including shopping, investing, and any other venture that uses electronic money or electronic data interchange.

g. Software programs that find Web sites and Web pages.

h. A business that has a permanent Internet connection and provides temporary connections to individuals and companies free or for a fee.

i. A specifically formatted electronic document that stores text, graphics, and other information on a Web site.

j. A specific software program that allows for the display of Web pages.

k. A special software pointer that points to the location of the computer on which specific information is stored and to the information itself.

l. A collection of linked Web pages, which typically starts with a home page.

CHECKPOINT Fill in the Blanks

Instructions: Fill in the blank(s) with the appropriate answer.

1. To create Web site databases, search services often use _____, _____, or _____.

2. Millions of people rely on _____ to buy products or services and conduct financial transactions on the Web.

3. The _____ sets the standard for HTML and HTTP.

4. _____ uses a television set as a monitor to allow access to the Internet.

5. On the Web, a hyperlink can be a _____, _____, or _____.

6. Yahoo!, AltaVista, Excite, and Lycos are _____ Web sites.

7. A popular type of handheld computer for managing personal information and accessing the Internet is a _____.

8. Data, instructions, and information can be sent over the telephone network using _____ lines or _____ lines.

9. A(n) _____ is the speed at which a line carries data or information.

10. Two widely used browsers today are _____ and _____.

CHECKPOINT Multiple Choice

Instructions: Select the letter of the correct answer for each question.

1. The communication standard to transmit data on the World Wide Web is _____.
   a. HTML
   b. HTTP
   c. URL
   d. DSL

2. A lead-in Web page, often containing multimedia and designed to catch the user's attention is called a _____ page.
   a. home
   b. Web
   c. splash
   d. table of contents

3. _____ is replacing telephone lines over the last mile, which significantly improves access to information on the Internet.
   a. HTTP
   b. The Internet backbone
   c. Cable
   d. The public switched telephone network (PSTN)

4. Short programs that can be included in an HTML document to add multimedia, animation, interactive forms, and scrolling text are called _____.

    a.   scripts and applets

    b.   PDAs and applets

    c.   servlets and ActiveX controls

    d.   both a and c

5. A language utilized to design Web pages specifically for handheld computers, PDAs, cellular telephones, and pagers is _____.

    a.   XML

    b.   HTML

    c.   WML

    d.   WAP

6. Tags added to a Web page that several search engines use to find new Web pages are called _____.

    a.   meta tags

    b.   robots

    c.   portals

    d.   spiders

7. To write a CGI program, use _____.

    a.   Extensible Markup Language

    b.   common gateway interface

    c.   a scripting language

    d.   Hypertext Markup Language

8. A private network for company employees often containing policies and procedures and database access is a(n):

    a.   Internet

    b.   ISDN

    c.   intranet

    d.   extranet

9. The type of address that most often appears in a URL on the Web is the _____.

    a.   IP address

    b.   protocol

    c.   domain name

    d.   both a and c

10. Text or graphics that link to other Web pages or to specific locations on the current Web page are called _____.

    a.   hyperlinks

    b.   PDAs

    c.   links

    d.   both a and c

CHECKPOINT Short Answer

Instructions: Write a brief answer to each question.

1. Describe the major features of the Internet and the World Wide Web.

2. Explain the differences between (a) dial-up and dedicated lines and (b) Internet service providers (ISPs) and online service providers (OSPs).

3. Describe the four main areas on which the Internet and the Web have had a significant impact.

4. Differentiate among personal, organization/topical, and commercial Web sites.

5. Explain three major areas to research before you begin to plan and create a Web site.

6. Describe briefly the following tools for creating Web pages and Web sites: HTML; scripts, applets, servlets, and ActiveX controls; scripting languages; XML; WML; Web authoring packages; and Microsoft Office applications.

7. Identify the primary responsibilities associated with each of the following Web design roles: writer/editor, multimedia developer, artist/graphic designer, Web page designer, Web programmer, and Webmaster.

AT ISSUE

Instructions: Write a brief essay in response to the following issues. Be prepared to discuss your findings in class. Use the Web as your research tool. For each issue, identify one URL utilized as a research source.

1. The vast majority of Web sites are created by responsible individuals and organizations for positive, legitimate purposes. Web sites that are inappropriate for children or are offensive to people of various ages, however, do exist. Such Web sites may contain graphic photos or video and distasteful language. Given that the Web is an open forum for expression and that the Constitution of the United States guarantees freedom of speech, what, if any, restrictions should be placed on these Web sites? Explain why the restrictions would or would not be justified, and who should make the decision as to which Web sites should be restricted.

2. Every day, millions of people purchase airline tickets, groceries, cars, clothing, gifts, and much more via e-commerce. Still, many people are hesitant to join the ranks of online shoppers. Discuss the advantages of online shopping and the reasons for some people's hesitancy. Identify what online businesses and credit card companies are doing and what could be done to encourage online shopping. Predict the future of e-commerce over the next five years, including what additional goods and services you would like to see available.

HANDS ON

Instructions: Complete the following exercises.

1. Surf the Web and identify a personal, organization/topical, and commercial Web site that impress you in a positive manner. Print the home page of each Web site, identifying the URL. Discuss what impressed you about the Web sites by responding to the following:

    a.   Describe the design elements.

    b.   Identify the information of value you found explaining how it was presented — for example, as photos, videos, text, or sound.

    c.   Rate the ease of finding the information.

    d.   Explain what would encourage you to make a return visit to each Web site.

2. Access the Web and utilize first a search engine and then an online directory to locate Web sites related to Web design. List the URLs of five Web sites you review. Identify what you consider to be the most informative Web design Web site, the reasons you believe the Web site was enlightening, and any useful resources provided.

CHAPTER 2
An Overview of Web Publishing

OBJECTIVES

After completing this chapter you will be able to:

- Explain the advantages of Web publishing

- Demonstrate timeliness in Web pages

- Compare Web publishing to print publishing

- Understand how to use basic design principles to create successful Web pages and Web sites

- Understand the effects of balance and proximity of Web page elements

- Describe the importance of contrast and focus on a Web page

- Recognize the impact of unity within a Web site

- Explain and apply specific attributes for writing effective Web content

- Recognize the characteristics of easily read Web pages

- Apply the inverted pyramid style of writing

- Differentiate between paragraph format and chunked format

- Describe the impact of color on Web pages

- Differentiate among warm colors, complementary colors, and cool colors

- Understand RGB color

- Define the technical issues about which a Web designer should be aware

- Discuss the legal and ethical issues in Web site development

- Recognize that some visitors to Web sites have special needs

- Describe the resources needed to create a Web site

INTRODUCTION

Chapter 1 introduced you to the exciting Web environment. In this chapter, you will discover the advantages of Web publishing and the fundamental design techniques necessary to publish successfully. Methods for meeting the Web audience's unique needs regarding textual content also will be discussed, as will the effective management of color and other important Web-related issues.

ADVANTAGES OF WEB PUBLISHING

Print is convenient. You can tuck a newspaper, magazine, or book under your arm, take it to your favorite reading place — an overstuffed chair, a backyard swing, or a park bench — and enjoy. Because print has been around a long time, it also is a very comfortable, trusted method of communication. Yet, Web publishing offers distinct advantages over print. These advantages include timeliness; interactivity; reduced production costs; and economical, rapid distribution.

Timeliness

Compared with print, timely content can be delivered more efficiently and economically via Web publishing. A print publication's content significantly determines how long the publication will be accurate, current, and valuable. The same is true for a Web publication. In fact, timely content on a Web site is crucial. Visitors look for Web sites with current and accurate information presented in a fresh, appealing manner. If they are unable to find it on your Web site, they are likely to leave and may not return. Popular, high-traffic Web sites that provide weather, news, stock market quotes, and other relevant topics are updated continuously; many on a daily basis or even more often as required (Figure 2-1). A Web site that you design might not need such frequent updating, but to ensure your success, you must supply changing and timely material.

Keeping a Web page or Web site up to date is not the lengthy or costly process involved with revising and reprinting a print publication. For example, suppose the chief executive officer (CEO) of your company suddenly resigned, and the senior vice president will assume the position.

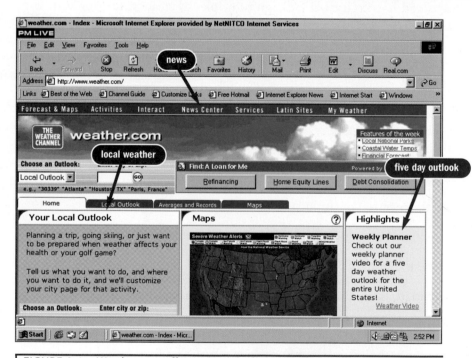

FIGURE 2-1   Weather.com offers visitors the latest weather conditions, maps, weather-related news and other timely, useful information.

The board of directors wants to assure customers that no interruption in service will occur. In minutes, from your hard drive you could open the source file of a currently published Web page and insert a press release explaining the change in management, along with a photograph of the new CEO. You then could upload the revised Web page from your computer to the host server using an FTP graphic interface program such as WS_FTP. **File Transfer Protocol (FTP)** is the common method for transferring files on the Internet.

By publishing news of the management change on the Web, you could reassure customers long before any print publication could be prepared and distributed. To ensure that you always consider timeliness in Web publishing, keep in mind the following Web Design Tip:

Web Design Tip
Plan to provide changing, timely content once your Web site is up and running.

Interactivity

Unlike print, a Web page offers the unique opportunity to interact with your audience. To encourage interactivity with your audience, make it convenient and easy. A simple way to ask your visitors questions and get information is to place an e-mail link to you on your Web site. Through e-mail, you can gather feedback about your Web site, develop a profile of your visitors, identify potential customers, or provide customer support (Figure 2-2). Once a visitor's e-mail address has been identified, you can follow up with additional e-mail, electronic newsletters, or print pieces. Use follow-up e-mail purposely and sparingly. Recipients often are overwhelmed by the number of e-mails sent to them. Make sure your e-mail is personal and targeted to your recipients' needs and interests so they will not regard it as **spam**, or junk, e-mail and delete it without even looking at it.

WEB INFO
For more information about adding interactivity to your Web pages, visit the Web Design Chapter 2 Web Info page (scsite.com/web/ch2/webinfo.htm) and then click Interactivity.

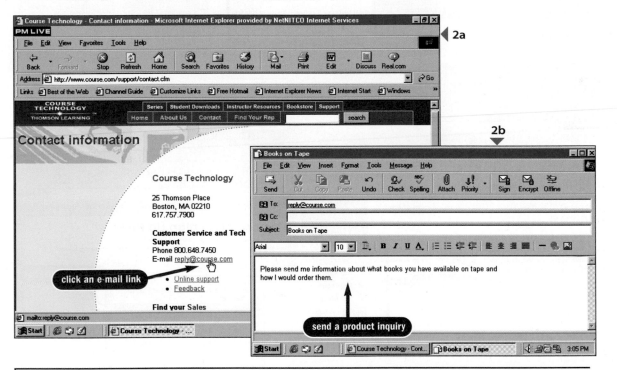

FIGURE 2-2   The e-mail link on this Web site allows potential customers to submit product inquiries.

A second popular method to encourage visitor interactivity is via forms. **Forms** are structured Web documents in which information can be typed or options selected. Common form elements include text boxes, check boxes, option buttons, and drop-down list boxes (Figure 2-3 on the next page). You can create forms with a text editor or a Web authoring package. After completing the form, your visitor needs only to click the Submit button to send the information to you. Forms frequently are utilized to quickly and easily order products, conduct surveys, and register for events. Recall that Chapter 1 identified other technologies that are required for forms to function and for the information to be processed.

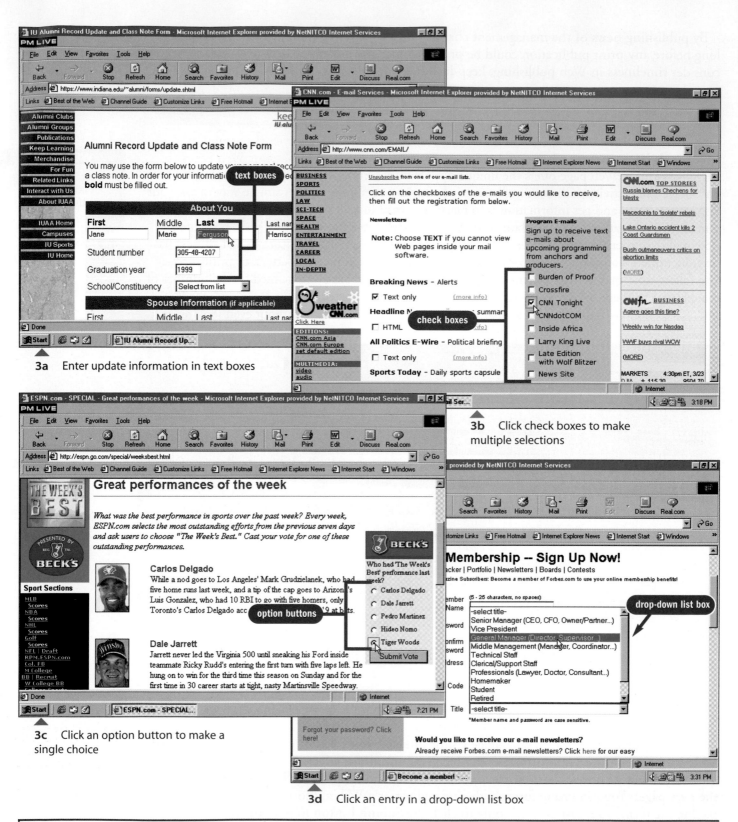

3a Enter update information in text boxes

3b Click check boxes to make multiple selections

3c Click an option button to make a single choice

3d Click an entry in a drop-down list box

FIGURE 2-3 Various applications of common form elements.

Incorporating interactivity into your Web site can be summarized in the following Web Design Tip:

Web Design Tip

Build into your Web pages simple and convenient ways for visitors to interact with you.

Reduced Production Costs

Compared with print, Web publishing is more cost effective. In the print environment, finances limit the extent to which you can design publications. For example, as a print designer, to stay within a budget, you may have to opt for a two-color, rather than a four-color, brochure, reduce the number and size of photographs, or eliminate design extras. It is unlikely that you would be instructed to design a great piece without giving cost any consideration.

On the Web, however, the situation is very different. As a designer of Web-deliverable materials, you can incorporate colorful designs, photographs, and text into your Web pages for considerably less cost. Some Web sites offer free downloads for animations, video, and sound clips, or you can purchase them on reasonably priced CD-ROMs.

Whenever you incorporate multimedia, you must consider file size, space limitations, and load time. You must prepare graphics and video and audio files for the best display and quality with quick load times. Find out from your Web site host the amount of space assigned your Web site and how much you will be charged if you utilize extra space. For example, a host may limit a Web site to 5 MB for a flat monthly fee, but add space for an additional cost. Take advantage of the economies of Web publishing as summarized in the following Web Design Tip:

Web Design Tip

When you design Web pages, do not limit your creativity to the print environment. Where appropriate, include color, photographs, animation, video, and sound clips in your Web design.

Economical, Rapid Distribution

Distributing information via the Web instead of print can be significantly faster and less expensive. For instance, imagine that as a volunteer for your community hospital, you are asked to publicize the upcoming health fair. Because you want to get the information out quickly to as many people as possible, you ask your mail distribution center what the cost would be to mail 1,000 brochures overnight or first-class. The answer might cause you either to ask for a bigger publicity budget or to look for additional or alternate ways to publicize the health fair.

The Web would be a very practical option for advertising the health fair. If the hospital has a Web site, you could publish the information as a special event and add it to the calendar. You also could query related Web sites, such as the community Chamber of Commerce or local health and fitness clubs, to publicize the health fair. E-mail also could be sent to last year's participants or other possible interested individuals or organizations. No charges would be involved, and the news about the event would be available almost immediately.

Remember that the Web can, with the same immediacy and cost, reach both global and local audiences. When you want to distribute information quickly, keep in mind the following Web Design Tip:

Web Design Tip

Consider using the Web when the need exists for economical and rapid distribution of information.

BASIC DESIGN PRINCIPLES

Print and Web publications both seek to convey a powerful message and leave a distinct impression. Successful publications from both media that accomplish these objectives combine creativity with the basic design principles of balance and proximity, contrast and focus, and unity. The following sections discuss how these principles apply specifically to Web pages.

WEB INFO

For more information about the basic design principles used for creating Web pages, visit the Web Design Chapter 2 Web Info page (scsite.com/web/ch2/webinfo.htm) and then click Design Principles.

Balance and Proximity

Arrange Web elements such as photographs, illustrations, and text **symmetrically**, which is centered or balanced, on a Web page or Web site to suggest a conservative, safe, and peaceful atmosphere. Avoid creating Web pages with too much symmetry, however. Such excess will produce boring, uninteresting Web pages. To create an intense, energetic mood, position your Web elements **asymmetrically**, or off balance. The content and purpose of your Web site should determine the mood. Figure 2-4 illustrates elements positioned symmetrically and asymmetrically and the resulting moods.

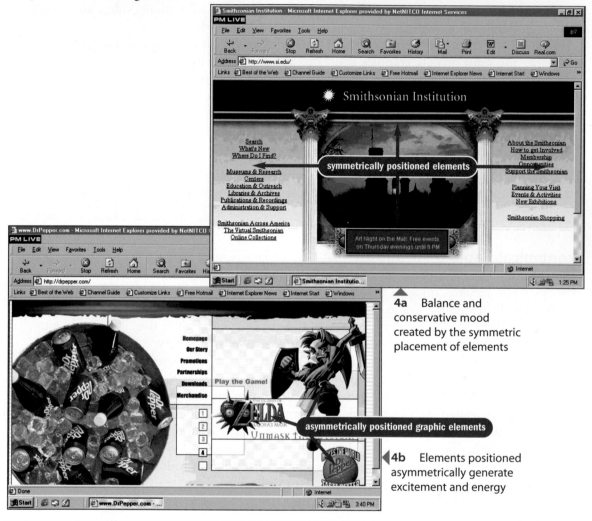

4a Balance and conservative mood created by the symmetric placement of elements

4b Elements positioned asymmetrically generate excitement and energy

FIGURE 2-4   By positioning elements symmetrically or asymmetrically on Web pages, you can create very different moods.

WEB INFO

For more information about white space on Web pages, visit the Web Design Chapter 2 Web Info page (scsite.com/web/ch2/webinfo.htm) and then click White Space.

Proximity, or closeness, is strongly associated with balance. Place elements that have a relationship close to each other. For example, position a caption near a photo, a company name with its mission statement, and headlines and subheads with body copy. Proximity visually connects elements that have a logical relationship, making your Web pages more organized (Figure 2-5). **White space**, the empty space around text and graphics, also can define proximity and help organize Web page elements, eliminate clutter, and make content more readable (Figure 2-6). You can create white space by adding line breaks, paragraph returns, paragraph indents, and space around tables and images. Keep in mind the following Web Design Tip:

Web Design Tip

Utilize proximity and white space to create effective organized Web pages.

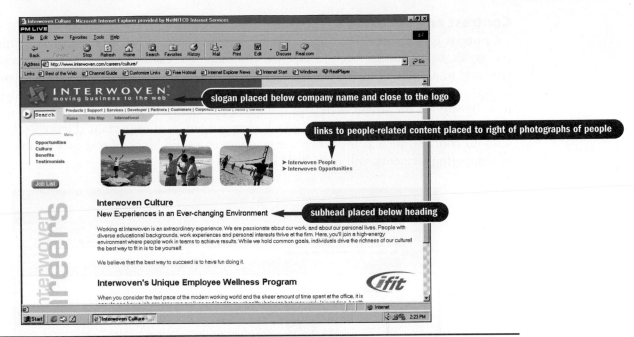

FIGURE 2-5   Elements that have a relationship should be placed close to each other.

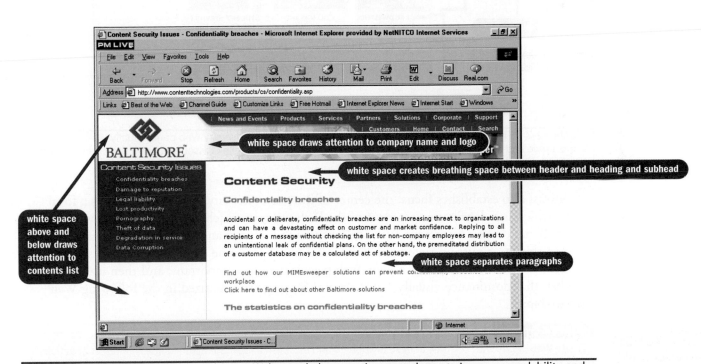

FIGURE 2-6   White space on the Baltimore Web page helps organize page elements, increases readability, and draws attention to certain elements.

Contrast and Focus

Contrast is a mix of elements to stimulate attention. You can achieve contrast by means of text styles, color choices, size of elements, and more. For example, a company name set in larger type and in a different font sets it apart from smaller subheads and body text. Similarly, a black background with purple text draws more attention than a cream background with light yellow text. By varying the size of Web page elements, you can establish a visual hierarchy of information that will show your visitors which elements are most important (Figure 2-7). Pages without contrast, such as those that are made up of a solid block of text or a jumble of competing elements, will draw little interest.

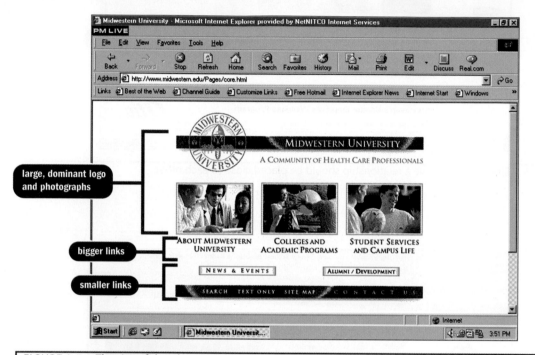

FIGURE 2-7 The size of the photos and logo on this Midwestern University Web page visually illustrate their importance and immediately draw attention. The significance of three links associated with the photos over the smaller links below is very clear.

Contrast also establishes **focus**, the center of interest or activity. A Web page needs a **focal point**, which is a dominating segment of the Web page, to which visitors' attention will be drawn. What do you want your Web site's visitors to focus on and to remember — a company name, a slogan or mission statement, a powerful photo, or some combination of these? Determine first what element on your Web page is the most important, and then use contrast to establish that dominance visually. Contrast and focus are summarized in the following Web Design Tip:

> **Web Design Tip**
> Create Web pages with contrast to elicit awareness and establish a focal point, the center of interest or activity.

Unity

Web pages and Web sites need **unity**, or a sense of oneness or belonging, to create and maintain a visual identity. Especially important to businesses and organizations, visual identity must be constant, not only throughout a Web site, but also with print publications, such as brochures, business cards, and letterheads. You can create unity on your Web site with consistency and repetition as illustrated in Figure 2-8.

WEB INFO

For more information about effectively utilizing consistency and repetition on Web pages, visit the Web Design Chapter 2 Web Info page (scsite.com/web/ch2/webinfo.htm) and then click Consistency.

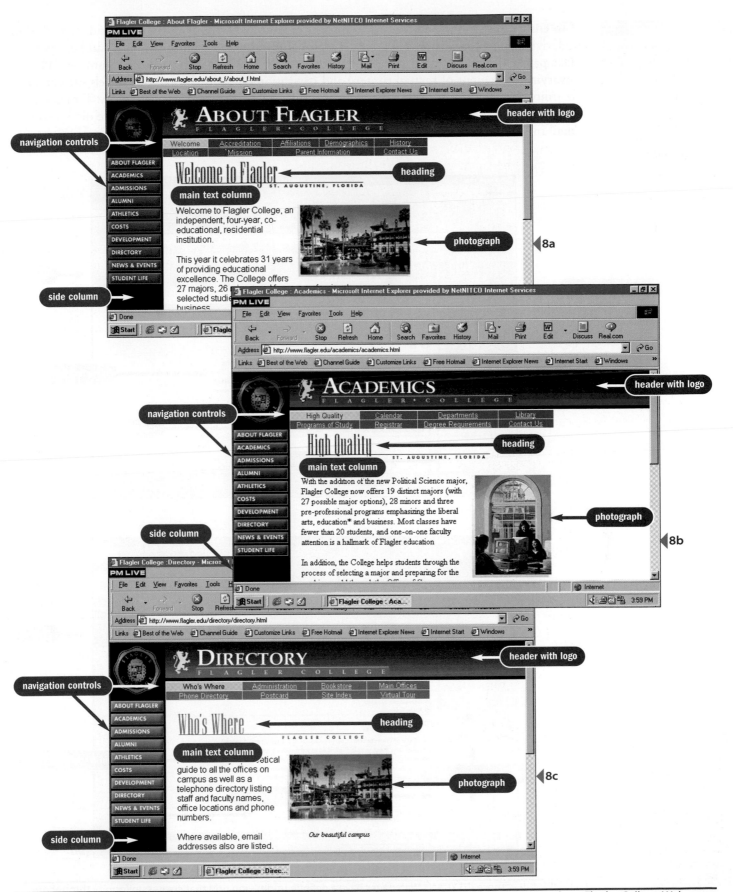

FIGURE 2-8   A sense of unity is created by means of consistent placement of elements and repetition on these Flagler College Web pages.

WEB INFO

For more information about using grids for placing page elements consistently, visit the Web Design Chapter 2 Web Info page (scsite.com/web/ch2/webinfo.htm) and then click Grid.

To ensure a uniform look for the Web pages in your Web site, you can use a grid. A **grid** is an underlying layout structure that arranges a page into rows and columns. A grid can help you place page elements consistently, as shown in the CITYBANK Web pages in Figure 2-9. The unvarying placement of textual content and navigation controls throughout a Web site can create unity and allow your visitors to locate information quickly and navigate easily. Tables and cascading style sheets (CSS), two additional methods for achieving continuity, are discussed in detail in later chapters.

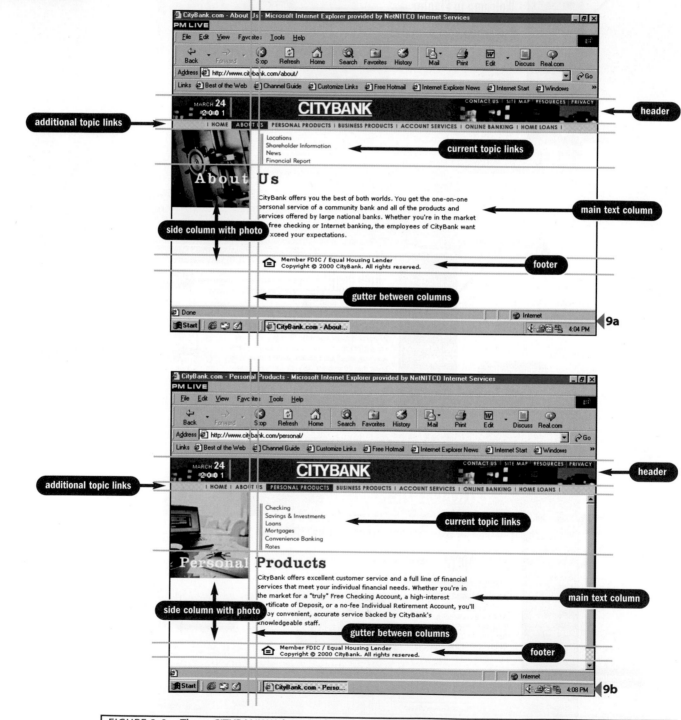

FIGURE 2-9   These CITYBANK Web pages have a definite underlying grid that creates uniformity throughout the Web site.

Alignment is the arrangement of objects in fixed or predetermined positions, rows, or columns. Mixing the alignment of elements causes Web pages to look inconsistent. When the elements on a Web page are aligned horizontally, they are arranged consistently to the left, right, or centered. Choose one method of alignment and use it regularly to ensure your Web pages have a common, structured look. Align elements vertically on your Web pages to assist readability and ensure an organized appearance (Figure 2-10).

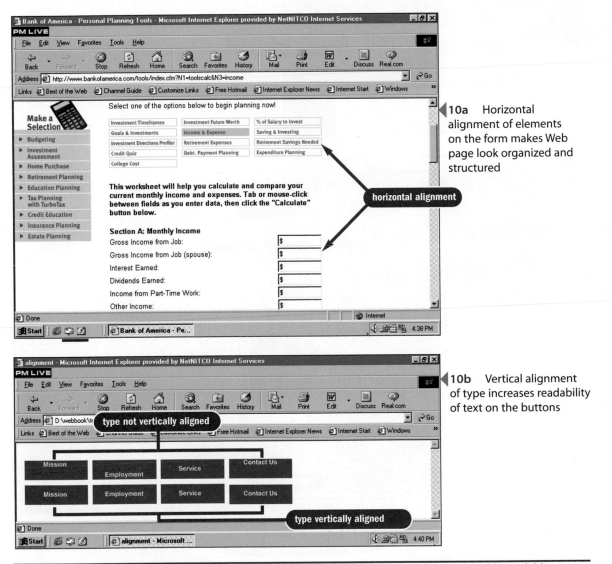

10a Horizontal alignment of elements on the form makes Web page look organized and structured

10b Vertical alignment of type increases readability of text on the buttons

FIGURE 2-10   Web pages with consistent alignment of elements look organized and are highly readable.

To further unify your Web site, use a common graphic theme and color scheme on all Web pages. The Coca-Cola Web site (shown in Figure 2-11 on the next page), for example, makes full use of the company's instantly recognizable logo, an appealing, consistent layout, and the accent color red against a beige background. This Web site builds on the company's already established visual identity portrayed on billboards and television and in newspaper and magazine advertisements. To establish and maintain a visual identity, create unity within your Web site by following this Web Design Tip:

Web Design Tip

Generate a sense of unity or oneness within your Web site by utilizing a grid, consistent alignment, a common graphic theme, and a common color theme.

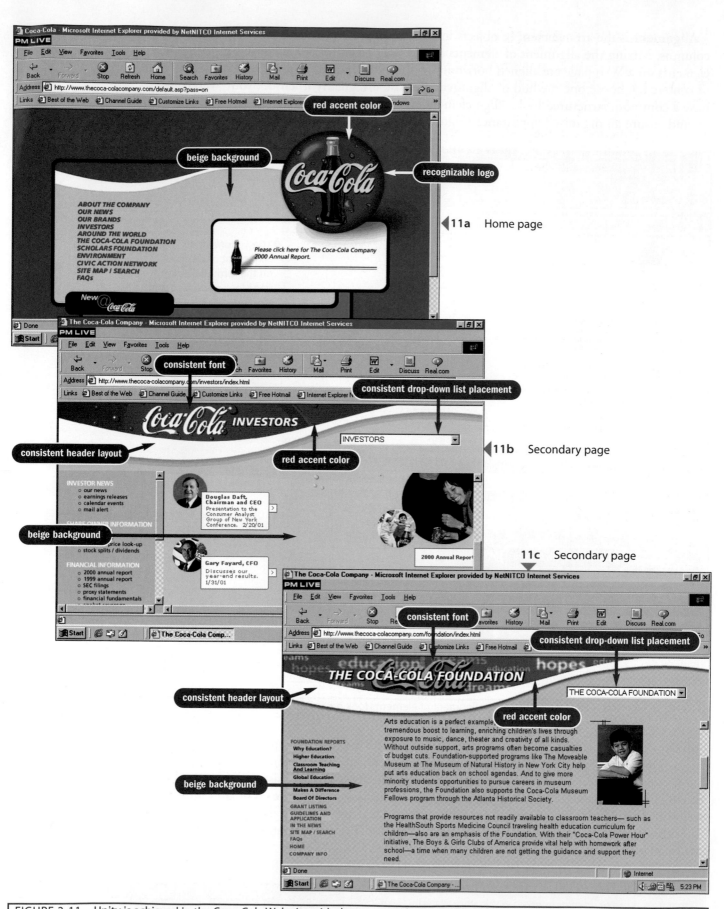

FIGURE 2-11 Unity is achieved in the Coca-Cola Web site with the company logo, consistent layout, and the attractive color scheme.

WRITING FOR THE WEB

People resort to the Web for a variety of reasons and circumstances. A student may surf the Web late at night after attending classes all day. A mother might find relaxation in sitting at her computer viewing Web sites after her toddler goes down for a nap. An executive might log on to the Web on his or her notebook computer on a business trip. Whether novice, expert, or somewhere in between in their level of expertise, members of the Web audience typically are looking for useful information that is accurate, easily read, understandable, and comprehensive in a concise package, and they want it fast to accommodate their limited time.

WEB INFO

For a list of guidelines about writing content for the Web, visit the Web Design Chapter 2 Web Info page (scsite.com/web/ch2/webinfo.htm) and then click Writing for the Web.

Accurate

When collecting content for your Web site, confirm its accuracy with reliable sources. Refer to respected subject experts, professional organizations, trade journals, and other resources with a proven track record. Once published, keep the content on your Web site timely. Information that does not appear current may be inaccurate, or be perceived as inaccurate. To demonstrate timeliness, indicate the last reviewed date on your Web pages, even if the content is not revised. Because visitors frequently print Web pages, include the last reviewed date to indicate the most current printout.

Typographical and spelling errors can embarrass you and challenge your Web site's credibility. If you publish your Web pages with such errors, your visitors might question how closely you checked your content and how committed you are to your purpose if you did not take the time to prevent these errors. To avoid these types of errors, write the text content for your Web pages in a word processing program first so that you can spell and grammar check. Proofread it, and then ask at least one other person to review it before you convert the text into a Web-ready document.

The following Web Design Tips will help you create accurate Web pages:

Web Design Tip

Establish credibility for your Web site by providing accurate and verifiable content. Include the last reviewed date to show timeliness.

Web Design Tip

Spell check and grammar check the textual portion of your Web site. After completing Web pages, set them aside for a day before proofreading for accuracy and completeness. Always have another person proofread your Web pages.

Easily Read

Members of the Web audience often scan Web pages quickly rather than taking the time to read every word. Make the information on your Web pages easy to scan by following these guidelines.

- Use headings, subheads, lists, and highlighted sections frequently (Figure 2-12). If you colorize these elements to draw attention, make sure the colors do not suggest a hyperlink. Blue is the default color for an active link, while purple is the default color for a visited link. Also, avoid underlining these elements, which would further suggest a hyperlink. Your visitors may become frustrated or annoyed if they repeatedly click such an element and nothing happens.

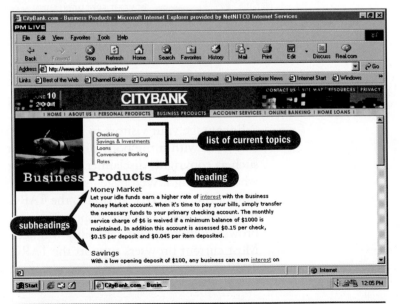

FIGURE 2-12   The list of current topic links, heading, and subheadings on this CITYBANK Web page make it easy to scan.

- Begin each paragraph with a topic sentence that summarizes the general idea of the whole paragraph. A visitor who scans only the first sentence of the paragraphs still will get the overall picture of your Web page's purpose.

To assist readability:

- Use type that is big enough to be read by most people, but not so large that it conveys an unsophisticated or child-like impression. The recommended range for type size is 10 to 14 point.
- Do not set type in all uppercase because it slows down reading.
- As a general rule for short blocks of text, headings, subheads, lists, and type on buttons, use sans serif type. **Sans serif type** is a geometric, straightforward looking type, having no serifs on its characters. The characters of **serif type** have **serifs**, which are short lines or ornaments that project from the primary stroke of a character. Helvetica, a sans serif type, and Times New Roman, a serif type, are illustrated in Figure 2-13.
- Enhance legibility of the type by choosing backgrounds that either are plain or subtle.

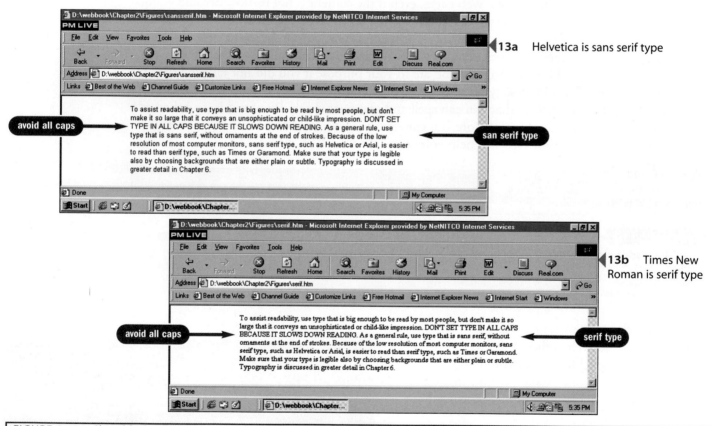

FIGURE 2-13   Short blocks of text set in sans serif type generally is easier to read than serif type on monitors.

Encourage your visitors to focus on the information on your Web page. Include only necessary links within the body of your content, and place any supplementary, non-navigational links such as copyright, disclaimer, or privacy statement at the bottom of the Web page. In addition, when creating a Web page using HTML or a Web authoring package, you can utilize one function of the TARGET attribute, the TARGET tag. If you add the **TARGET tag** to a hyperlink, the linked Web page will display in a new browser window rather than displaying in the current browser window. This capability will keep your visitor in visual contact with your Web site. Most current browsers support the TARGET attribute. Figure 2-14 shows how to insert the TARGET tag in an HTML document using a text editor, and a TARGET tag in action.

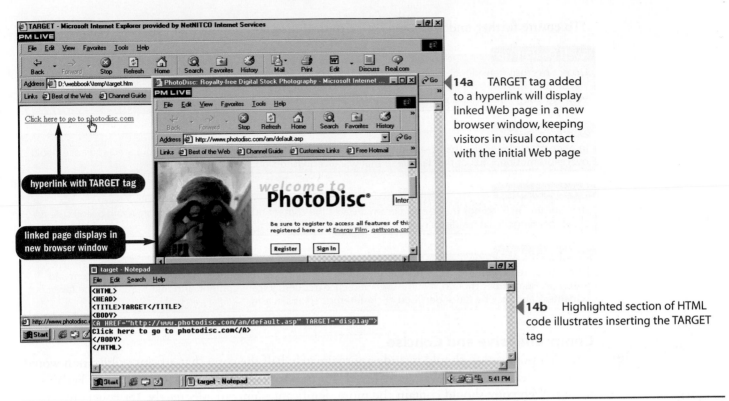

14a TARGET tag added to a hyperlink will display linked Web page in a new browser window, keeping visitors in visual contact with the initial Web page

14b Highlighted section of HTML code illustrates inserting the TARGET tag

FIGURE 2-14   The TARGET tag can be an effective means of maintaining contact with Web site visitors

The following Web Design Tips summarize how you can improve the readability of your Web site:

Web Design Tip

Encourage visitors to spend time on your Web site by providing Web pages that are easy to scan and easy to read.

Web Design Tip

Include only necessary links within the body of your content, and place supplementary, non-navigational links such as copyright, disclaimer, or privacy statements at the bottom of the Web page.

Understandable

So that visitors quickly will understand the general idea behind the content on a Web page, write your copy in an **inverted pyramid style** (Figure 2-15). This style places the conclusion first, followed by details, and then any background information.

Writing your Web content in inverted pyramid style quickly increases your visitors' understanding of your Web site's purpose and message. Inverted pyramid style resembles an upside-down triangle, with the summary or conclusion at the top and the background information at the base. The summary or the conclusion is called the **lead**, and the details are called the **body**. Inverted pyramid is a classic, time-honored newswriting style.

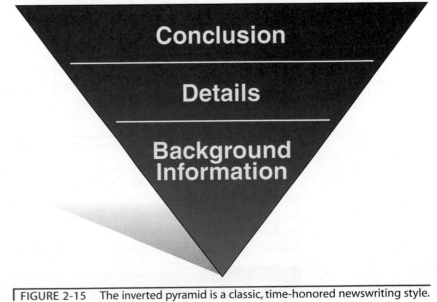

FIGURE 2-15   The inverted pyramid is a classic, time-honored newswriting style.

To ensure further understanding, practice the following Web Design Tips:

Web Design Tip

Do not overuse transitional words or phrases, such as similarly, as a result, or as stated previously. These transitions will have no significance to a visitor who is skimming the Web page's content or who has arrived at your Web page via clicking a link at another Web site.

Web Design Tip

In general, use language that is straightforward, contemporary, and geared toward an educated audience. Avoid overly promotional, full-of-fluff language that will divert visitors quickly.

Web Design Tip

Use wording in headings that clearly communicates the content of a Web page or section. Avoid overly cute or clever headings. Such headings typically confuse or annoy visitors.

Web Design Tip

Be cautious regarding the use of humor. Small doses of humor correctly interpreted can enliven content and entertain. Remember, though, that the Web audience frequently scans content, and that humor can be taken out of context and may be misunderstood or misinterpreted as sarcasm.

Comprehensive and Concise

A Web publication should include approximately half the copy that a print publication would contain. The majority of Web users prefer not to read long passages of text onscreen. For this reason, Web copy should contain the more significant points to adequately, yet concisely, cover the subject. By chunking information on your Web pages, visitors will be able to scan sections, each of which focuses on a specific topic. For example, consider the same information presented in Figure 2-16 in **paragraph format** and **chunked format**. Most visitors to a Web page prefer reading the chunked format.

Paragraph Format

Lakeland College is one of North America's most prestigious liberal arts colleges, located in sunny California. Getting to t... easy. We are located just 25 miles north of Los Ar... visitors find the Pasadena Freeway the most conve... route to travel. The college is just three miles west... Lakeland College is well known throughout Nort... of distinguished fine arts, theatre, and radio and T... proud to offer more than 50 undergraduate and g... Our students enjoy the convenience of both our v... learning classes. Many of our current students and... many benefits of attending Lakeland College. The... benefits include Lakeland's award winning faculty... which often are lower than comparable institution... afforded our faculty, staff, and students by our we...

Chunked Format

Lakeland is a prestigious, North American liberal arts college.

Location
- 25 miles north of Los Angeles, California
- 3 miles west of the Pasadena Freeway

Academic Programs
- Distinguished fine arts, theatre, and radio/TV programs
- 50+ undergraduate and graduate degree offerings
- Weekend and distance learning classes

Benefits
- Award-winning faculty
- Competitive tuition rates
- Secure, well-lit campus

FIGURE 2-16   Paragraph format versus chunked format.

Consider using hyperlinks for any additional information, such as historical backgrounds or related topics. Lengthy text articles not intended to be read onscreen should appear in their entirety without any hyperlinks. This allows visitors to print the article or save it as a file. Be aware that various Web browsers may insert misplaced or unwanted Web page breaks. The following Web Design Tip emphasizes the importance of being concise with text:

Web Design Tip

Consider using the chunked format, rather than the paragraph format, to reduce long passages of text.

UNDERSTANDING COLOR ON THE WEB

Color can be a powerful design tool for creating attractive, effective Web sites. If color is used excessively, inappropriately, or without a basic comprehension of how monitors project color, however, the results can be unappealing and unproductive. To utilize this design tool effectively, you must understand the impact of color on the Web, and the color system by which monitors project color.

Impact of Color

Use color to enhance your Web site's purpose and personality. Choose an attractive color scheme for your Web site and make such elements as headlines, backgrounds, and navigation buttons reflect colors from this scheme. You can make good choices for your Web site without being a color theory expert simply by observing how others effectively use color and by becoming aware of commonly accepted principles and conventions. Visit different Web sites and note the impression colors and color combinations have on you. Did one Web site have a calming effect, while another made you feel tense or excited? The color wheel shown in Figure 2-17 illustrates the colors that generally can be categorized as warm or cool, along with the colors that complement others. **Warm colors** tend to be associated with activity and power, while **cool colors** suggest tranquility and peace.

WEB INFO

For more information about using the color wheel, visit the Web Design Chapter 2 Web Info page (scsite.com/web/ch2/webinfo.htm) and then click Color Wheel.

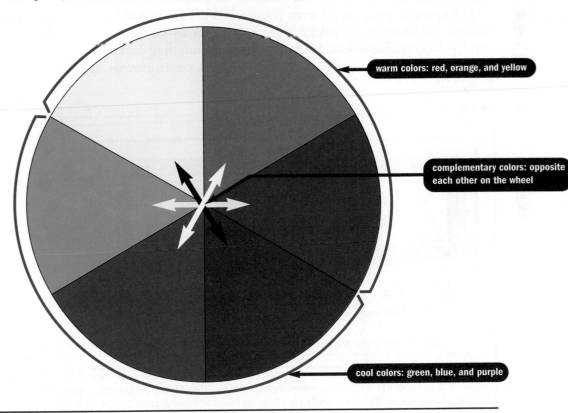

warm colors: red, orange, and yellow

complementary colors: opposite each other on the wheel

cool colors: green, blue, and purple

FIGURE 2-17   The color wheel.

Over time, certain colors have come to symbolize particular qualities. For example, white represents good or purity, black — bad, red — passion, and purple — royalty. Consider the qualities generally associated with different colors when selecting colors for your Web site. If you are targeting your Web site to a specific global audience, research any color associations for that country. Consider this Web Design Tip when choosing colors for your Web pages:

Web Design Tip

Knowing how people perceive colors helps you emphasize parts of a Web page. Warmer colors (red and orange) tend to reach toward the reader. Cooler colors (blue, green, and violet) tend to pull away from the reader.

Choice of colors for your Web site is not restricted to the six colors in the color wheel. The following RGB color section discusses available options.

RGB Color

Color is projected from monitors using an **RGB system**, which combines channels of red, green, and blue light. The light from each channel can be emitted in various levels of intensity. These levels are called **values** and are measured from 0–255. When values from the channels are combined, different colors result. For example, combining values 205 (red), 102 (green), and 153 (blue) produces a dusty rose color.

Because each light channel can emit 256 levels of intensity, an RGB system can produce more than 16.7 million possible colors (256 red x 256 green x 256 blue = 16,777,216). The actual number of colors that a monitor will display depends upon the monitor's capability. For example, an 8-bit monitor can display 256 colors, a 16-bit monitor 65,536 colors, and a 24-bit monitor 16.7 million colors. A **bit** (binary digit) is the smallest unit of data a computer can store.

Most monitors support at least 8-bit color. Browsers on both PCs and MACs share 216 of the 256 colors. These 216 colors often are referred to as a **browser-safe palette**, or **Web palette**. If your graphics include colors in addition to the 216 colors, the browser will **dither**, or substitute, colors within its 216 choices that resemble the proposed color. Dithering can cause the illustrations to appear spotty and uneven (Figure 2-18). This does not apply to photographs. Being limited to a browser-safe palette is not an issue for 24-bit color monitors, because they can display 16.7 million colors. Many current Web authoring packages or graphics and illustration programs offer browser-safe palettes. You also can create browser-safe colors in many graphics programs.

WEB INFO

For more information about the browser-safe palette for using color in Web pages, visit the Web Design Chapter 2 Web Info page (scsite.com/web/ch2/webinfo.htm) and then click Browser-Safe Palette.

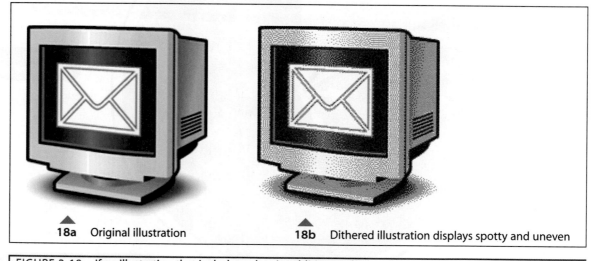

18a Original illustration   **18b** Dithered illustration displays spotty and uneven

FIGURE 2-18 If an illustration that includes colors in addition to the browser-safe palette is viewed with a monitor that supports 8-bit color, the browser will substitute colors that come close to the proposed colors. This substitution is called dithering, and may cause an illustration to appear spotty and uneven.

If you are using a text editor to create a Web page, you can specify a browser-safe color for a Web page element by entering the color's hexadecimal code, which is the equivalent of the color's RGB values. The hexadecimal system utilizes 16 symbols the letters A–F and digits 0–9 to signify values. For example, the hexadecimal code for the dusty rose color with the RGB values of 205:102:153 is FF6099. If you are using a Web authoring package with a browser-safe palette, you need not understand the hexadecimal system in detail; the software will determine and enter the hexadecimal code for you. Just be aware that expressing RGB color values in hexadecimal is the most accurate means to specify color in HTML.

To ensure that visitors to your Web site will see the colors you choose properly, keep in mind the following Web Design Tip:

Web Design Tip
Use a Web authoring package with a browser-safe palette to create your Web pages. If you use a text editor to create Web pages, make use of the color's hexadecimal code.

NOTEWORTHY ISSUES

Successful Web publishing further includes recognizing certain technical, legal and ethical, accessibility, and resource issues, as well as the design techniques that can effectively manage them.

Technical

Before creating your Web site, you should understand a few technical issues relating to good design. These issues include bandwidth, browser variables, and monitor resolution.

BANDWIDTH   **Bandwidth**, which is the quantity of data that can be transmitted in a specific time frame, is measured in bits per second (bps). If you have a 56 K (57,600 bps) modem, you would have double the bandwidth capability of a 28 K (28,800 bps) modem. This means that your 56 K modem will provide a quicker Internet connection. The speed of the user's and the ISP's or OSP's Internet connections, the amount of traffic on the Internet at a specific time, and the size of the Web page influence how quickly a Web page loads.

As a designer, you have control over only the file size of the Web page, including all its elements such as text, graphics, animations, and so on. Because a visitor generally will wait no longer than five to ten seconds for a Web page to load before moving on to another Web site, you need to make choices regarding which elements to include on your Web pages. For example, to speed load time you might choose fewer graphics; or you could provide **thumbnails,** which are miniature versions, that link to larger photos. In addition to making such choices, you must optimize elements for quick load time. For example, you can reduce file sizes using an image editing program such as **Adobe Photoshop.** To speed up the loading of Web pages, follow this Web Design Tip:

Web Design Tip
Create fast-loading Web pages by restricting the number and file size of Web page elements.

BROWSER VARIABLES   In Chapter 1, you learned that Netscape Navigator and Microsoft Internet Explorer are today's most widely used browsers. Navigator and Internet Explorer are **graphical display browsers,** which, along with text, can display graphics such as photographs, clip art, and animations. Most visitors will view your Web site with a graphical display browser. Keep in mind, however, that a few visitors may be using a **non-graphical display browser,** such as Lynx, which displays only text.

Some visitors may choose to turn graphics off when using a graphical display browser so they can avoid the load time for graphics. To provide a description of the graphic that is not visible to visitors who have graphics turned off, add an **ALT tag** to the <IMG SRC> ATTRIBUTE when you insert images into your Web pages using a text editor. A Web authoring package also will allow you to provide a description of a graphic for visitors who have graphics turned off (Figure 2-19 on the next page). Additionally, you may want to consider developing a **text-only version** of your Web site, which contains no graphic elements.

WEB INFO
For more information about how bandwidth influences the speed at which Web pages load, visit the Web Design Chapter 2 Web Info page (scsite.com/web/ch2/webinfo.htm) and then click Bandwidth.

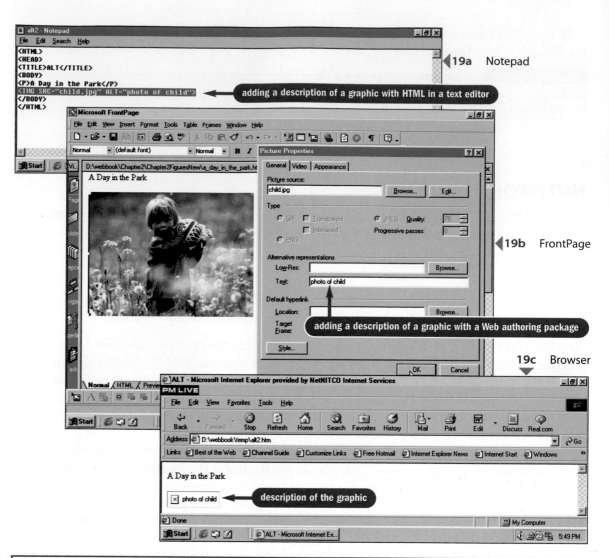

FIGURE 2-19 Via a text editor or a Web authoring package, you can provide a description of a graphic for visitors who have graphics turned off.

WEB INFO

For more information about monitor resolution, visit the Web Design Chapter 2 Web Info page (scsite.com/web/ch2/webinfo.htm) and then click Resolution.

MONITOR RESOLUTION A Web page displays differently depending on the resolution setting of the user's monitor. **Resolution** is the measure of a monitor's sharpness and clarity, related directly to the number of pixels it can display. A **pixel**, short for picture element, is a single point in an electronic image. On a PC monitor, 96 pixels per inch is the approximate default number. The pixels on a monitor are so close together that they appear connected.

Resolution is expressed as two numbers: the number of columns of pixels and the number of rows of pixels that a monitor can display. At higher resolutions, the number of pixels increases while their size decreases. Page elements appear large at low resolutions and decrease in size as resolution settings increase.

Common resolution settings that you can choose in the Control Panel are 640 x 480, 800 x 600, and 1024 x 768. You can access the Control Panel by clicking the Start button on the Windows taskbar at the bottom left of your screen, and then choosing Settings and Control Panel. Resolution settings represent the total number of pixels displayed on the screen. For some time, the recommended practice has been to design Web pages for the lowest common denominator setting of 640 x 480. Today, many argue that the lowest common denominator is 800 x 600 and that Web pages should be designed for this setting (Figure 2-20). The reality is that if you design Web pages to be viewed at higher resolutions, a user viewing the Web pages at 640 x 480 is forced to scroll to see the entire Web page.

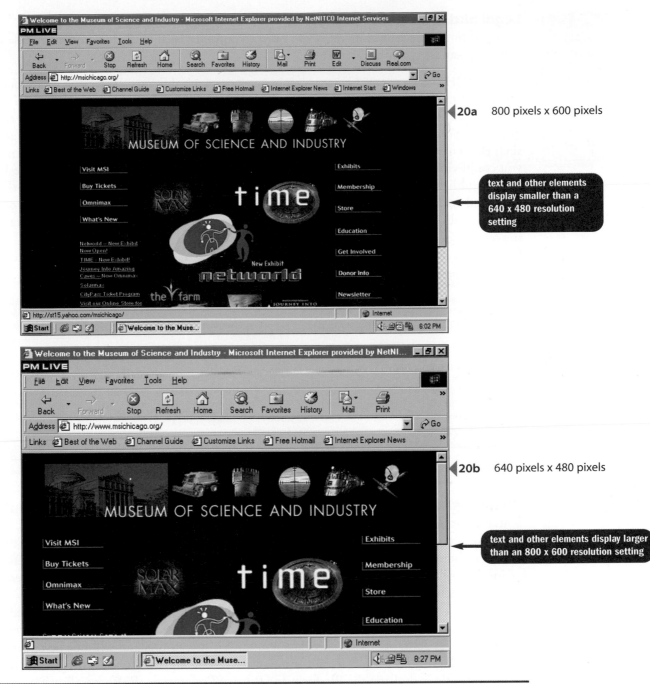

20a 800 pixels x 600 pixels

text and other elements display smaller than a 640 x 480 resolution setting

20b 640 pixels x 480 pixels

text and other elements display larger than an 800 x 600 resolution setting

FIGURE 2-20 Monitor resolution settings affect the display of a Web page.

As the lowest common denominator debate continues, some designers choose to continue to design for 640 x 480. Others design for the higher settings and indicate on their Web pages the best screen resolution with which to view the Web site. Still others create Web pages with relative table widths that adjust automatically to different monitor settings as explained in the following Web Design Tip:

Web Design Tip

To avoid screen resolution issues with tables, use percentages instead of pixels to define width. A table, for example, defined at 90% instead of a fixed width of 600 pixels will display on 90 percent of the monitor's screen area at various resolution settings.

WEB INFO

For more information about legal and ethical issues in Web publishing, visit the Web Design Chapter 2 Web Info page (scsite.com/web/ch2/webinfo.htm) and then click Legal and Ethical Issues.

Legal and Ethical

In addition to technical matters, you need to consider legal and ethical issues. These include copyright, and privacy and security.

COPYRIGHT   At some time, you might see a great graphic on a Web page that would be perfect for your Web site. To get it, all you need to do is right-click the picture and then click the Save Picture As command. Or perhaps you hear a great music file on a Web site and think the visitors to your Web pages would enjoy it, too. Simply because it is relatively easy to acquire such elements on the Web, however, does not make it right. By doing so without permission, you could violate the creator's **copyright**, or ownership of intellectual property. In the United States, published and unpublished works are protected by copyright, whether or not they are registered with the U.S. Copyright Office. In general, the law states that only the owner may print, distribute, or copy the property. To reuse the property, permission must be obtained from the owner. Copyright protection extends to the Web.

As a Web designer, you should practice the following Web Design Tips regarding copyright:

Web Design Tip

Make sure that your Web site elements, such as photos, illustrations, animations, video, and sound files are free of copyright restrictions by creating or buying your own. If you want to use elements belonging to someone else, obtain written permission to do so. Always assume that an element is copyrighted, even if no such evidence appears.

Web Design Tip

Protect your own works. If someone else is going to design and maintain your Web pages, obtain a written statement that you hold the copyright to the Web site's content. Put a copyright notice on your Web pages, which includes the word Copyright or the symbol ©, the publication year, and your name (for example, Copyright 2002 Trillium Consulting or © 2002 Trillium Consulting). You also may want to include an acceptable use policy, which tells visitors how they may or may not use your Web site's content. For example, you may permit visitors to print your text, but not allow them to download your graphics.

PRIVACY AND SECURITY   With the increased volume of e-commerce, personal and confidential information is transmitted regularly using Web sites. Social Security numbers, credit card and bank account numbers, addresses, and telephone numbers are a few examples of the sensitive data disclosed in Internet transactions. Two legitimate concerns of both consumers and businesses are about how the information is being used and the steps being taken to ensure that it remains secure and out of the hands of unauthorized parties.

Including a privacy statement that typically explains how any information submitted will be used is one way to ease the concerns of your Web site visitors. For example, the information will be used only to gather demographic data about Web site visitors and will not be released to any third party. Figure 2-21 illustrates a commercial Web site's privacy and security statement. The W3C currently is drafting the **Platform for Privacy Preferences (P3P)** specification. P3P will make it possible for browsers to determine automatically the privacy policies of a Web site and inform the user, or submit the information based on defined user preferences. P3P makes use of specific keywords and values.

To provide security for transmission of personal or confidential information and for credit card transactions, e-commerce Web sites use encryption. **Encryption** is a process that changes data so that it cannot be understood should someone unauthorized try to access it. Through **decryption**, a process which changes the data back to its original format, the information becomes understandable.

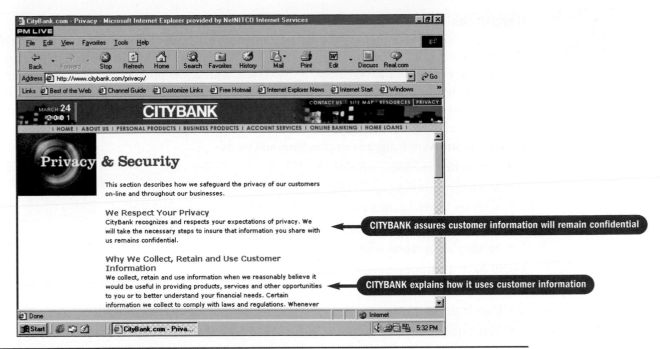

FIGURE 2-21   CITYBANK Web site's privacy and security statement.

Netscape created the protocol **Secure Sockets Layer (SSL)** to help safeguard confidential information transmitted on the Web. Both Netscape Navigator and Internet Explorer support SSL, which uses a specific type of encryption. URLs for Web pages requiring SSL begin with https instead of http. The following Web Design Tips summarize privacy and security:

Web Design Tip
If your Web site gathers information, include a privacy statement to ease visitors' concerns.

Web Design Tip
To provide security, encrypt confidential information.

Accessibility

In addition to considering technical, legal, and ethical issues, you need to think about access to your Web site by visitors with special needs. The World Wide Web Consortium (W3C) supports advancing Web usability for individuals with special needs. To this end, the **Web Accessibility Initiative (WAI)** was created. Along with other initiatives, the WAI is encouraging accessibility through technology, guidelines, and research. Currently, the WAI Guidelines are specifications, not regulations, that many organizations have chosen to adopt.

Access for people with various types of special needs is a serious concern. Because the Web is a highly visual environment, however, people with special visual needs such as lost or impaired vision and color blindness, encounter the most access problems. The W3C Web site (w3.org) can answer many of your questions regarding accessibility. It also offers links to resources and tools such as **Bobby**, a free Web tool that analyzes Web page accessibility, and **TOM (Text-only Maker)**, which can help make Web pages more accessible. Accessibility is summarized in the following Web Design Tip:

Web Design Tip
Utilize resources and tools to make your Web pages more accessible to people with special needs.

WEB INFO

For more information about access to Web pages for people with special needs, visit the Web Design Chapter 2 Web Info page (scsite.com/web/ch2/webinfo.htm) and then click Accessibility.

Resources

To determine the scope of and the development time frame for your Web site, think about the resources you have or could acquire. After assessing current and attainable resources, you may decide to design a basic three-page Web site with a few photos that you can complete in a week, or a significantly more complex Web site that will require months to develop. The type of Web site you are designing will determine which of the following resources you will need to consider.

Hardware/Software (upgrade or purchase one or more):

- Computer, monitor, printer
- Modem, Internet connection
- Scanner, digital camera (still or video), video capture capability
- Web authoring, graphics, illustration, or animation software
- Stock photographs, clip art

If you have a corporate infrastructure:

- Is it adequate?
- Can it support e-commerce?
- What about security?

Staffing

- Do you have enough staff to develop and maintain a Web site?
- Will any need specialized training?
- Should any development or maintenance of the Web site be outsourced?

Budget

- What will the initial Web site development cost?
- How much should be budgeted for maintenance?
- Does funding exist for initial and ongoing training?

Managerial/Administrative Support

- Will upper management document its support of the Web initiative?
- Will upper management signify its approval of a Web site policy and make it known to the organization?
- Will upper management commit to long-term funding of the Web initiative?

CHAPTER SUMMARY

Print publishing deservedly has been a time-honored, trusted communication method. Even so, print cannot match the benefits of the Web for current, interactive content and for efficient, cost-effective production and distribution of information. Web and print publications are similar in their intent to deliver a powerful message and leave a distinct impression. Achieving these objectives via Web publications requires combining creativity with the fundamental design principles of balance and proximity, contrast and focus, and unity. The Web audience quickly wants to find accurate, easily read, understandable, comprehensive, and concise information that they can use. Writing content with these attributes requires applying specific techniques. Color can powerfully enhance a Web site's message and personality. Persuasive, effective color use involves studying other Web sites, being aware of accepted color principles and conventions, and understanding RGB color. Successful Web publishing further includes recognizing certain technical, legal and ethical, accessibility, and resource issues, as well as the design techniques that can manage them effectively.

KEY TERMS

Instructions: Use the following terms from this chapter as a study review.

Adobe Photoshop (2.19)
alignment (2.11)
ALT tag (2.19)
asymmetrically (2.6)
bandwidth (2.19)
bit (2.18)
Bobby (2.23)
body (2.15)
browser-safe palette (2.18)
chunked format (2.16)
color wheel (2.17)
contrast (2.8)
cool colors (2.17)
copyright (2.22)
decryption (2.22)
dither (2.18)
encryption(2.22)
File Transfer Protocol (FTP) (2.2)
focal point (2.8)
focus (2.8)
forms (2.3)
graphical display browsers (2.19)
grid (2.10)
hexadecimal system (2.18)
inverted pyramid style (2.15)

lead (2.15)
non-graphical display browser (2.19)
pixel (2.20)
paragraph format (2.16)
Platform for Privacy Preferences (P3P) (2.22)
privacy statement (2.22)
proximity (2.6)
resolution (2.20)
RGB system (2.18)
sans serif type (2.14)
Secure Sockets Layer (SSL) (2.23)
serif type (2.14)
serifs (2.14)
spam (2.3)
symmetrically (2.6)
TARGET tag (2.14)
text-only version (2.19)
thumbnails (2.19)
TOM (Text-only Maker) (2.23)
unity (2.8)
values (2.18)
warm colors (2.17)
Web Accessibility Initiative (WAI) (2.23)
Web palette (2.18)
white space (2.6)

CHECKPOINT Matching

Instructions: Match each term with the best description.

_____ 1. bandwidth

_____ 2. focus

_____ 3. asymmetric

_____ 4. RGB system

_____ 5. white space

_____ 6. resolution

_____ 7. sans serif type

_____ 8. contrast

_____ 9. symmetric

_____ 10. unity

_____ 11. proximity

_____ 12. serif type

a. Centered or balanced.
b. The empty space around text or graphics.
c. The measure of a monitor's sharpness and clarity.
d. Closeness.
e. A sense of oneness or belonging.
f. A color system that combines red, green, and blue light.
g. Type consisting of characters with short lines or ornaments that project from the primary strokes of characters.
h. A mix of elements to stimulate attention.
i. Off balance.
j. The center of interest or activity.
k. Geometric, straightforward looking type.
l. The quantity of data that can be transmitted in a specific time frame.

Instructions: Fill in the blank(s) with the appropriate answer

1. If you vary the size of Web page elements, you will establish a visual _____ of information that will show which elements are most _____.

2. To demonstrate the timeliness of your Web site's content, indicate the last _____ date on your Web pages.

3. E-commerce Web sites frequently use _____ to process data so it cannot be read by unauthorized individuals and _____ to reformat the data so that it is understandable.

4. If you use colors to create a graphic outside of the browser-safe palette, a browser may _____ the graphic.

5. If you take and use a video file without obtaining the owner's permission, you may be violating _____.

6. E-mail that is unsolicited, junk mail commonly is referred to as _____.

7. _____ is the type that displays most clearly for short blocks of text.

8. Visitors to a Web page generally prefer reading text in _____ format rather than _____ format.

9. Elements that are centered are _____ placed, while those off balance are _____ placed.

10. Ensure that type is legible by choosing backgrounds that are either _____ or _____.

Instructions: Select the letter of the correct answer for each question.

1. To make a linked Web page display in a new browser window, utilize one function of the _____.
    a. META tag
    b. TARGET attribute
    c. HTML tag
    d. either a or b

2. To transfer files on the Internet, a designer most commonly would use _____.
    a. HTTP
    b. protocol
    c. encryption
    d. FTP

3. The measure of a monitor's sharpness and clarity is called _____.
    a. pixel
    b. resolution
    c. decryption
    d. bit

4. To stimulate attention on a Web page, utilize _____.

    a. contrast

    b. focal point

    c. forms

    d. balance

5. A specification that will enable browsers automatically to determine the privacy policies of a Web site and inform the user, or submit the information based on defined user preferences is _____.

    a. RGB

    b. P3P

    c. W3C

    d. SSL

6. A consistent color scheme and repetition of Web page layout will create a sense of _____.

    a. focus

    b. white space

    c. unity

    d. proximity

7. Color is projected from monitors using a(n) _____ system, which combines red, green, and blue light.

    a. hexadecimal

    b. CMYK

    c. RGB

    d. encryption

8. The quantity of data that can be transmitted in a specific time frame is a _____.

    a. bit

    b. pixel

    c. bandwidth

    d. serif

9. A dominating segment of a Web page that draws attention is called _____.

    a. focus

    b. focal point

    c. white space

    d. grid

10. A protocol created by Netscape to secure confidential information transmitted on the Web is _____.

    a. TOM

    b. SSL

    c. IRC

    d. WAI

CHECKPOINT Short Answer

Instructions: Write a brief answer to each question.

1. Explain briefly the four Web publishing advantages that print publishing cannot match.

2. Identify the four basic design principles that help Web pages deliver a powerful message and leave a distinct impression.

3. Describe briefly how to incorporate each of the four basic design principles into a Web page.

4. Explain why writing for the Web environment is different from writing for print.

5. Identify the features of effective written Web content.

6. What effects can color have on a Web site?

7. Explain what a browser-safe palette is and how it relates to monitors.

8. Describe the impact of each of the following issues on Web design:
   a. Bandwidth
   b. Monitor resolution
   c. Copyright
   d. Privacy and security
   e. Accessibility
   f. Resources

9. Briefly explain RGB color.

10. Differentiate between paragraph format and chunked format.

AT ISSUE

Instructions: Write a brief essay in response to the following issues. Be prepared to discuss your findings in class. Use the Web as your research tool. For each issue, identify one URL utilized as a research source.

1. This chapter discussed the advantages that Web publishing offers over print publishing. E-books, which are electronic versions of books, are a relatively new technology that continues the debate of Web versus print publishing. Explain how an e-book works, the different types currently available, advantages and disadvantages, and their impact on print publishing.

2. Wireless handheld devices that provide Internet access are another popular, recent technology. Such devices include personal digital assistants (PDAs), cellular telephones, and Web pagers. Describe the capabilities and limitations of these devices regarding Internet access and display of Web pages. Predict the effect these devices will have on Web design over the next two years.

HANDS ON

Instructions: Complete the following exercises.

1. The importance of writing for the Web environment and audience was stressed in this chapter. Surf the Web and find a Web page of a personal, organization/topical, or a business/commercial Web site that, in your opinion, did not adequately prepare its textual content for the Web environment and audience. Print the original Web page and then rewrite the content applying the appropriate guidelines and suggestions presented in this chapter.

   Also emphasized in this chapter was how color can be a powerful design tool for creating attractive, effective Web sites. Surf the Web and identify a Web site that utilizes an appealing, well-chosen color scheme in its design. Describe how the color scheme is applied throughout the Web site, and the mood conveyed by the colors.

2. Privacy, copyright, and accessibility by individuals with disabilities are three Web-related concerns of individuals, organizations, and businesses today. Explain public opinion and your personal opinion regarding one of these issues. Visit the World Wide Web Consortium (W3C) Web site and identify its position and any current or proposed specifications regarding the issue. Surf the Web to identify a Web site that is addressing this issue successfully and explain the methods being used.

SECTION 1 CASE STUDY

The Case Study is an ongoing development process in Web design using the concepts, techniques, and Web Design Tips presented in each section. In Section 1, you are to select the type of Web site and a topic of interest and complete the Assignment.

In Section 1, you will begin the process of designing your own personal, organization/topical, or commercial Web site. As you progress through the chapters, you will learn further how to utilize design as a tool to create effective Web pages and Web sites. At each section's conclusion, you will receive instructions for completing each segment of the ongoing design process.

The following are suggestions for Web site topics. Choose one of these topics or create your own. Select a topic that you find interesting, feel fairly knowledgeable about, or are excited about researching.

1. **Personal Web Site**

   A hobby or special interest:

   - Collecting Beanie Babies, stamps, coins, rare books

   - Gardening, kickboxing, mountain climbing, breeding show dogs

   - Archery, rollerblading, football, waterskiing

2. **Organization/Topical**

   Increase support and membership for:

   - A community watch program, 4-H club, Girl Scouts, Meals On Wheels, American Red Cross, Boys & Girls Clubs of America

(continued)

SECTION 1 CASE STUDY

(continued)

Promote awareness of:

- Endangered animals, physical fitness, black and white photography, interactive video games

3. **Commercial**

Start up a business or expand an existing business with a Web presence.

Selling a service:

- Catering, financial counseling, lawn maintenance, painting, installing computer networks

Selling a product:

- Microchips, boutique items, surgical equipment, antiques, tennis racquets

Assignment

Instructions: Complete the assignment relating to the details of the Case Study.

Your completed Web site, which will consist of five to ten Web pages, will be evaluated primarily regarding the application of good design. As your first step, develop a one-page document using a text editor or a word processing package in response to the following:

1. Identify which type of Web site you will design: (a) personal, (b) organization/topical, or (c) commercial; the topic; and the title you will give your Web site.

2. List three or more general goals for your Web site. (You will fine-tune these goals into a specific purpose in the next section.)

3. List any elements other than text — for example, photos, animations, or music — that you could include on your Web site to support your general goals.

4. Identify the design tools you think you will need, including software, hardware, and any specialty equipment.

5. Identify any other issues you will consider in the design of your Web site.

CHAPTER 3

Developing a Design Plan for a Web Site: Part 1

OBJECTIVES

After completing this chapter you will be able to:

- Develop Part 1, the first four steps, of the six-step design plan for a Web site

- Define a Web site's purpose

- Write a purpose statement for a Web site

- Identify the audience

- Determine the goals and needs of the audience

- Discuss common content elements

- Describe and apply methods for choosing content that will add value and further the objectives of a Web site

- Explain repurposing content for Web usage

- Describe the content typically found on different types of Web sites

- Discuss the impact photographs can add to a Web site

- Explain the difference between multimedia and interactive multimedia

- Describe how animation can be utilized effectively

- Explain the difference between downloadable and streaming media

- Differentiate among Web site structures

- Understand the specific functions of Web pages

INTRODUCTION

Chapters 1 and 2 introduced you to Web design, including tools, roles, research methods, and principles. You also became aware of important techniques for writing text for Web pages and managing color in the Web environment. Now in Chapter 3, you will begin to develop a design plan for your Web site. Why do you need a design plan? Would you hire a builder for your getaway vacation home before seeing blueprints? Would you take a trip to Europe without setting up a travel itinerary? A Web site is a similar investment to which you will devote significant time and other resources. Any investment, if it is to succeed, requires detailed planning. To develop a solid design plan for your Web site, you should follow six major steps. Figure 3-1 illustrates the six-step process. Chapter 3 discusses Steps 1 through 4 and Chapter 4 discusses Steps 5 and 6.

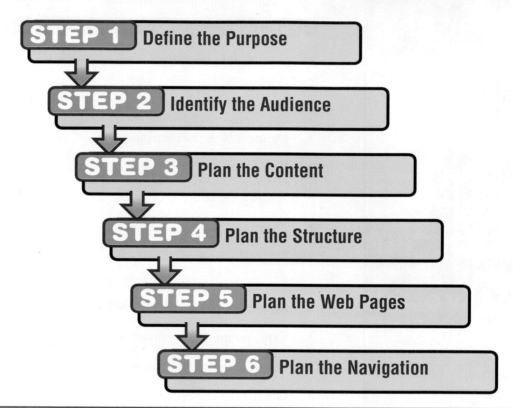

FIGURE 3-1   Follow these six steps to develop a solid design plan for your Web site.

STEP 1: DEFINE THE PURPOSE

The initial step in the development of a solid design plan is to define the purpose of the Web site. To accomplish this, you must decide on a specific topic or theme, and then list the goals for your Web site.

Decide on a Topic for the Web Site

Many Web sites are planned around the interests of the designer. If you have not yet decided on a topic for your Web site, brainstorm by listing five possible topics. For example, say you are a financial planner interested in designing a Web site to enhance the growth of your business. Your list might include topics such as money, banking, securities, loans, or credit. Next, choose the top two possibilities you believe have the greatest potential to make an interesting, worthwhile Web site. Then, decide on one of these two interests: the one on which you feel the most knowledgeable or the one about which you are willing to spend the time to learn more.

Being a financial planner, you decide on the topic of money. Money is too broad a topic, however. A Web site topic must be neither too broad nor too narrow. To narrow the topic of money, consider a few of its many aspects: earning, spending, inheriting, or investing. After careful consideration, you conclude the topic of your Web site to be investing money.

List the Goals of the Web Site

Know what it is that you want your Web site to accomplish. Do you want to communicate information, educate, entertain, or sell a product or service? It is likely that you want to accomplish more than one of these goals with the design of your Web site. If you do, prioritize these goals as you define the purpose. As you develop your design plan, choose content, and create the Web site, keep the purpose of your Web site at the forefront of your planning.

With the topic of investing money decided, you want to determine what your Web site's goals are. Should it:

- Convey information about investing?
- Educate investors?
- Tell amusing stories about investing?
- Facilitate investing online?

When designing a Web site, include a **purpose statement** that communicates the intention of the Web site. Figure 3-2 illustrates the investment Web site's purpose statement: to communicate investment information and educate customers on investing their money for a secure retirement.

WEB INFO

For more information about developing a design plan for a Web site, visit the Web Design Chapter 3 Web Info page (scsite.com/web/ch3/webinfo.htm) and then click Design Plan.

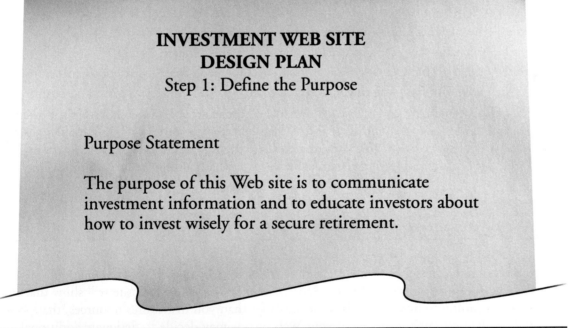

**INVESTMENT WEB SITE
DESIGN PLAN**
Step 1: Define the Purpose

Purpose Statement

The purpose of this Web site is to communicate investment information and to educate investors about how to invest wisely for a secure retirement.

FIGURE 3-2   After choosing a specific topic and deciding what you want your Web site to accomplish, you can define your purpose as exemplified by the investment Web site's purpose statement.

The following Web Design Tip summarizes the necessary requirements for defining the purpose of a Web site:

Web Design Tip
Defining the purpose of a Web site requires a distinct site topic that is neither too broad nor too narrow, and a clear understanding of what the site should accomplish.

STEP 2: IDENTIFY THE AUDIENCE

The second step in your design plan is to identify the audience. Although anyone in the world with Internet access potentially could be a member of your Web site's audience, trying to design for such a vast audience simply is not practical. Even if you greatly reduce the scope, but fail to target your audience, you will include unwanted information for some and omit content needed by others.

Consider again the investment Web site, the purpose of which is to communicate investment information and educate investors. As the designer, which investors do you want to educate? Do you want to explain how to invest money to people who want to buy their first home? Or, are your strategies geared to investors who want to guarantee their children's college education, or for those who want a comfortable, secure retirement? Realizing that each type of investor has specific goals and needs requiring a unique investment plan and strategies, you target your audience as people who want to invest for a comfortable, secure retirement.

Define the Goals and Needs of the Audience

WEB INFO

For more information about determining the goals and needs of a Web site audience, visit the Web Design Chapter 3 Web Info page (scsite.com/web/ch3/webinfo.htm) and then click Audience.

Whatever the purpose of your Web site, identify your audience and consider its specific goals and needs. To define goals and needs, develop a preliminary **audience profile** by considering the following:

- Who would be most interested in your message, and why would they be interested?
- What are they expecting to gain from your Web site?
- Are they seeking entertainment or answers?
- Do they need quick facts or in-depth explanations?
- Do they have any biases regarding your message?
- What do they have in common — age, income, education, careers, lifestyles?
- What is their level of computer experience?
- Are they expecting the latest technology or are they intimidated by it?
- Are they experienced Web site navigators, or do they need basic instructions and icons?
- Are they international — requiring research of cultural differences, norms, and customs?

The extent to which you consider your audience's needs and goals in your Web site's design will determine its degree of usability. If your Web site is not perceived as highly usable, visitors will choose to patronize other Web sites that do meet their goals and needs. Testing your Web site for usability before publishing is extremely important, as summarized in the following Web Design Tip:

> **Web Design Tip**
>
> To create a Web site with a high degree of usability, identify the goals and needs of its audience.

If you have limited resources and a tight time frame for initial Web site development, identify your audience's top two goals and needs. After meeting those, your Web site will show that its purpose is beginning to be realized. If someone other than you distributes resources, that person — based on the preliminary success of your Web site — may decide to designate additional resources to meet other audience goals and needs. After creating your Web site, continually gather feedback from your audience to fine-tune and add to this preliminary profile. You may discover that your audience has more goals and needs than originally anticipated.

In some cases, a Web site may have more than one audience. If your Web site falls into this category, you need to prioritize which audience is the most important to reach. Avoid trying to reach too many different audiences. Attempting to do so will result in a very confusing Web site that visitors will find difficult to navigate.

You will be able to determine the major objectives for your Web site as a result of defining its purpose and identifying the audience. Stating objectives for a Web site is similar to setting up goals for a business, in that doing so gives structure and direction. Follow this Web Design Tip regarding objectives for a Web site:

> **Web Design Tip**
> Refer to your objectives constantly during the planning and creating phases. Include content that will contribute to the stated objectives. Test to see if you have met your objectives before making the Web site live.

Figure 3-3 illustrates a profile of the audience and the major objectives for the investment Web site.

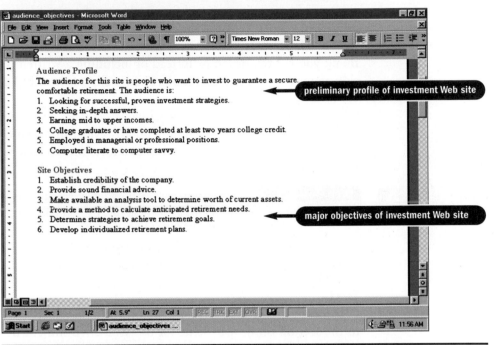

STEP 3: PLAN THE CONTENT

Step 3 of the design plan is to consider the different types of content you could include in your Web site. Content is so critical to the success of a Web site that Chapter 5 and Chapter 6 are devoted exclusively to the specifics of content. This section serves as an introduction to the types and usages of Web content.

FIGURE 3-3 Identify your audience and develop a preliminary audience profile. In addition to the profile, this example lists the objectives for the investment Web site.

Value-Added Content

Base your choice of content on how effectively it would contribute to the objectives of your Web site. Content that furthers Web site objectives adds value, not merely volume. Overall, **value-added content** will be relative, informative, and timely; accurate and high-quality; and usable. As a designer of an investment Web site, you must ensure that the Web site contains value-added content by following the Web Design Tips below:

> **Web Design Tip**
> Develop relative, informative, and timely content. Include the latest research on investing in dot-com companies, tax tips, or advice on selecting a broker.

> **Web Design Tip**
> Ensure that content is accurate and high quality. Keep current with the advice of respected financial journals and leaders, and include professional looking charts and graphs based on credible data.

WEB INFO

For more information about choosing content that adds value to a Web site, visit the Web Design Chapter 3 Web Info page (scsite.com/web/ch3/webinfo.htm) and then click Value-Added Content.

Then, study your audience profile and offer content it wants and can use. For example, include a financial calculator to determine current worth, or the top-ten investment strategies. Keep in mind the following Web Design Tip:

Web Design Tip

To advance the defined objectives of a Web site, choose content that adds value, that is, content that is relative, informative, and timely; accurate and high-quality; and useable.

In general, original content prepared for the Web is preferred. If you have no option but to use existing content designed for another medium, such as print, you should **repurpose,** or modify it for the Web. For example, in place of the static order form that customers would have to print, fill out, and fax to you, generate an online form that returns a confirmation and a thank you for the order; or instead of including a written paragraph stating the company mission statement, incorporate a short audio clip of the CEO explaining the company's commitment to its customers.

Repurposing content frequently involves editing or segmenting video and audio, abbreviating and rewriting text, and rescanning photos. Most importantly, it requires creative thinking with the Web environment and audience as a foremost consideration, as illustrated in the following Web Design Tip:

Web Design Tip

Do not duplicate content created for print on Web pages. Repurpose the content so it will add value.

An introduction to various Web site content elements including text, photographs, animation, video, audio, and dynamically generated content follows.

Text

Text typically is the primary component of a Web site. To ensure quality textual content, refer to the section on how to write for the Web environment in Chapter 2 and the following general guidelines for repurposing text from print publications.

- Abbreviate the amount of text significantly. Remember, visitors typically do not like to read long passages of text onscreen.
- Chunk information into logical sections for readability.
- Add hyperlinks to explanatory or detailed information.
- Use the active voice and a friendly tone.
- Remove transitional words and phrases such as, as stated previously, similarly, and as a result. The transitions no longer may be relevant and are of little use to a visitor who is scanning the content.
- Do not use Web clichés such as Click here to register. Instead, use Register online.

The following is a list of content that often appears as text on personal, organization/topical, and commercial Web sites.

Personal

- Hobbies/personal interests
- Personal opinions/beliefs

- Biographies
- Resumes
- Links to other Web sites

Organization

- Mission statement
- Organizational goals
- Ways to become a member or support the organization

- Links to organizational publications
- Calendar of events

Topical
- Facts/opinions
- Statistics
- Articles by subject experts
- Links to related Web sites

Commercial
- Company history
- Products/services
- Technical support/customer service
- Job opportunities
- Annual/quarterly reports
- Credit applications
- Order forms
- Contact information including e-mail, telephone, and fax
- Privacy/security statements

As a designer for an investment Web site, you need to consider the guidelines outlined for the commercial Web site. The text content most crucial to your Web site is products and services, history of the company, technical support or service information, contact information, and privacy and security statements. Depending on the products and services you are offering, you may want to include online ordering forms, credit applications, employment opportunities and annual or quarterly reports.

Photographs

After text, **photographs** are the most commonly included content element on Web sites. Photos can personalize and familiarize the unknown. For example, say your company tells you that you will be transferred in one month to Indianapolis, Indiana. You begin feeling a little nervous about the prospect of moving until you visit Web sites suggested by the relocation department. One realtor's Web site shows you homes in Indianapolis currently on the market in your price range (Figure 3-4). Suddenly, this move seems manageable after all.

WEB INFO

For more information about using photographs on Web sites, visit the Web Design Chapter 3 Web Info page (scsite.com/web/ch3/webinfo.htm) and then click Photographs.

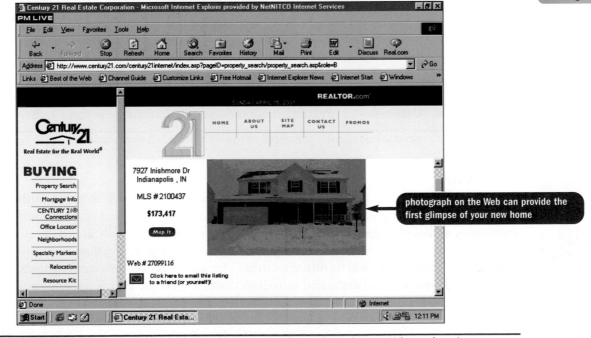

FIGURE 3-4   Photographs on a Web site can personalize and familiarize the unknown. When relocating to another city, for example, you can review homes currently on the market.

The use of photographs can help you deliver a message and/or prompt an action beyond the capabilities of text alone. For example, consider a motorcycle enthusiast who wants to buy a new bike and is trying to decide how much money to spend. As this person surfs the Web, think of the impression that viewing the Harley-Davidson Web site makes on this individual (Figure 3-5). The photo of the rider on the Harley rounding the curve of an open road with the late afternoon sun reflecting off the bike's chrome can convince the visitor to buy.

When choosing photographs for your Web site, select high-quality, relative pictures that will add value. For the investment Web site, photos of successful investors or new investors in an investment strategies class would illustrate your business and financial expertise in action as summarized in the following Web Design Tip:

Web Design Tip

Photographs on Web pages can powerfully communicate and motivate. Select relatable, high-quality photographs that will further the Web site objectives.

FIGURE 3-5   Consider the potential of the photo on this Web site to sell motorcycles.

Multimedia

Multimedia can add action, excitement, and interactivity to your Web pages. Although definitions vary, multimedia typically is regarded as some combination of text, graphic images, animation, audio, or video. These elements can be utilized individually as well as combined.

The Web site of the United States Air Force contains extensive information organized in a multimedia format to appeal to future recruits. This Web site uses interactive games, animated graphics, fighter-jet sound clips, and movies to create a Web site that is dynamic and informative (Figure 3-6).

Viewers are intrigued and entertained by multimedia presentations, which require considerable investments of time and other resources if originally developed. The following Web Design Tip suggests sources for multimedia:

Web Design Tip

Utilizing development tools and techniques, designers can create original multimedia, or they can purchase ready-made elements on CD-ROM or download them from many Web sites.

WEB INFO

For more information about using multimedia in Web design, visit the Web Design Chapter 3 Web Info page (scsite.com/web/ch3/webinfo.htm) and then click Multimedia.

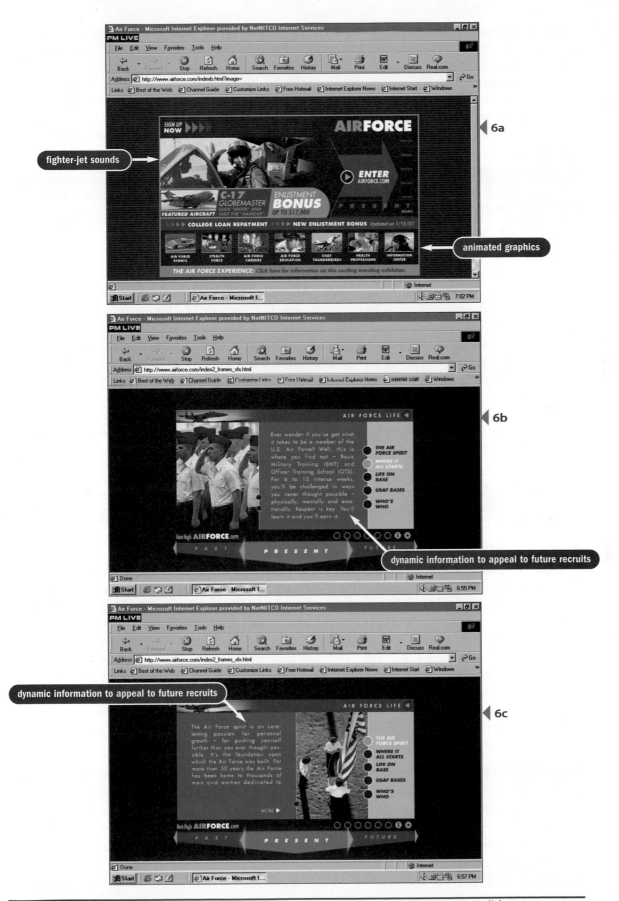

FIGURE 3-6   Utilizing multimedia created with Macromedia's Flash, the U. S. Air Force accomplishes some impressive recruiting.

Multimedia presentations also can be **interactive**. Instead of passively viewing the presentation, the viewer actively participates, for example by clicking or moving the mouse or entering text. Multimedia and other technologies often require the use of a **plug-in**, which is a software program that allows certain content to function within the Web page. **Helper applications**, forerunners to plug-ins, allowed for the functionality, but it took place in another browser window. Hundreds of plug-ins for video and audio, animations, presentations, and more are available on the Web. The following Web Design Tip offers a suggestion regarding plug-ins:

> **Web Design Tip**
>
> If plug-ins need to be downloaded to access multimedia on a Web site, provide a link on your Web pages to the download Web site.

WEB INFO

For more information about using animations in Web design, visit the Web Design Chapter 3 Web Info page (scsite.com/web/ch3/webinfo.htm) and then click Animations.

Animations

Animations are widely used on the Web to attract attention and enliven Web pages with rotating objects, scrolling text, or advertising banners. The most prevalent format is **animated GIF** that gives the appearance of moving pictures. The animated GIF format is discussed in detail in a later chapter. Using animations adds interest and appeal to your Web pages. It can allow you to demonstrate a process effectively, for example, showing step-by-step procedures. An example of a sequence of animations is illustrated in Figure 3-7. These Web pages are designed to instruct the visitor how to add names and numbers to the phone book of a cellular telephone.

When including animations, use them subtly and sparingly. Excessive amounts of animations on Web pages can become distracting and annoying. Overuse of spinning, gyrating, flashing elements can cause your visitors to leave your Web site in a hurry. Use the following Web Design Tip as a guideline for using animations:

> **Web Design Tip**
>
> Limit the use of animation on Web pages so it is effective, yet allows visitors to focus on the content.

WEB INFO

For more information about using audio in Web design, visit the Web Design Chapter 3 Web Info page (scsite.com/web/ch3/webinfo.htm) and then click Audio.

Audio

Audio frequently is utilized as an extremely effective, low-bandwidth alternative to video. Audio can vary in both form and intensity — from a child's whisper to the president's State of the Union Address, or from a heavy metal band to the Mormon Tabernacle Choir. The human voice and music can persuade, inspire, personalize, motivate, or soothe.

Audio also enhances recall. Perhaps you remember the speeches of the great orators Martin Luther King, Jr. and John F. Kennedy. Do their powerful words bring to mind images of the 1960s? Does a lyric that keeps playing in your head remind you of a significant life event?

Think of the ways that audio — with its capability of evoking emotion, prompting action, and triggering memory — could benefit your Web site. Imagine, for example, the persuasive effect of a glowing testimonial about your product from a satisfied customer, or the recall possibilities of a catchy jingle. Include audio using the following Web Design Tip:

> **Web Design Tip**
>
> Incorporate audio into a Web site to personalize a message, enhance recall, set a mood, or sell a product or service.

Web audio and video can be categorized as either downloadable media or streaming media. **Downloadable media** must be downloaded in its entirety to the user's computer before it can be heard or seen. **Streaming media**, on the other hand, begins to play as soon as the data begins to **stream**, or transfer, in.

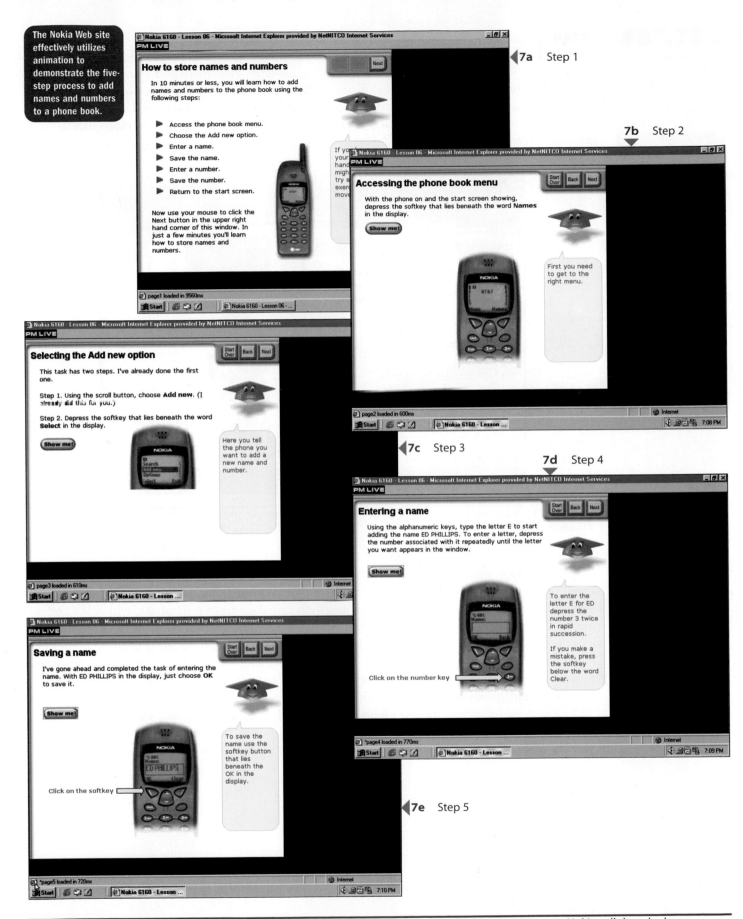

The Nokia Web site effectively utilizes animation to demonstrate the five-step process to add names and numbers to a phone book.

FIGURE 3-7   This Web site illustrates a sophisticated use of animation to teach people how to program a Nokia cellular telephone.

WEB INFO

For more information about using video in Web design, visit the Web Design Chapter 3 Web Info page (scsite.com/web/ch3/webinfo.htm) and then click Video.

Video

Typically, **video clips** incorporate the powerful components of movement and sound (Figure 3-8). Of all the cutting-edge technologies, however, efficiently delivering quality video via the Web has presented the most difficult challenges. The primary problem is the extremely large size of video files, resulting from the enormous amounts of data required to depict the audio and video. The choice for designers is to limit the size of downloadable video files or to generate streaming video.

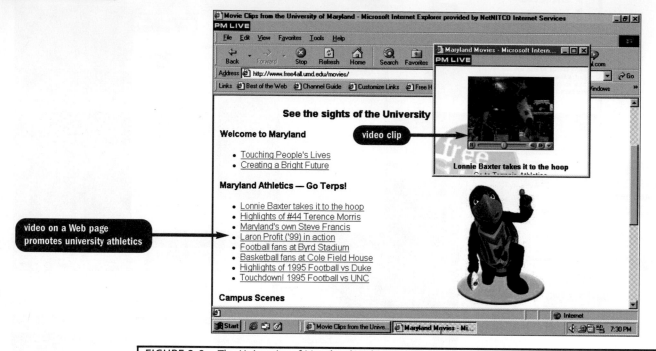

FIGURE 3-8 The University of Maryland Web site utilizes a video clip to promote the university's athletic program.

Dynamically Generated Content

Dynamically generated content, unlike static information, updates periodically and can be served up to your Web site visitor triggered by a specific event, such as the time of day or user input. Dynamically generated content frequently is called up from a **database**, which is a collection of data arranged so the contents can be updated and used in various ways. Microsoft developed **Active Server Page (ASP) technology**, which is one method for generating content dynamically. Figure 3-9 shows an Active Server Page, which dynamically draws degree programs from a university database. An **Active Server Page** is a special kind of HTML document with embedded commands created using **scripting languages**, such as VBScript or JScript, or ActiveX Data Object program statements. These commands allow interactivity and custom information delivery. ASP Web pages need to be served up by a Microsoft Web server, but can be viewed on current, popular browsers, such as Netscape and Internet Explorer.

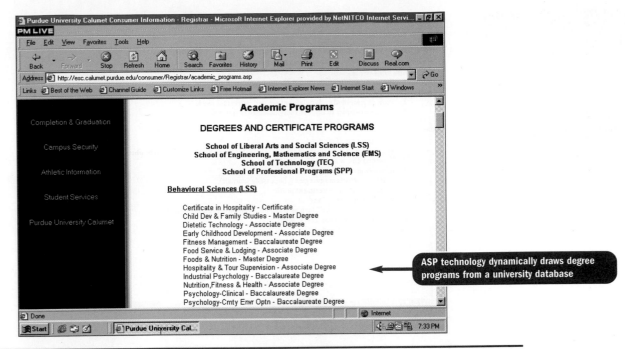

FIGURE 3-9   An Active Server Page (ASP) with dynamically generated content

To decide whether to include multimedia or dynamically generated content, ask yourself the following questions:

1. Will it add value to my Web site and further the objectives I have defined?

2. Does it match my audience profile?

3. Are visitors expecting cutting-edge technology?

4. Will visitors feel that experiencing the content is worth the time if they must download a special player or plug-in?

If you cannot answer yes to these questions, do not include dynamically generated content. Just because cutting-edge technology is available is never a valid reason to use it. If you can answer yes, however, then take advantage of this powerful content to enhance your Web site. Make sure you optimize the media for effective Web delivery by keeping in mind the following Web Design Tip:

Web Design Tip

Including cutting-edge technology on Web pages just because you can never is a valid reason to do so. Incorporate multimedia and/or dynamically generated content only for legitimate reasons.

At this point, add to your design plan a simple list of general information that would add value and further your Web site's objectives. Identify possible sources for the content, keeping in mind the issue of copyright discussed in Chapter 2. Figure 3-10 on the next page illustrates the value-added content list for the investment Web site.

After you define the purpose, identify the content, and plan the content, you are ready to plan the structure of your Web site. A Web site is composed of a series of Web pages. Each Web site structure typically begins with a home page. The home page is the first Web page a visitor sees when accessing your Web site. Through the home page, a visitor can navigate to additional Web pages in your Web site.

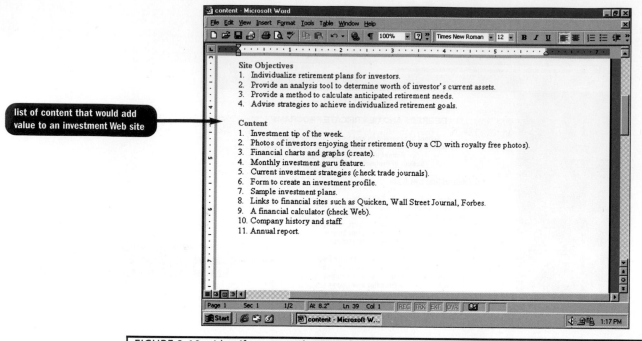

list of content that would add value to an investment Web site

FIGURE 3-10   Identify content elements that will add value to your Web site, and possible sources to acquire the content as exemplified by this list of content for the investment Web site.

STEP 4: PLAN THE STRUCTURE

With the purpose defined, the audience identified, and the content planned, Step 4 in the development of the design plan is to plan the structure.

Outline Your Web Site

The Web site's **outline** will serve as a blueprint and define its major navigational paths. To outline, some designers use a flowchart, a storyboard, or a text outline. Choose the method that you find most flexible and comfortable.

Structure your information to achieve the objectives you have defined. Linear/tutorial, random, and hierarchical are three types of structural themes utilized for organizing Web site information. **Linear/tutorial structure** organizes and presents information in a specific order (Figure 3-11a). A training Web site could utilize this structure to ensure that steps will not be missed or performed out of sequence. The linear/tutorial structure controls the navigation of users by progressing them one Web page at a time. Linear/tutorial structure also is appropriate for information that needs to be viewed in a historical or chronological order; for example, a Web site that analyzes the invention and growth of the World Wide Web.

Random structure presents information without a specific order. From the home page, visitors can choose any other Web page freely according to their interests. The arrows from the home page shown in Figure 3-11b illustrate how a visitor to this type of Web site could navigate to different Web pages without a precise order. Web sites with topics such as predatory creatures of South America or famous Latin guitarists are examples of Web sites in which random structure can be used effectively. Use random structure for small Web sites only. Larger, complex Web sites organized in this manner cause confusion and frustration for visitors.

A **hierarchical structure** organizes information into categories and subcategories (Figure 3-11c). Information found in organizational and topical Web sites usually is well suited to hierarchical structure.

A university Web site, for example, might structure its information as follows:

• A category of academics with subcategories of majors and departments
• A category of athletics with subcategories of teams and schedules
• A category of students with subcategories of current and prospective students and alumni

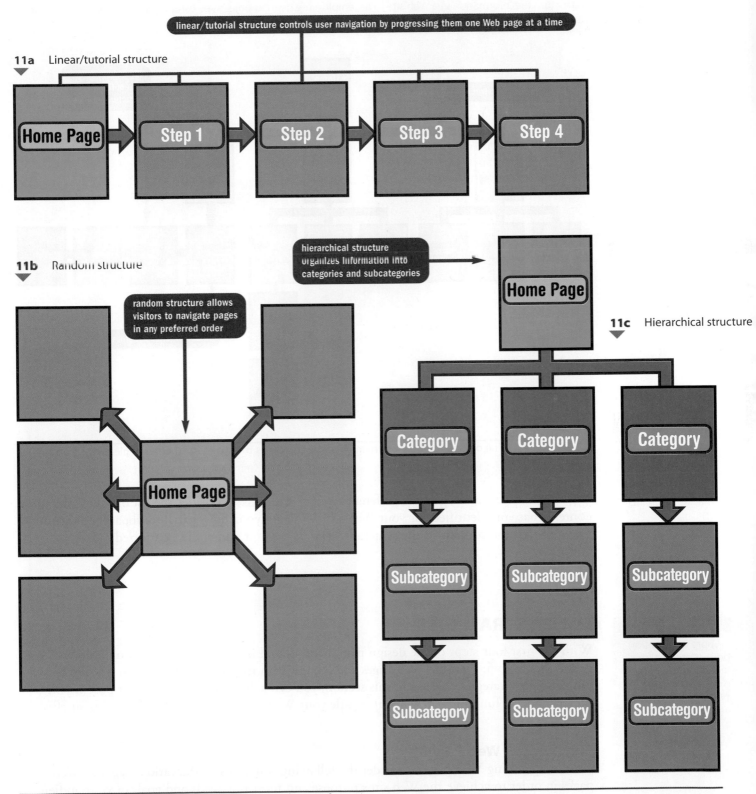

FIGURE 3-11   Structural themes for organizing Web site information.

Larger Web sites frequently use a combination of structural themes rather than using a single method to organize information. Figure 3-12 illustrates the combined structural themes utilized to create the outline structure for the investment Web site. The following Web Design Tip summarizes the key points regarding planning the structure of a Web site:

> **Web Design Tip**
>
> Structure the information in a Web site to accomplish the defined objectives, establish primary navigation paths, and maximize the Web site's usability.

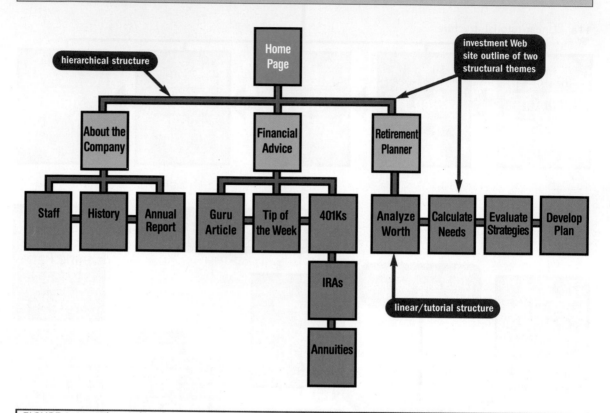

FIGURE 3-12 The outline for the investment Web site combines the structural themes of hierarchical and linear/tutorial.

With an understanding of the different types of structures, consider the list of value-added content that you identified for your Web site. Utilizing your flowchart, storyboard, or text outline, position the content in the structure where it fits best and could be utilized most effectively.

OTHER STRATEGIES

With the first four steps of the design plan incorporated into the development of your Web site, prepare for Step 5: Plan the Web Pages and Step 6: Plan the Navigation covered in Chapter 4. Utilizing the strategies covered in this section, you can achieve the Web site's purpose if you understand the functions of Web pages, title your Web pages effectively, and develop an effective file system.

Functions of Web Pages

Before planning Web pages, consider the following functions of the various types of Web pages in order to achieve the Web site's purpose and meet the needs and goals of your audience.

WEB INFO

For more information about strategies for creating home pages, visit the Web Design Chapter 3 Web Info page (scsite.com/web/ch3/webinfo.htm) and then click Home Page.

HOME PAGE A **home page** is the first Web page your visitor will see. It represents the Web site topic and requires interest and appeal to ensure a good experience. It should:

- Indicate clearly to visitors the kind of Web site they have accessed. A business Web site, for example, should identify the company name and the product or service offered. Sometimes a company name and logo is so well known that it is synonymous with a product or service. If your company is small and does not enjoy the advantage of instantaneous recognition, clearly indicate the product or service.

- Draw visitors into your Web site, conveying that something they need or want can be realized by going deeper into the Web site.

- Serve as an entry to the major content of the Web site via elements such as text hyperlinks, buttons, or **image maps**, which are graphics that have specific designated areas that when clicked link to other locations or Web pages (Figures 3-13a and 3-13b).

- Offer some type of **search function**, a method by which visitors quickly can find the information they seek. A Web site **directory** is another common method to help visitors find information (Figure 3-13a).

- Contain a dynamic area that provides constantly changing, interesting content such as Tip of the Day, Today's News, What's New, or Hot Topics.

- Provide one or more methods of contact, such as an e-mail link, telephone and fax numbers, and mailing addresses.

- Establish the visual identity for your Web site. Organizations and companies spend a large amount of time and money defining, creating, and maintaining a positive, recognizable image. For example, Nike is the company for premiere athletic shoes, and the American Red Cross is the organization that provides relief during disasters. Visual elements such as a graphic, logo, typeface, and a color scheme used alone or in combination can symbolize an image, such as the Nike swoosh or the red cross (Figures 3-14a and 3-14b on the next page). A visual identity can be established and maintained by consistently using the elements on billboards, brochures, business cards, stationery, advertisements, and Web sites.

- Be different enough to stand out as the initial Web page but connect visually with secondary Web pages.

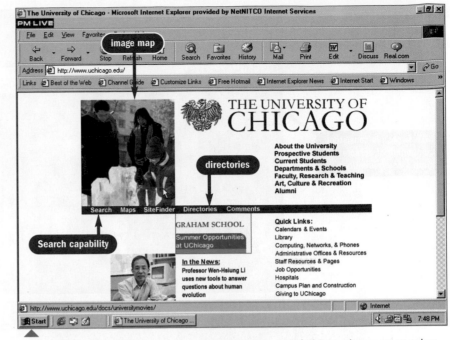

13a When clicked the image map on the University of Chicago home page takes you deeper in the Web site. The Web page also offers a search capability and directories to help visitors quickly find information.

13b When an image map is clicked on the home page, a Web page deeper in the Web site displays; also included is further navigation using Search and directories.

FIGURE 3-13 The University of Chicago Web site utilizes image maps, search capabilities, and directories to navigate further into the Web site.

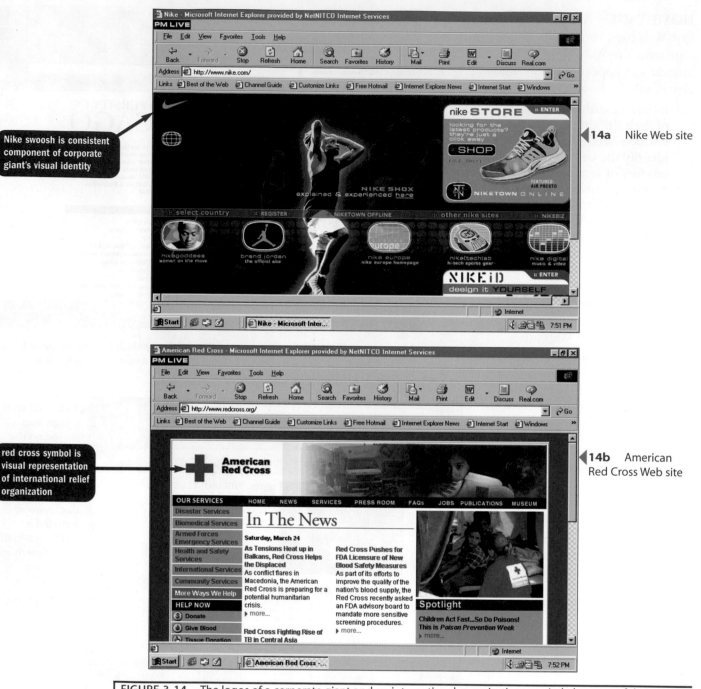

Nike swoosh is consistent component of corporate giant's visual identity

14a   Nike Web site

red cross symbol is visual representation of international relief organization

14b   American Red Cross Web site

FIGURE 3-14   The logos of a corporate giant and an international organization are vital elements of their visual identity.

SPLASH PAGE   A **splash page** provides an element of interest that draws visitors into your Web site with a desire to see more. It should:

- Capture the visitor's attention and draw them in to the Web site. A splash page typically contains few elements yet employs powerful multimedia such as graphics, sound, and movement (Figure 3-15). Members of the Web audience give splash pages mixed reviews. Those who seek entertainment and/or appreciate the latest technology, applaud them. Others consider them a nuisance, and an obstacle to accessing Web site content.

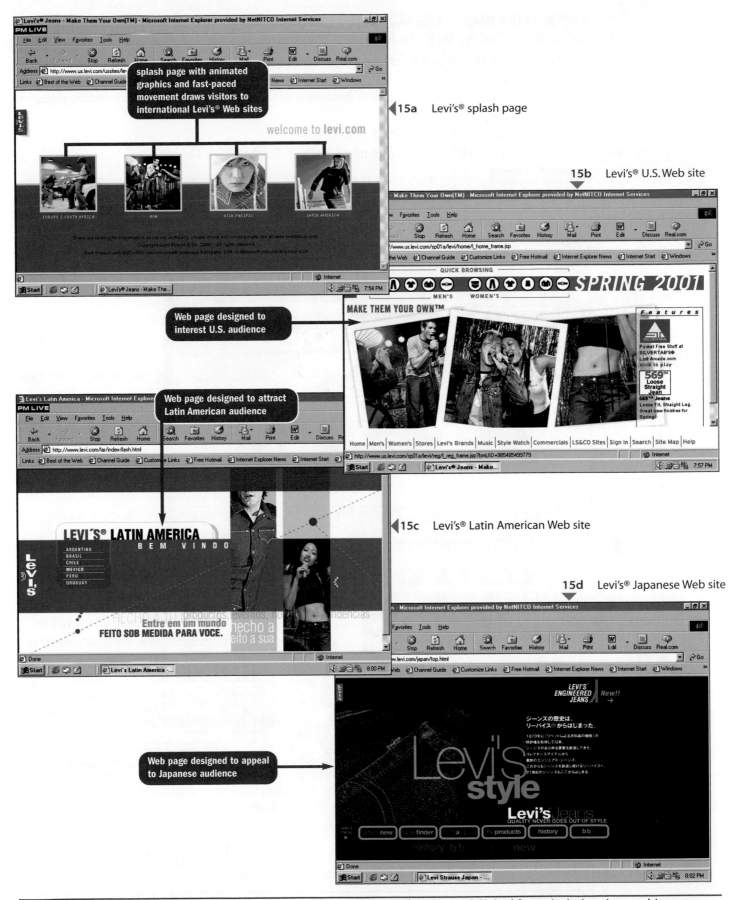

15a   Levi's® splash page

15b   Levi's® U.S. Web site

15c   Levi's® Latin American Web site

15d   Levi's® Japanese Web site

FIGURE 3-15   The splash page on the Levi's® Web site entices visitors into the company's United States, Latin American, and Japanese Web sites.

SECONDARY PAGE A **secondary page** connects and combines the Web site and establishes continuity within the Web site. It should:

- Have a look that shows a definite visual connection with the home page and other secondary pages, which will further the sense of unity within the Web site.
- Clearly display the Web site name, because some visitors may not access secondary pages via the home page.
- Provide a link to the home page (Figure 3-16).

Functions of Web pages are summarized in the following Web Design Tip:

Web Design Tip

To fulfill a Web site's purpose and meet its audience's goals and needs, home, splash, and secondary Web pages should perform typical functions. Become familiar with these functions before beginning to plan Web pages.

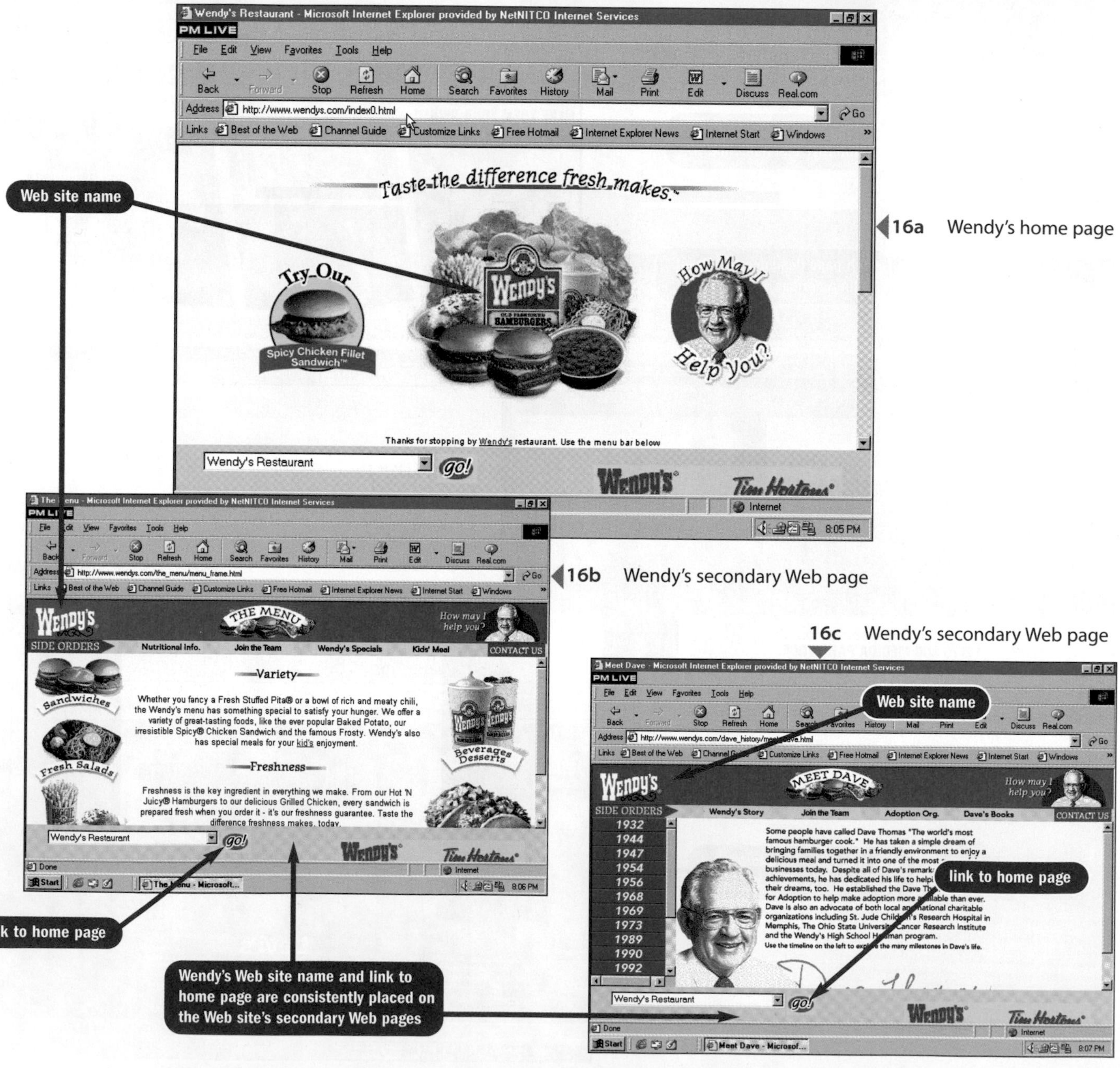

Web site name

16a Wendy's home page

16b Wendy's secondary Web page

link to home page

Wendy's Web site name and link to home page are consistently placed on the Web site's secondary Web pages

16c Wendy's secondary Web page

Web site name

link to home page

FIGURE 3-16 These secondary pages at Wendy's Web site visually connect with the home page and each other. The Web pages also clearly display the Web site name and provide a link back to the home page.

Titling Your Web Pages

When you create your Web pages, plan to make the title of each Web page attention getting, relevant, and accurate for the following reasons. The **title**, which appears on the title bar in the browser, may be the first element your visitor sees as the Web page loads. Also, if your visitor bookmarks your Web page, the bookmark will reflect the title. If the bookmark has no relevance to the actual content of the Web page, your visitor might not remember why the Web page was bookmarked initially. Title Web pages appropriately using the following Web Design Tip:

WEB INFO

For more information about choosing titles for Web pages, visit the Web Design Chapter 3 Web Info page (scsite.com/web/ch3/webinfo.htm) and then click Web Page Title.

> **Web Design Tip**
> Give Web pages accurate and pertinent titles that will draw the attention of visitors.

The title of a Web page differs from the file name of your Web page. The **file name** is the name you give the Web page when you save it to your local hard drive, for example index.htm. If you create your Web page in a text editor, you insert the title in the <HEAD> section as follows.

<HTML>

<HEAD>

<TITLE>Index</TITLE>

</HEAD>

If you use **Microsoft FrontPage**, a popular Web page authoring and site management program to design your Web pages, it will create a title for your Web page automatically. You can change the title in FrontPage by right-clicking the Web page and editing the Web page properties (Figure 3-16).

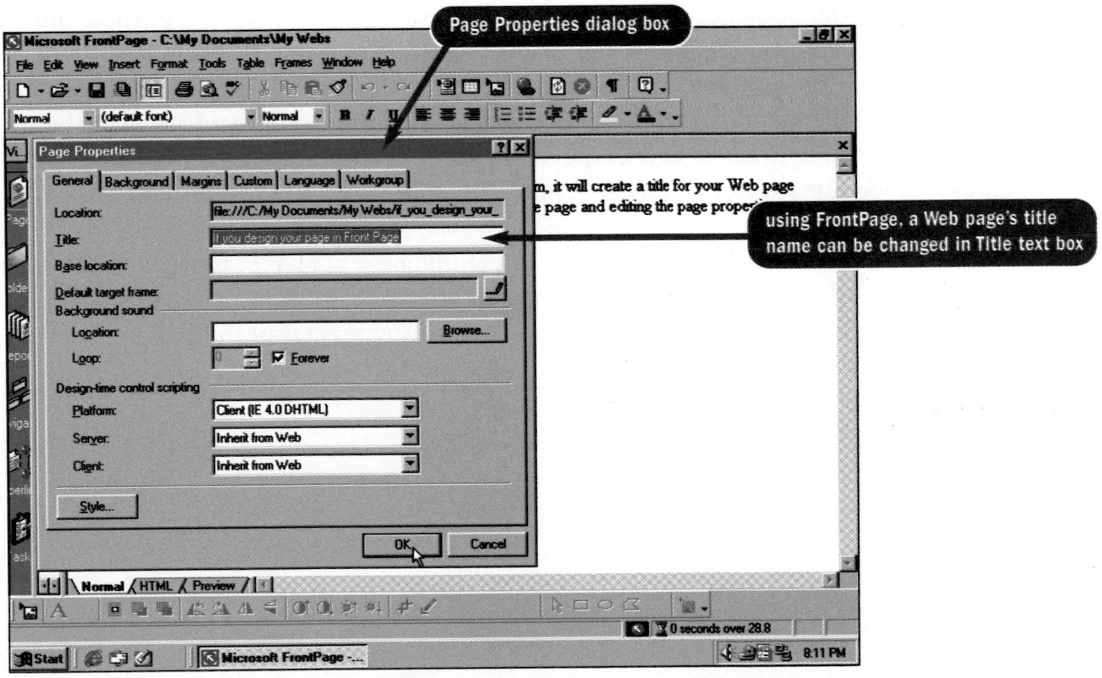

FIGURE 3-17   Changing the title name of a Web page is an easy process using FrontPage.

Develop a File System

Plan an organized file system for your Web site. Keeping organized will help you work more effectively, minimize the risk of losing or misplacing Web site elements, and facilitate the publishing of your Web site to an ISP or OSP. If your Web site is small — fewer than 30 total files including HTML, graphic, audio, video, and so on — create one folder on your local disk for all the files. If your Web site is large — more than 30 total files — create separate, logical subfolders; for example, include subfolders for HTML, photographs, audio, and video files. For both small and large Web sites, create a subfolder in which you can place original files such as word processing files or graphic files that you later will transform into Web-usable formats. Organize according to the following Web Design Tip:

> **Web Design Tip**
>
> Organize the files of a Web site systematically to maximize productivity, reduce the possibility of lost content, and facilitate publishing the Web site.

Whatever file system you create, regularly back up your files, preferably at a location separate from your hard drive. If your backup is in another location on your hard drive and your hard drive crashes, you will lose both your original and backup files. Instead, use an external device, such as a Zip® or Jaz® drive. The larger storage capacity of Zip® or Jaz® disks is preferable over other, smaller storage media. In most instances, one or two Zip® or Jaz® disks will hold your entire Web site file system.

CHAPTER SUMMARY

A Web site demands a considerable investment of time and other important resources. To ensure a Web site's success, a detailed design plan is essential. Step 1 is to define the purpose of the Web site, which entails choosing a specific topic and deciding what you want your Web site to accomplish. Identifying the audience is Step 2. A preliminary audience profile should be developed to consider audience needs and goals. As a result of defining the purpose and identifying the audience, you can determine the major objectives for your Web site. Step 3 of the design plan is to plan the content the Web site will contain. Content types include text, photographs, animations, video, audio, and dynamically generated content. Step 4, to plan the structure, will facilitate planning Web pages and the Web site navigation interface. Common Web site structures include linear/tutorial, random, and hierarchical. Web pages should perform certain functions to help achieve the Web site's purpose and meet the audience's needs and goals. Consideration of these functions assists in planning the actual Web pages. As a Web site develops, an organized file system will help the designer work more effectively, minimize the risk of losing or misplacing elements, and smooth the process of publishing the Web site to an ISP or OSP.

KEY TERMS

Instructions: Use the following terms from this chapter as a study review.

Active Server Page (3.12)
Active Server Page (ASP)
   technology (3.12)
animations (3.10)
animated GIFs (3.10)
audio (3.10)
database (3.12)
directory (3.17)
downloadable media (3.10)
dynamically generated
   content (3.12)

helper applications (3.10)
hierarchical structure (3.14)
home page (3.17)
image maps (3.17)
interactive (3.10)
linear/tutorial structure (3.14)
Microsoft FrontPage (3.21)
multimedia (3.8)
outline (3.14)
photographs (3.7)
plug-in (3.10)

purpose statement (3.3)
random structure (3.14)
repurpose (3.7)
scripting languages (3.12)
search function (3.17)
secondary page (3.20)
splash page (3.18)
stream (3.10)
streaming media (3.10)
text (3.6)
video clips (3.12)

CHECKPOINT   Matching

Instructions: Match each term with the best description.

_____ 1. Active Server Page (ASP)

_____ 2. helper applications

_____ 3. interactive multimedia

_____ 4. dynamically generated content

_____ 5. downloadable media

_____ 6. linear/tutorial structure

_____ 7. image maps

_____ 8. plug-in

_____ 9. random structure

_____ 10. repurpose

_____ 11. streaming media

_____ 12. database

_____ 13. hierarchical structure

a. Information served to a visitor triggered by a specific event, such as time of day or user input.

b. Modifying content designed for one medium to be used in another.

c. Organization by categories and subcategories.

d. Media that displays as it transfers in.

e. Graphics that have specific designated areas that when clicked link to other locations or Web pages.

f. A program that allows certain content to function within a Web page.

g. A program that allows certain content to function in another browser window.

h. Information presented in no specific order.

i. An experience involving a combination of media such as graphics, audio, video, and animations, in which the viewer participates.

j. A collection of data arranged so the contents can be updated and used in various ways.

k. Media that must be downloaded in its entirety to a user's computer in order to be seen or heard.

l. A Web page that uses a Microsoft developed technology to generate content dynamically.

m. A specific order of organization.

CHECKPOINT Fill in the Blanks

Instructions: Fill in the blank(s) with the appropriate answer

1. The purpose of a Web site should be neither too _____ nor too _____.

2. To define the goals and needs of a Web site's audience, develop a _____.

3. As a result of defining the purpose and identifying the audience, you will be able to determine the major _____ for your Web site.

4. Content designed for another medium, such as print, should be _____ for the Web.

5. Most animations that you will find on the Web are in the _____ format.

6. _____ can be an extremely effective low-bandwidth alternative to video.

7. A primary problem with video files is their _____.

8. _____ can be established and maintained through the consistent use of elements on billboards, brochures, business cards, stationery, advertisements, and Web sites.

9. If a Web page is bookmarked for future reference, the bookmark will reflect the _____ of a Web page.

10. As a Web site develops, a(n) _____ will help a designer work more effectively, minimize the risk of losing or misplacing elements, and facilitate the publishing of a Web site.

CHECKPOINT Multiple Choice

Instructions: Select the letter of the correct answer for each question.

1. The extent to which you consider your audience's needs and goals will determine the Web site's degree of _____.

   a. structure
   b. visual identity
   c. usability
   d. ASP

2. Content that furthers Web site objectives, adds _____, not volume.

   a. appeal
   b. excitement
   c. value
   d. elements

3. Which of the following is not a guideline for repurposing text from print publications?

   a. abbreviate the amount of text significantly
   b. chunk information into logical sections for readability
   c. use passive voice and a formal tone
   d. remove transitional words and phrases

4. Photographs on a Web site can _____.

    a. personalize and familiarize the unknown

    b. deliver a message

    c. prompt an action

    d. all of the above

5. Multimedia presentations frequently require the use of a _____.

    a. database

    b. plug-in

    c. helper application

    d. either b or c

6. The delivery of quality _____ over the Web has presented the most difficult challenges.

    a. audio

    b. animations

    c. photographs

    d. video

7. An outline of the structure of a Web site will _____.

    a. serve as a blueprint for the Web site

    b. define the Web site's major navigational paths

    c. determine the Web site's major objectives

    d. both a and b

8. Value-added content is _____.

    a. relative, informative, and timely

    b. accurate and high-quality

    c. usable

    d. all of the above

9. After text, _____ are the most commonly included content elements on Web sites.

    a. animations

    b. photographs

    c. audio clips

    d. video clips

10. Which of the following typically is not found on an organization's Web site?

    a. mission statement

    b. calendar of events

    c. hobbies or personal interests

    d. goals

CHECKPOINT Short Answer

Instructions: Write a brief answer to each question.

1. Define and explain the difference between multimedia and interactive multimedia.

2. Identify the first four steps of a developing a Web site design plan.

3. What is the basic guideline for choosing content for a Web site?

4. Explain the process for identifying a Web site's audience.

5. How should you utilize the major objectives you have determined for your Web site?

6. Discuss the functions of a home page, a splash page, and secondary pages.

7. Describe three types of Web site structures.

8. Explain the advantages and disadvantages of streaming media.

9. Discuss the following content types identifying one way each type can add value to a Web site: text, photographs, animations, video, audio, multimedia, and dynamically generated content.

10. Explain the difference between a plug-in and a helper application.

AT ISSUE

Instructions: Write a brief essay in response to the following issues. Be prepared to discuss your findings in class. Use the Web as your research tool. For each issue, identify one URL utilized as a research source.

1. Napster and clone applications, such as Gnutella and Wrapster, gained controversial popularity, especially on university campuses. After installing this software, a person can go online, access MP3 files of musical performances, download, and, with the right equipment, burn the files on a CD. Some entrepreneurs make a profit by selling these CDs to friends. The Record Industry Association of America (RIAA) has charged the Napster company with copyright infringement. Napster supporters contend that the software allows the protest of the high pricing of CDs by record companies. The situation further is complicated because some students are using their university accounts to acquire the software. Discuss the technical, legal, and moral issues raised by software such as Napster. Suggest possible solutions for this issue.

2. The Web-connected car has a bright future according to many. Clarion Corporation's Clarion AutoPC was the first radio/CD player with voice-activated capability to deliver Internet information, such as news, stock quotes, and e-mail. Motorola has since introduced its prototype, iRadio. Leading car manufacturers predict the devices allowing car-based Internet access will be standard equipment in a few years. One manufacturer's cars will offer a screen for browsing only when such a car is parked. Opportunities for Internet access have multiplied: computers at work and home, notebook computers to take on vacation, handheld computers, cellular telephones, and now Web-connected cars. Discuss the pros and cons of the growth of Internet accessibility.

HANDS ON

Instructions: Complete the following exercises.

1. Access the Web, locate a good example of a personal, organization/topical, and a commercial Web site, and indicate the respective URLs. Identify what you believe to be the purpose and audience of each Web site. For each URL, describe briefly the content included to help achieve the Web site's purpose and meet the needs and goals of the audience.

2. Find one Web site organized according to each of the following structures: linear/tutorial, random, and hierarchical. Identify the URLs and create an outline that illustrates the specific structure of each Web site.

CHAPTER 4

Developing a Design Plan for a Web Site: Part 2

OBJECTIVES

After completing this chapter you will be able to:

- Develop Part 2, Steps 5 and 6, of the six-step design plan for a Web site
- Discuss methods to organize information on Web pages effectively
- Establish a visual connection between a home page and secondary pages
- Describe the impact of a color scheme on a Web site
- Identify the tool options for developing a consistent Web site layout
- Explain how to utilize a layout grid
- Describe the basic components of a table
- Discuss how tables can be used to create page templates
- Differentiate between absolute width and relative width
- Explain the advantages and disadvantages of style sheets
- Differentiate between external and internal style sheets
- Explain the advantages and disadvantages of frames
- Identify guidelines for creating a well-designed Web site navigation system
- Explain user-based and user-controlled navigation
- Differentiate between a relative URL and an absolute URL
- Describe the common types of navigation elements

INTRODUCTION

You have learned the connection between a detailed design plan and a successful Web site. Chapter 3 introduced you to the first four of the six steps required to develop a solid design plan: Step 1: Define the Purpose, Step 2: Identify the Audience, Step 3: Plan the Content, and Step 4: Plan the Structure. Continuing with the development of a design plan, Chapter 4 introduces the remaining two steps, which are Step 5: Plan the Web Pages and Step 6: Plan the Navigation.

STEP 5: PLAN THE WEB PAGES

With your knowledge of the Web site's purpose and audience and an understanding of the required content and structure, the next step is to organize Web page information and establish a visual connection between your home page and secondary pages with the proper layout and color scheme.

WEB INFO

For more information about organizing information on Web pages, visit the Web Design Chapter 4 Web Info page (scsite.com/web/ch4/webinfo.htm) and then click Organization.

ORGANIZE INFORMATION

As you learned in Chapter 2, for some time, the recommendation has been to design Web pages for the lowest common denominator setting of 640 x 480 pixels. Many Web designers argue that the lowest common denominator for screen resolution today is 800 x 600 pixels, and they propose designing Web pages for that setting.

As the lowest common denominator debate continues, some designers choose to continue to design for 640 x 480 pixels. Others design for the higher settings and indicate on their Web pages the best screen resolution with which to view the Web site. Still others create Web pages with relative table widths that adjust automatically to different screen settings. The following concepts for organizing information apply to whatever resolution setting for which you choose to design.

The initial, visible screen area of a Web page is very valuable space because it provides the first glimpse of your Web site and the opportunity to convince visitors that your offering is important and well organized. When organizing information for the visible screen area, keep in mind the following Web Design Tips:

> **Web Design Tip**
> A home page and a splash page must utilize the initial, visible screen area advantageously to achieve their objectives: to provide information about the Web site's purpose and to grab visitors' attention and draw them into the Web site.

> **Web Design Tip**
> Secondary pages need not fit so rigidly within the initial, visible screen area. While organizing these pages, keep in mind the original screen dimensions so you do not force visitors to scroll horizontally to view them. If downward scrolling is necessary, ensure a smooth and logical flow of information.

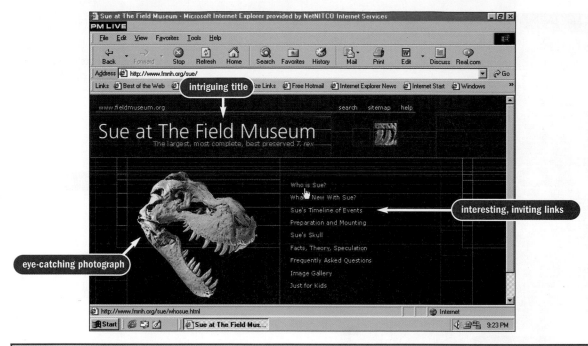

FIGURE 4-1   The home page of the Sue at The Field Museum Web site, featuring Sue the *Tyrannosaurus rex*, utilizes the invisible screen area effectively.

Generally, create Web pages no longer than two screens of information. This guideline is based on the fact that most people find reading and remembering the context of information beyond two screens difficult, which supports abbreviating and chunking text on Web pages. If you limit page lengths to two screens, your visitors will not need to scroll excessively, and more readily will comprehend the information.

If for some reason you cannot limit a Web page to two screens, provide links at the top to select areas within the page so information can be accessed readily. Also, provide links within the Web page that take visitors back to the top. The following Web Design Tips offer guidelines regarding the quantity of information on Web pages:

Web Design Tip

If information is designed to be read online, limit the pages to two screens, and provide any necessary links to additional information.

Web Design Tip

The exception to the two screen length recommendation is for Web pages you intend to be printed and read offline. These Web pages should display in their entirety and contain no unnecessary links.

ESTABLISH A VISUAL CONNECTION

Chapter 3 explained the need for a home page and secondary pages to have a visual connection. You can achieve this connection by creating a consistent look and feel, which unifies and strengthens the Web site's visual identity, and reassures visitors as they navigate (Figure 4-2 on the next page). If pages are inconsistent in appearance, visitors may feel confused, or even possibly believe a link has taken them to an entirely different Web site.

WEB INFO

For more information about creating a consistent look and feel for your Web pages, visit the Web Design Chapter 4 Web Info page (scsite.com/web/ch4/webinfo.htm) and then click Visual Connection.

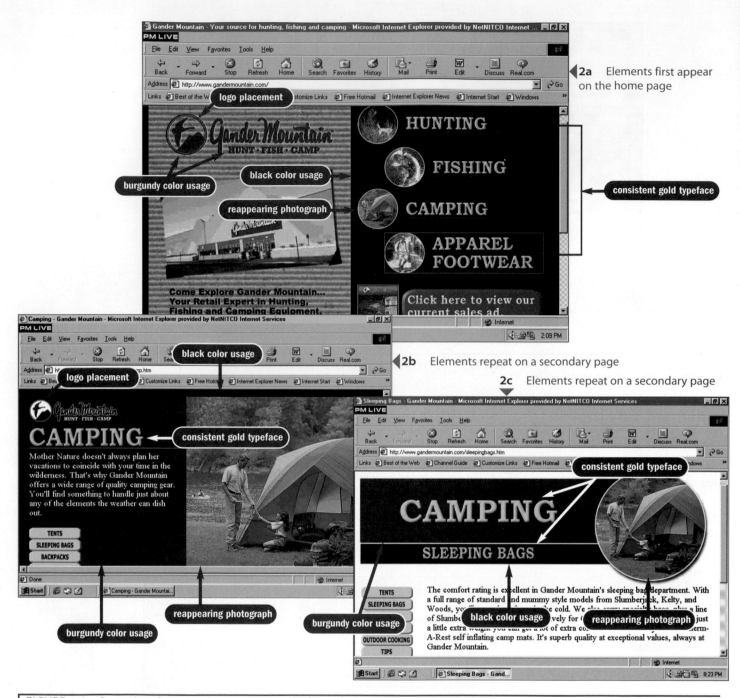

FIGURE 4-2   Repeating elements gives a consistent look and feel to Gander Mountain's home and secondary pages.

The consequences of and the remedy for over applying consistency are explained in the following Web Design Tip:

Web Design Tip

Be careful not to over apply consistency to the extent that your pages become boring and uninteresting. The key is to balance harmony with elements that contrast, enliven, and intrigue.

Understanding and applying the suggestions that follow regarding color scheme and layout are fundamental to establishing and maintaining a visual connection among Web pages.

Color Scheme

Chapter 2 discussed how a well-chosen color scheme creates unity within a Web site. An accepted guideline for a color scheme is offered in the following Web Design Tip:

Web Design Tip

As a general rule, limit the number of colors in your scheme to three. Additional colors lessen the effectiveness of the color scheme.

As you consider options, remember the power of color to influence moods, as well as the importance of choosing browser-safe colors. Review the section on color in Chapter 2 to recall the principles of color on the Web. To build a visual connection throughout your Web site, apply the color scheme to the background, text, and graphic elements included on your Web pages. Figure 4-3 illustrates the attractive color scheme chosen for the Heinz Web site. The red, green, and taupe text and graphic elements stand out against the white background. The complementary colors in the photographs add additional visual appeal.

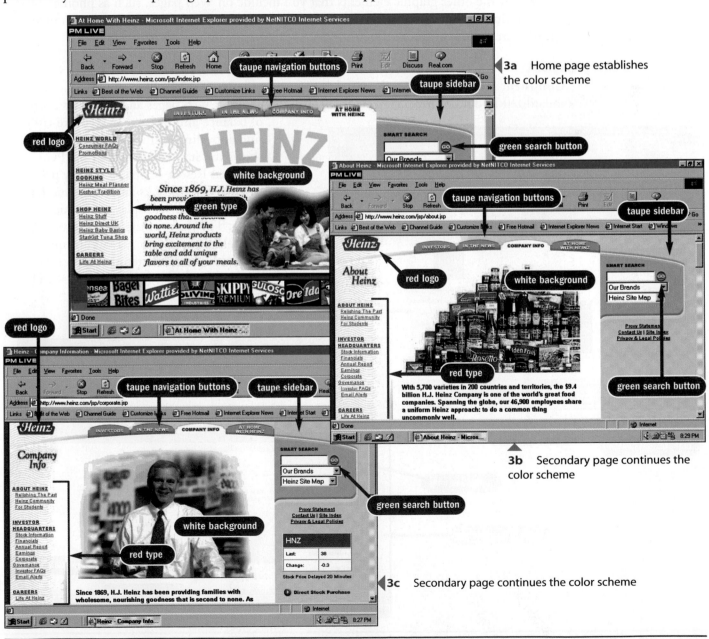

FIGURE 4-3   The Heinz Web site utilizes an effective color scheme of red, taupe, and green on a white page background to create a sense of unity.

Choose a background color that increases the legibility of any text that displays on top of it. Avoid, for instance, placing purple text on a lime green background. The combination both hinders online reading, and causes significant eyestrain. Black or blue text on a light-colored background would be a better choice. Follow the suggestions regarding text and color in these Web Design Tips:

Web Design Tip

Test the results of different blends of background and superimposed text on onscreen legibility. Consider also the results when pages are printed. Imagine, for instance, the output of a Web page with white text on a yellow background using a monochrome printer.

Web Design Tip

In addition to legibility and printout quality, choose a text color(s) for titles, headlines, subheads, and so on that enhances the Web site's mood, complements the background, and attracts the appropriate amount of attention.

Remember the other graphic elements that you include on Web pages, such as photographs and illustrations, typically will add more color. Choose photos and illustrations that complement or match your color scheme.

Layout

Consistent **layout** of pages and page elements creates unity within a Web site. A logical, standardized layout ensures a clear, visible connection among Web pages and generates a sense of balance and order that Web site visitors find appealing and reassuring. Figure 4-4 shows the standard layout of the PGA National Resort & Spa secondary pages. The navigation links and search mechanism consistently display at the top of pages. The body of the page shows a predictable three-column layout: column one — main textual content; column two — a panoramic photo; column three— a Did you Know? information bulletin.

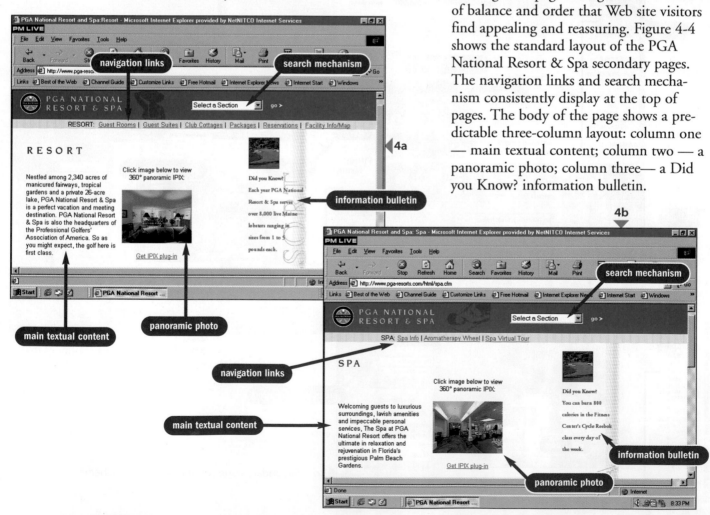

FIGURE 4-4   The PGA National Resort & Spa's home and secondary pages.

Grids

Many designers utilize a **grid**, which is an underlying layout structure that arranges a page into rows and columns. A grid is for layout purposes only and does not display when a Web page actually is viewed with a browser. With a grid, you consistently can set margin width, alignment of elements, and more.

To establish a basic layout grid for the pages of your Web site, consider the elements that will regularly display on your pages, for example major text blocks, photos, navigation controls, and headings. Sketch your grid or utilize the onscreen grid capability offered in some Web authoring packages (Figure 4-5). As you develop the pages for your site, utilize the basic grid layout. To this grid you carefully can add variations that generate interest and variety without upsetting the essential balance and order. The benefit of using a grid is stated in the following Web Design Tip:

Web Design Tip

Developing and utilizing a basic layout grid will help unify your Web site by establishing a visual connection among your Web pages.

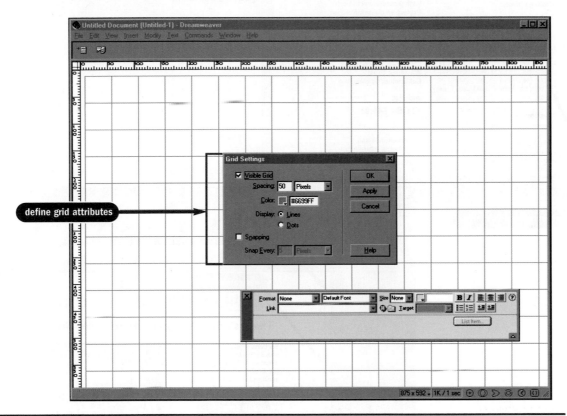

FIGURE 4-5   The onscreen grid feature offered by a Web authoring package can help you align elements and achieve a consistent layout.

WEB INFO

For more information about using tables to define layout, visit the Web Design Chapter 4 Web Info page (scsite.com/web/ch4/webinfo.htm) and then click Tables.

Tables

A **table** contains cells, which align into rows and columns. The original intended usage for **HTML tables** was to display rows and columns of data (Figure 4-6a). Designers more frequently utilize tables to create page templates. You can use tables to physically apply the basic layout grid that you establish for your Web pages. Many pages found on the Web use a two-column table to define the layout. In this popular format, the left column usually is narrower than the right column. Navigation links frequently display in the left column (Figure 4-6b).

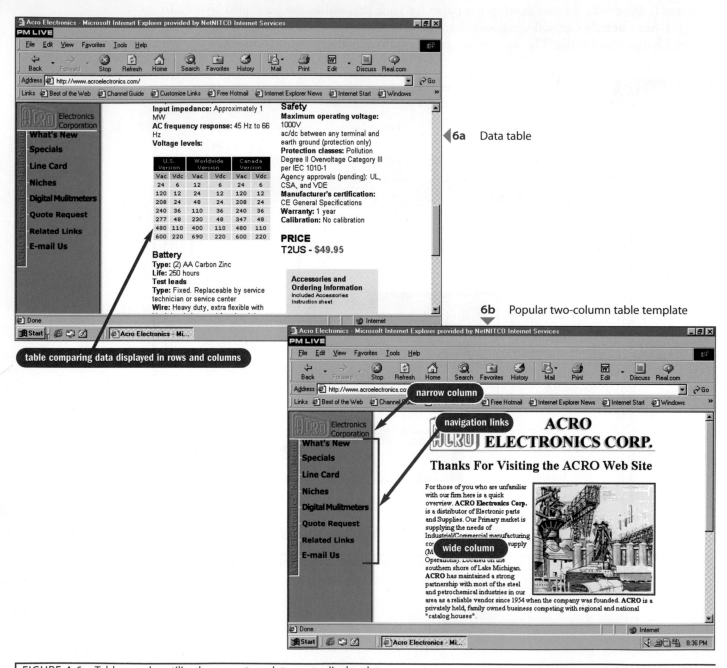

6a Data table

6b Popular two-column table template

table comparing data displayed in rows and columns

narrow column

navigation links

wide column

FIGURE 4-6 Tables can be utilized as page templates or to display data.

Using tables, you can position text and other elements according to the rows and columns. Tables can display borders or be borderless. Borders and cells can be colorized. By specifying a number of pixels with the **cell spacing** attribute, you can regulate the space between cells. With the **cell padding** attribute and a pixel number, you can regulate the space between a cell's content and its borders. Figure 4-7 illustrates cell padding and cell spacing. You can create simple or complicated tables by inserting table tags into an HTML document in a text editor, or by using the table-generation capability built into Web authoring software.

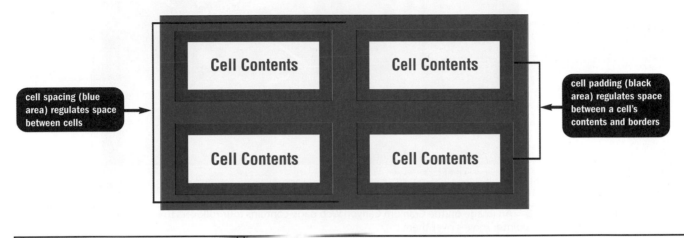

FIGURE 4-7 The cell spacing and cell padding attributes of a table.

You can specify the width of a table either by absolute or relative width. To define by **absolute width** using a text editor or Web authoring software, enter the number of pixels for the table's width. A table specified this way would display only at that exact width even if a browser window were resized. To define by **relative width**, enter a percentage instead of a pixel number. A table specified this way would resize in relation to the size of a browser window.

If you specify the width of a table by absolute width, you can ensure that the user's view of the table contents will be the same as your view. A table defined by absolute width also displays more quickly than a table defined by relative width because the browser does not have to calculate the width. The advantage of defining a table by relative width is adaptability to various browser window sizes. The disadvantage to using relative width is browsers set at different window sizes will fit the table contents as needed, for example, wrapping text in an undesired manner. Consequently, you cannot guarantee the user's view of the table contents will be identical to your view if you define a table by relative width.

Segmenting an image and reconstructing it with tables is a specialized use of a layout tool. You might use this process so only specific parts of the image will be animated or act as a rollover. A **rollover** is a technique utilizing JavaScript that changes a page element when the mouse pointer moves over it. A section of an image acting as a rollover, for example, may display a box with additional information (Figure 4-8). You also may want to split an image and reconstruct it in order to add a caption in a specific location. Previously, segmenting and reconstructing an image was a fairly complex process. Now, Web image editing and optimizing software such as **Macromedia Fireworks** and **Adobe ImageReady** simplify the segmenting process and automatically generate the table code that reconstructs the image.

WEB INFO

For more information about segmenting and reconstructing images using tables, visit the Web Design Chapter 4 Web Info page (scsite.com/web/ch4/webinfo.htm) and then click Segmenting and Reconstructing.

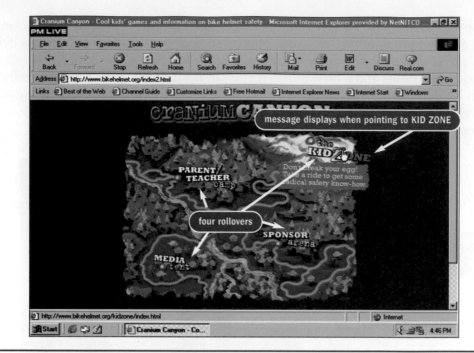

FIGURE 4-8 An image on the Cranium Canyon Web page contains four rollovers that display messages when the mouse pointer moves over them.

Follow the recommendations regarding tables in this Web Design Tip:

Web Design Tip

Before you actually create any table, sketch it. Determine the number of rows and columns and the content you will place in the cells. Calculate the overall width of the table and the necessary width for each column. If you plan carefully, you will not find tables intimidating; rather, you will view them as manageable, powerful layout tools.

WEB INFO

For more information about using style sheets for establishing consistency on Web pages, visit the Web Design Chapter 4 Web Info page (scsite.com/web/ch4/webinfo.htm) and then click Style Sheets.

Style Sheets

Print designers enjoy the freedom and appreciate the tools that allow them to layout and control the appearance of documents. Web designers, on the other hand, criticize HTML for affording few options to control the look of Web pages. The world Wide Web Consortium (W3C) responded to this criticism with a multi-featured specification for HTML, **cascading style sheets (CSS)**. This specification allows Web designers to attach to their HTML documents style sheets that contain specific information regarding the appearance of Web pages. **Styles** can define the height, width, positioning, and alignment of elements; set margins; indicate page breaks; and specify other layout features.

Style sheets allow you to define several attributes all at once to all elements sharing the same HTML tag. A style consists of an HTML tag and a definition(s), which defines the element's appearance. For example, by defining one style, you could specify that text on your Web pages will wrap around all images on only one side (Figure 4-9). Without styles, you would have to insert the proper HTML code around each image in your pages. By centralizing information, styles both can simplify the process of making changes and save a designer considerable time.

You can apply styles with internal or external style sheets. Use an **internal style sheet** for individual pages, especially if they contain large amounts of text. Internal style sheets become part of the coding of a Web page. <STYLE> is placed within the <HEAD> segment of an HTML document, followed by the tag to which the style is to apply. Within curly braces ({ }), the tag properties are listed, separated by semicolons. </STYLE> ends the style sheet.

Use an **external style sheet** if you have numerous Web pages that you want to be consistent in appearance. An external style is a separate text file to which you can link your Web pages. Within the text file, an HTML tag is indicated, followed by the tag properties separated by semicolons within curly braces. The text file, the external style sheet, is saved in text-only format with a **.css extension**. A link can be placed within the <HEAD> segment of pages to which the style sheet is to apply.

The following Web Design Tip makes a recommendation regarding style sheet usage:

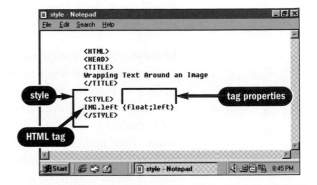

FIGURE 4-9   A style that defines how text will wrap around images on a Web page.

Web Design Tip

Style sheets are considered an up-and-coming technology, because no current browser supports all style specifications. If you decide to use style sheets, test how your specifications display in different browsers before publishing your Web pages.

Chapter 3 began the development of the investment Web site to illustrate the first four steps of a solid design plan. To incorporate Step 5: Plan the Web Pages for the investment Web site, you would establish the visual connection using the guidelines for choosing a color scheme to create unity and a layout using grids and tables. Figure 4-10 shows the plan for the investment Web pages, documenting the details in a Word document.

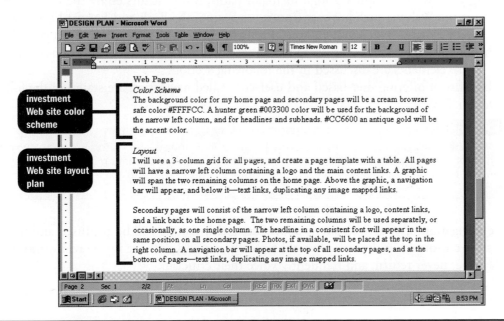

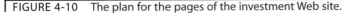

FIGURE 4-10   The plan for the pages of the investment Web site.

STEP 6: PLAN THE NAVIGATION

With the organization, color scheme, and layout determined, the final step in developing a design plan is to plan the navigation system to ensure the success of your Web site. Not only will a well-designed navigation system pull the visitors' attention down the home page, but also it will draw them deeper into your Web site and give them a sense of context. To allow direction and flexibility, the navigation design should be both user-based and user-controlled.

User-Based Navigation

Your navigation will be **user-based** if you followed the guidelines for creating the outline structure in Step 4: Plan the Structure presented in Chapter 3. The major navigational paths for a Web site discussed in Step 4 are determined by its outline structure. Effective Web site outlining organizes information to achieve the Web site's primary objectives, which are designed to meet the needs and goals of the audience. In the investment Web site model, a combination of linear/tutorial and hierarchical structures, which became the Web site's major navigational paths (shown in Figure 3-12 on page 3.16 in Chapter 3), organize the information to achieve the following objectives:

1. Establish credibility of the company.

2. Provide sound financial advice.

3. Make available an analysis tool to determine the worth of current assets.

4. Provide a method to calculate anticipated retirement needs.

5. Advise strategies to achieve retirement goals.

6. Develop individualized retirement plans.

User-Controlled Navigation

To ensure that your navigation design is **user-controlled**, you need to offer options to navigating your Web site only through its major paths. Most visitors enjoy the freedom to move about the Web via such browser features as Search, the Back and Forward buttons, History, and Favorites (Figure 4-11). You can offer similar navigating options on your Web site via such elements as text, buttons, image maps, menus, a site index, a Search feature, and frames. These elements are discussed in the following section.

The benefits of offering user-based and user-controlled navigation are stated in the following Web Design Tip:

Web Design Tip

If your Web site's navigation design is both user-based and user-controlled, your visitors will be able to move to different locations on a page or to other pages in your Web site to find useable information quickly and easily. A positive experience on your Web site equals satisfied customers who may return and express their approval to others.

If the navigation of your Web site is poorly designed, visitors will be confused and frustrated. Dissatisfied customers in the virtual world typically respond as those in the real world do: they quickly leave, never return, and frequently voice their criticism.

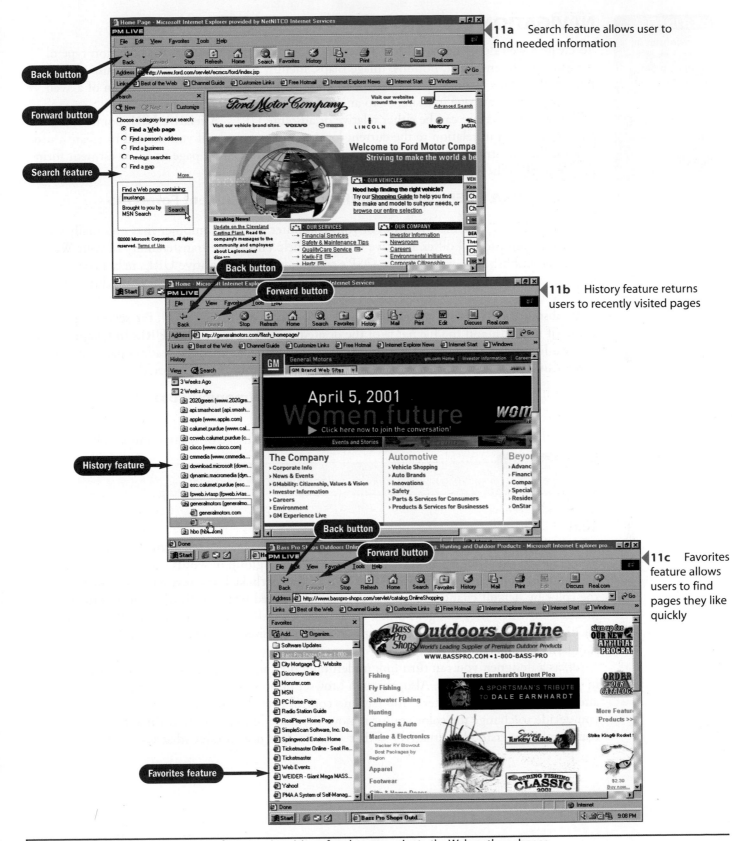

11a Search feature allows user to find needed information

11b History feature returns users to recently visited pages

11c Favorites feature allows users to find pages they like quickly

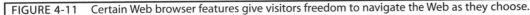

FIGURE 4-11   Certain Web browser features give visitors freedom to navigate the Web as they choose.

WEB INFO

For more information about the types of navigation elements used to create a well-designed navigation system, visit the Web Design Chapter 4 Web Info page (scsite.com/web/ch4/webinfo.htm) and then click Navigation Elements.

NAVIGATION ELEMENTS

To create a well-designed navigation system for your Web site, consider the common type of navigation elements: text, buttons, image maps, menus, a site index, a Search feature and frames. By means of linking, these elements can take a visitor to a different section of a Web page, to a different page in a site, or to another Web site.

The links you create can be either relative or absolute URLs. A **relative URL** points to another location in relation to the current location. For example, if you wanted to create a text link on the investment Web site from the investment guru feature page to an investment form profile page in the same directory, the relative URL would be

<A HREF="investmentform.htm">Investment Form</A>

In all likelihood, the file structures of your computer and the computer that eventually will host your Web site will differ. Relative URLs can help ensure the transferability of your Web site when you publish it to your ISP's or OSP's computer. Because relative URLs tells a browser to look for a linked page in relation to its current location, the browser will have no difficulty locating the page.

An **absolute URL** points to another location by specifying the protocol, the server, a path name (if needed), and the file name of the desired page. You can review URLs in Chapter 1. To create a link from the investment guru feature page to a recommended reading page on the American Association for Retired Persons' Web site, the absolute URL would be

http://www.aarp.com/moneyguide/moneybooks.html

The following Web Design Tip offers guidelines for the usage of relative and absolute URLs:

Web Design Tip
Use relative URLs for Web pages within your site, and absolute URLs for pages located on another server.

Text

Linked text undoubtedly is the most commonly used navigation element. By default, unlinked text on Web pages is black. When a word or a group of words is linked, the default appearance is blue and underlined. When linked text is clicked, the text remains underlined, but the color by default changes to purple. A blue, underlined text link clearly indicates to visitors a location to which they can go. Purple, underlined text tells visitors they previously visited this location. These defaults, with rare exceptions, are recognized instantly as a link. Utilizing these standard defaults contributes to a well-designed navigation system.

Yet, as a designer, you can turn link underlining off and change the color of hyperlinked text in your HTML documents. Also, through browser options, a visitor can hide underlining and alter colors of hyperlinked text. You have no control over the options a visitor may choose. If you decide to change the color and/or remove the underlining from hyperlinked text, substitute commonly understood alternatives so that a visitor does not wonder what text to click.

Recognized alternatives include text that changes color or becomes highlighted when the mouse pointer moves over it. The rollover effect can be created by adding a specific JavaScript to a Web page either via a text editor or Web authoring software. Another accepted convention is text placed at the top of a page separated by vertical bars or enclosed within square brackets as shown in Figure 4-12.

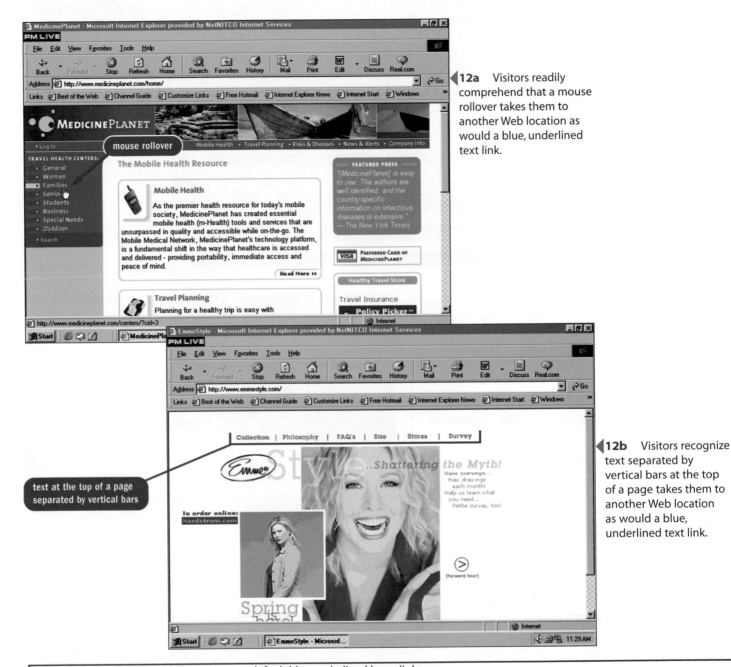

12a Visitors readily comprehend that a mouse rollover takes them to another Web location as would a blue, underlined text link.

12b Visitors recognize text separated by vertical bars at the top of a page takes them to another Web location as would a blue, underlined text link.

FIGURE 4-12   Recognized alternatives to default blue underlined hyperlinks.

Buttons

Buttons are the second most common navigation elements for Web sites. You will find an infinite variety of sizes, styles, colors, and shapes on Web pages. Besides linking to another location, some buttons when clicked change color or highlight, make clicking or other sounds, or depress as an actual button would. Typically, you create the links by a process called image mapping, which is discussed in the next section. You can generate special effects by adding specially designed scripts to HTML code in a text editor, or using Web authoring software with these capabilities.

Buttons can be downloaded from the Web, purchased on a CD-ROM, found within Web authoring programs, or created using such image editing programs as Adobe Photoshop. You can construct what appears to be a button bar through an innovative use of tables. Figure 4-13 illustrates a button bar and the HTML code that was used to produce it. A button bar created this way will load quickly and display even if a visitor has turned off graphics in the browser.

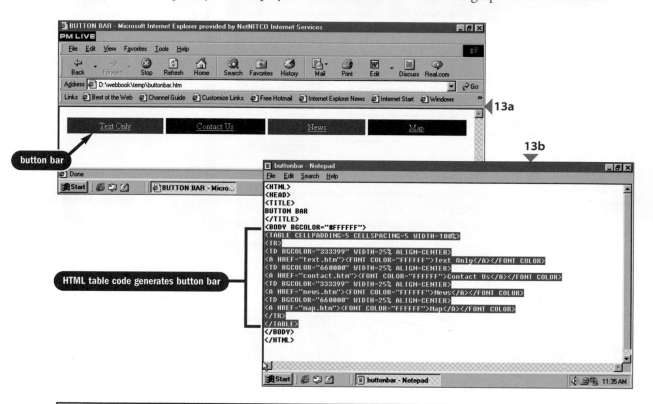

FIGURE 4-13   A button bar created with table code.

Adhere to the recommendations in the following Web Design Tip regarding buttons and a well-designed navigation system:

Web Design Tip

If you utilize buttons as a navigation element, do not allow their size or appearance to detract from more important content. Their role is to serve as a link, not be a focus. Also, ensure that their look matches the mood of the Web site. For example for an antique dealer's Web site, you would choose a classic, conservative button style, not a neon, translucent style.

In addition to buttons, **icons**, which are small, symbolic images, can serve as links. Figure 4-14 illustrates icons commonly found on Web sites. Use icons subtly and sparingly. Excessive or overly cute icons tend to make Web pages look amateurish and distract from the content.

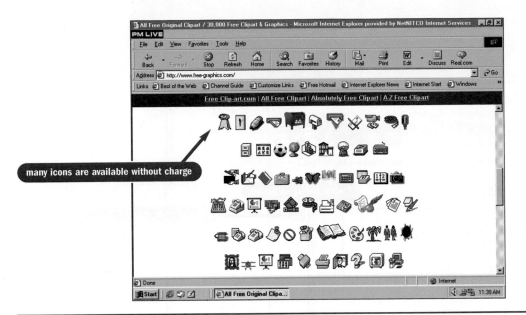

FIGURE 4-14   Many Web sites offer free icons ready to download.

Image Maps

Image maps, sometimes referred to as clickable maps, were introduced in Chapter 3 as graphics having specific designated areas that when clicked link to other locations or pages. Photographs and illustrations frequently are used as image maps. The designated hot areas that link to URLs are defined by x and y coordinates. The coordinates define the pixel distance from the graphic's left corner. Image mapping capabilities are included in several Web authoring packages, as well as in specialty image mapping software such as **MapEdit**.

Image maps can be either client-side or server-side. In a **client-side image map**, the mapping information resides in the HTML document and is processed by the user's browser. Browser versions Netscape Navigator 2.0 and Internet Explorer 3.0 and higher process client-side image maps. Older Web browsers support only server-side image maps. With a **server-side image** map, a CGI script processes the mapping information, which resides on a server. The following Web Design Tip explains an advantage and disadvantages of utilizing server-side image maps:

Web Design Tip
Although all Web browsers can process server-side image maps, they are more complicated to create than client-side image maps, increase demands on a server, and typically have slower response times than client-side image maps.

Optimize the file size of photos and illustrations that you use for image maps so load time will not be hampered. As with buttons, choose photos and illustrations for image mapping that accurately represent the content they link to and enhance the Web site's mood.

Menus

Menus, whether they are pull-down, pop-up, or scrolling, offer visitors several options from which to choose. Typically, a visitor selects an option and then either double-clicks the selection or clicks a Go or View button to travel to another location on the same Web page, a page within the Web site, or to another site on the Web (Figure 4-15 on the next page). When using menus, keep in mind the following Web Design Tip:

Web Design Tip
The main advantage of menus is that they allow you to offer many navigation options in a relatively small amount of space.

WEB INFO
For more information about using image maps in a navigation system, visit the Web Design Chapter 4 Web Info page (scsite.com/web/ch4/webinfo.htm) and then click Image Maps.

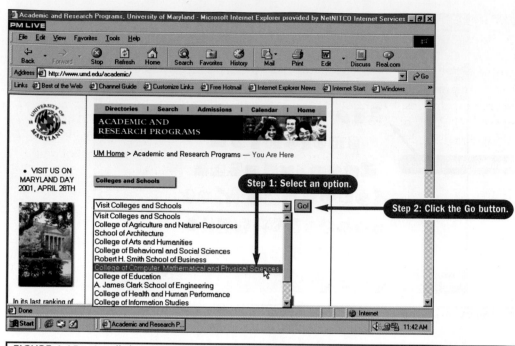

FIGURE 4-15 A pull-down menu on the University of Maryland Web site helps visitors find colleges and schools.

Site Index

If your Web site is very large or complex, a **site index** can help your visitors readily find information. A site index contains hyperlinked text to specific locations within the Web site. You can organize the index either alphabetically, or by an outline of the site, similar to a table of contents (Figure 4-16). Site indexes generally are preferred over **site maps**, which are graphic representations. This preference is based on the argument that the information in site maps often is too condensed to be of real value. Conversely, a site map with detailed information creates an inefficient, oversized graphic.

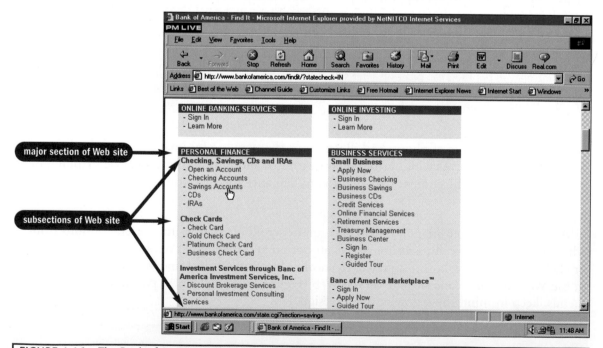

FIGURE 4-16 The Bank of America Web site index is organized according to the site structure.

Search Feature

A **Search feature** is very popular Web navigation tool, especially for large, complex Web sites such as those of universities and major corporations or organizations. Chapter 1 introduced you to the search engines utilized by such sites as Yahoo! and AltaVista to provide search services. The process for locating specific information is similar with both large- and small-scale search capabilities: a user enters keywords into a search box and clicks the Search button (Figure 4-17). A list of Web pages containing the keywords will display. Microsoft FrontPage offers designers the ability to build a Search feature into Web pages, provided that the Web site is on a server with specific FrontPage server features. The advantage of incorporating a Search feature into a Web site is stated in the following Web Design Tip:

WEB INFO

For more information about incorporating a Search feature in Web site navigation, visit the Web Design Chapter 4 Web Info page (scsite.com/web/ch4/webinfo.htm) and then click Search Feature.

Web Design Tip

A Search feature can give visitors the much desired flexibility and control to navigate a Web site in the manner they choose.

17a Initiate a search for specific information by clicking link to the Search feature

17b Enter keywords related to desired information and click Search button

FIGURE 4-17 Visitors can utilize the Search feature to find information quickly on the U.S. Fish & Wildlife Service Web site.

Frames

Frames divide a Web page into sections and can be utilized both as a page design tool and a navigation element. On the surface, frames may seem not much different from tables. They are similar in that they can be used to layout a page, and can have borders or be borderless. A table or several tables may display on one Web page; however, within each frame you can place a different Web page. **Scrolling** is another distinct feature of frames. You can scroll down one frame, which may or may not have a scroll bar, and the other frame(s) will remain fixed (Figure 4-18).

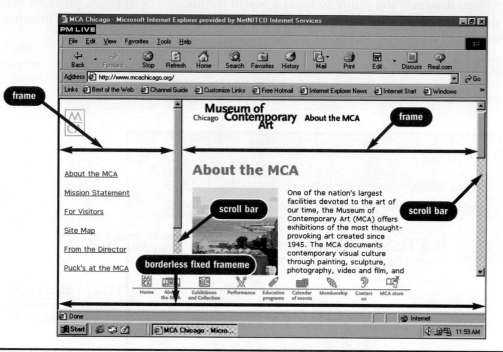

FIGURE 4-18 The Chicago Museum of Contemporary Art home page is comprised of frames.

WEB INFO

For more information about the pros and cons of using frames in Web site navigation, visit the Web Design Chapter 4 Web Info page (scsite.com/web/ch4/webinfo.htm) and then click Frames.

Frames, like splash pages, receive mixed reviews. On the plus side, frames can facilitate navigation. In a two-frame page, for example, the left column could contain navigation links. The other column, sometimes called the contents frame, could be used to display linked pages. As a result, visitors could view pages with the navigation links always visible.

On the negative side, frames can hamper navigation, especially regarding use of a browser's Back button. If visitors are unsure of what frame they are in, the results of clicking the Back button can be annoying. Similarly, visitors may think they bookmarked a page, only to be unable to find the page later. In fact, they bookmarked the wrong page because they did not realize what frame they were in. In addition, several frames on one page can be very confusing and significantly decrease the visible area for the most important content. Frames are best suited for larger monitors. A page created with frames is almost non-functional on the small screens of personal digital assistants (PDAs).

HTML Version 4.0 specifies frames, and popular Web authoring packages make frame creation very easy (Figure 4-19). Make sure that you understand the pros and cons of frames, and take into consideration that some visitors might be viewing your Web pages with browsers that do not support frames.

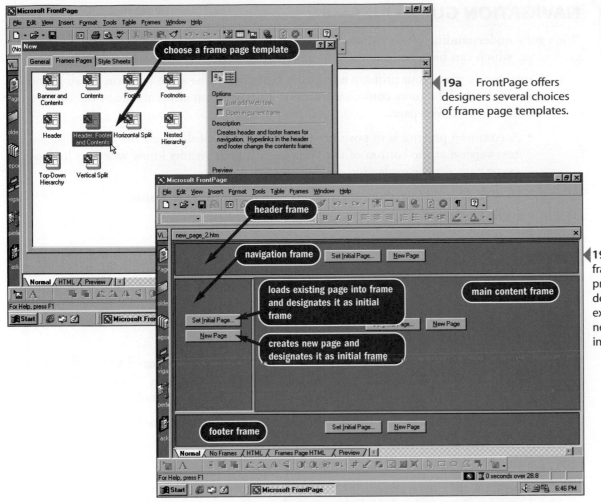

19a FrontPage offers designers several choices of frame page templates.

19b Within each frame, FrontPage provides options for designating an existing page or a new page as the initial frame.

FIGURE 4-19 Microsoft FrontPage makes creating a frame page simple.

To incorporate Step 6: Plan the Navigation for the investment Web site model created in Chapter 3, as the designer, you would include both user-based navigation and user-controlled navigation to offer visitors direction and flexibility. The outline prepared in Chapter 3 directly affects the major navigational paths. Figure 4-20 illustrates the navigation design for the investment Web site.

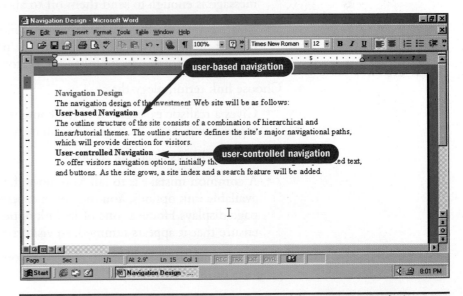

FIGURE 4-20 The plan for the navigation design of the investment Web site.

WEB INFO

For more information about navigation guidelines and elements, visit the Web Design Chapter 4 Web Info page (scsite.com/web/ch4/webinfo.htm) and then click Navigation Guidelines.

NAVIGATION GUIDELINES

With your understanding of the common types of navigation elements, consider the following guidelines, which can help you create a well-designed navigation system for your Web site.

1. Consistently place your primary navigation elements in the same location on all pages of your Web site. The more common locations for navigation elements are at the top, bottom, or the side of a Web page.

   - A common practice is to position a graphic version of the elements at the top, and a text version at the bottom of the Web page. If your visitors know where to look on every page for the navigation controls they will:

      - Feel confident about their ability to navigate your Web site.
      - Find their information readily and effortlessly.
      - Become satisfied customers.

2. All secondary pages should include:

   - A link back to the home page. A visitor should be able to return from any secondary page to the home page, which typically will make available the primary content links for your site. If your Web site should be viewed sequentially, then secondary pages should have links to the next and previous pages.

   - A logo or other type of **site identifier**. A visitor may have accessed a secondary page from a search engine, and not from your Web site's home page. A logo or site identifier will indicate where the visitor is in relation to the Web as a whole.

   - A page title displayed in the address bar that is relative and descriptive of the Web page contents.

3. Ensure that links on your Web pages are:

   - Functional. Check external links frequently. If a page has been moved or renamed and you have not updated the link, your visitor will encounter the **HTTP 404 error message** that indicates the page could not be found. For some visitors, one such message is enough to send them off to another site.

   - Relative and worthwhile. Include only links that are worth clicking. The content behind them should relate directly to the pertinent subject matter, and be substantive, additional information useful to the visitor.

4. Choose link terminology that:

   - Gives a realistic expectation of the content to be found if the link is visited. Do not use vague terminology. Be clear and accurate to avoid frustrating or disappointing your visitors.

5. Indicate to visitors clear link options:

   - A common mistake is to fail to remove the link to the current page from the list of available link options. You may have experienced visiting a Web site on which the home page displays Home as one of its link options. As a rule, remove such a link entirely, or ensure that it appears dimmed, so visitors are not confused.

6. If you use graphics as navigation elements, consider visitors who may have turned graphics off in their browsers:

   - Use the **ALT attribute**, which provides a description of the image that is not displayed.

   - Provide text links in addition to the linked graphic elements.

A well-designed navigation system will ensure the success of your visitors to move throughout your Web site with ease. Figure 4-20 shows an example of a Web site that uses proper navigation conventions.

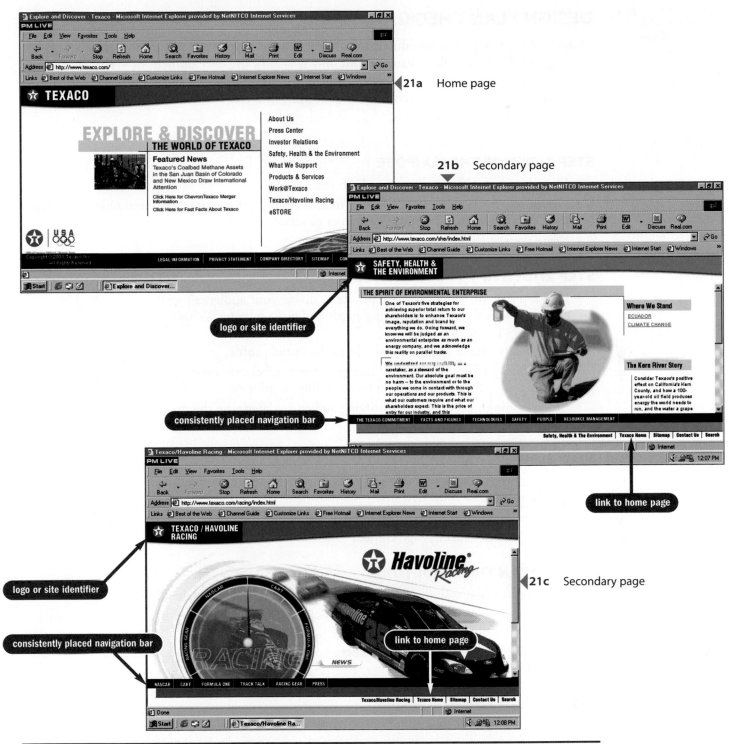

FIGURE 4-21   Texaco's secondary non-sequential Web pages follow the guidelines for navigation.

The following Web Design Tip explains the critical need for a Web site to have a well-designed navigation system:

Web Design Tip

At any time, visitors can click the Back or Forward button in the browser window that takes them to a Web site they previously have visited. Just as quickly, they can type another URL, jump to a search engine, or choose a bookmark. A well-designed navigation system that allows visitors to find usable information quickly and easily will encourage them to stay longer on your Web site and return in the future.

DESIGN PLAN CHECKLIST

Chapter 3 and Chapter 4 introduced the critical need to develop a solid six-step design plan for creating a Web site. Detailed planning not only is vital in the development of a Web site, but also in any other similar investment to which time and other significant resources will be dedicated. To ensure a successful Web site, the following checklist provides a reference for you in the development of your design plan.

STEP 1: DEFINE THE PURPOSE

- Identify the specific topic of your Web site.
- Decide what you want your Web site to accomplish; for example, to communicate information, educate, entertain, or sell a product or service.
- Write your purpose statement.

STEP 2: IDENTIFY THE AUDIENCE

- Develop a preliminary audience profile to define your audience's goals and needs. The extent to which you consider their needs and goals in your Web site's design will determine its degree of usability.
- Continually gather feedback and add to the initial profile.
- If resources are limited, identify and meet your audience's top two goals and needs. Then focus on additional goals and needs according to priority.
- After defining purpose and identifying audience, determine the major objectives for your Web site.

STEP 3: PLAN THE CONTENT

- Select content that contributes to the Web site objectives. Such content adds value, not merely volume to your Web site.
- Repurpose content designed for another medium before including it on your Web pages.
- Do not include cutting-edge content just because you can.

STEP 4: PLAN THE STRUCTURE

- Consider the best way to structure your information to achieve the Web site objectives.
- Choose a structural theme for your site — linear/tutorial, random, or hierarchical — or a combination of structural themes.
- Determine the positions in your structure where the content fits best and could be utilized most effectively.

STEP 5: PLAN THE WEB PAGES

- Organize your information.
- Establish a visual connection between your home page and secondary pages.
- To create unity within your Web site, choose a uniform color scheme and utilize a consistent page layout.

STEP 6: PLAN THE NAVIGATION

- Create a navigation design that is both user-based and user-controlled, offering both major navigational paths and options to navigating the paths.
- Choose navigation elements that your visitors readily will understand and that match the Web site's mood.
- Consistently place navigation elements in predictable, logical locations.

CHAPTER SUMMARY

This chapter identifies the remaining steps to creating a design plan to ensure your Web site's success. Step 5 is to plan how to organize page information and establish a visual connection between a home page and secondary pages. The initial, visible screen area must be used advantageously. Design a home page so the most important information fits within these parameters. Also consider the screen area when designing secondary pages. Ensure that visitors never have to scroll horizontally to view pages, and that the information on secondary pages flows smoothly and logically. A visual connection between a home page and secondary pages strengthens a Web site's identity and reassures visitors. A uniform color scheme and a consistent layout created with such tools as grids, tables, and style sheets, will establish a strong visual connection.

Step 6 is to plan a well-designed, site navigation system that is both user-based and user-controlled, offering both major navigational paths and options to navigating the paths. Such a system allows visitors to find usable information quickly and easily. Common types of navigation elements include text, buttons, image maps, menus, a site index, a Search feature, and frames. Frames are a unique type of navigation element. Before using frames, take into consideration their advantages, disadvantages, and the viewing capabilities of visitors. This chapter concludes with general guidelines for creating a well-designed navigation system and a design plan checklist.

KEY TERMS

Instructions: Use the following terms from this chapter as a study review.

.css extension (4.11)	linked text (4.14)
absolute URL (4.14)	Macromedia Fireworks (4.9)
absolute width (4.9)	MapEdit (4.17)
Adobe ImageReady (4.9)	menus (4.17)
ALT attribute (4.22)	relative URL (4.14)
buttons (4.16)	relative width (4.9)
cascading style sheets (CSS) (4.10)	rollover (4.9)
cell padding (4.9)	scrolling (4.20)
cell spacing (4.9)	Search feature (4.19)
client-side image map (4.17)	server-side image map (4.17)
external style sheet (4.11)	site identifier (4.22)
frames (4.20)	site index (4.18)
grid (4.7)	site maps (4.18)
HTML table (4.8)	style sheets (4.10)
HTTP 404 error message (4.22)	styles (4.10)
icons (4.16)	table (4.8)
image maps (4.17)	user-based (4.12)
internal style sheet (4.11)	user-controlled (4.12)
layout (4.6)	

CHECKPOINT Matching

Instructions: Match each term with the best description.

_____ 1. absolute width

_____ 2. external style sheet

_____ 3. client-side image map

_____ 4. icons

_____ 5. rollover

_____ 6. relative URL

_____ 7. server-side image map

_____ 8. cell spacing

_____ 9. cascading style sheets (CSS)

_____ 10. frames

_____ 11. internal style sheet

_____ 12. absolute URL

_____ 13. table

_____ 14. cell padding

_____ 15. relative width

a. Specifying a number of pixels with this attribute, you can regulate the space between cells.

b. This attribute and a pixel number regulates the space between a cell's contents and its borders.

c. A text-only file containing style information to which other Web pages can be linked.

d. Small, symbolic images that can serve as links.

e. Specifies how wide a table should be in pixels.

f. CGI script processes the mapping information in this image map.

g. Specifies how wide a table should be in percentages.

h. A style sheet placed within the <HEAD> segment of an HTML document.

i. A technique utilizing JavaScript that changes a page element when the mouse pointer moves over it.

j. HTML specification that allows Web designers to attach to their HTML documents style sheets that contain specific information regarding the appearance of pages.

k. Points to another location in relation to the current location.

l. Points to another location by specifying the protocol, the server, a path name (if necessary), and the file name of the desired page.

m. An image map in which the mapping information resides in the HTML document and is processed by the browser.

n. Sections of a Web page that can hold different pages.

o. Contains cells, aligned into rows and columns.

CHECKPOINT   Fill in the Blanks

Instructions: Fill in the blank(s) with the appropriate answer

1. A well chosen color scheme and a consistent layout will create _____ within a Web site.

2. As a rule, create Web pages no longer than _____ screens of information.

3. Choose a background color to increase the _____ of superimposed text.

4. A well-designed site navigation system is both _____ and _____.

5. Designers often utilize tables as _____ for their Web pages.

6. A browser will display a table more quickly if its overall width is specified in _____ rather than _____.

7. Use a(n) _____ style sheet for single Web pages with large amounts of text. If the same style sheet is to apply to numerous Web pages, create a(n) _____ style sheet and _____ pages to it.

8. Within each frame, you can place a different _____.

9. Use _____ URLs within a Web site and _____ URLs for Web pages located on another server.

10. The default appearance of an active text link is _____ and _____. The default appearance of a visited text link is _____ and _____.

CHECKPOINT   Multiple Choice

Instructions: Select the letter of the correct answer for each question.

1. Frames are best suited for viewing with _____.
    a. PDAs
    b. small monitors
    c. handheld computers
    d. large monitors

2. If information is to be read online, you should limit the pages to _____ screens.
    a. ten
    b. two
    c. twenty
    d. five

3. With style sheets, you can specify attributes to all page elements sharing the same _____.
    a. URL
    b. tag
    c. frame
    d. ALT attribute

4. A well-designed navigation system for a Web site is _____.

    a. user-based

    b. user-created

    c. user-controlled

    d. both a and c

5. The space between a cell's content and its borders is _____.

    a. cell padding

    b. absolute width

    c. CSS

    d. cell spacing

6. A table defined by _____ typically will display faster.

    a. relative width

    b. relative URL

    c. absolute width

    d. absolute URL

7. _____ can help ensure the transferability of your Web site when you publish it to your ISP's or OSP's computer.

    a. Internal style sheets

    b. Server-side image maps

    c. Absolute URLs

    d. Relative URLs

8. All secondary pages should include a _____.

    a. link to the home page

    b. logo or site identifier

    c. descriptive, relative page title

    d. all of the above

9. Segmenting and reconstructing an image with _____ is a unique and specialized use of a layout tool.

    a. frames

    b. grids

    c. tables

    d. style sheets

10. Organize information on Web pages so visitors will not have to scroll _____.

    a. down

    b. excessively

    c. horizontally

    d. both b and c

CHECKPOINT   Short Answer

Instructions: Write a brief answer to each question.

1. Briefly describe the initial visible screen area's impact on the organization of information on a home page and its secondary pages.

2. What is the value of having a visual connection between a home page and its secondary pages?

3. How do you apply a color scheme to establish a strong visual connection?

4. Identify and briefly describe tools that can be utilized to create a consistent layout.

5. Explain the advantages and disadvantages of style sheets.

6. Explain user-based and user-controlled navigation.

7. Discuss the common types of navigation elements.

8. Differentiate between:

    a.   Absolute width and relative width

    b.   A relative URL and an absolute URL

9. What are the advantages and disadvantages of using frames in a Web site?

10. Explain briefly the general guidelines for navigation for the following:

    a.   Placement of navigation elements.

    b.   Elements to include on secondary pages.

    c.   Links: functionality, value, terminology, and options.

    d.   Visitors who have turned off graphics.

AT ISSUE

Instructions: Write a brief essay in response to the following issues. Be prepared to discuss your findings in class. Use the Web as your research tool. For each issue, identify one URL utilized as a research source.

1. Cascading style sheets (CSS), a multi-featured specification for HTML, offers designers an expedient, powerful method to control the layout of Web pages. Yet, as of this writing, style sheets are considered an up-and-coming technology because no current browser supports all style specifications. Identify the current level of support for style sheets by leading browsers and the W3C recommendations for style sheet usage. Explain why you will or will not utilize cascading style sheets to design your Web site.

2. This book introduced the lowest common denominator debate regarding the monitor resolution setting for which Web pages should be designed. Presently, the debate continues between a 640 x 480 pixel setting and an 800 x 600 pixel setting. Identify the current resolution setting for which Web pages should be designed according to the experts. Include statistics that validate the current recommendation. Specify the impact of resolution settings on the design of your Web pages.

HANDS ON

Instructions: Complete the following exercises.

1. Surf the Web and locate one personal, organization/topical, and commercial Web site that you believe exemplifies a strong visual connection between the home page and its secondary pages. Identify the three URLs and the elements in each that effectively contributed to the strong connection.

2. Locate three Web sites from which you can download buttons, icons, photographs, or illustrations that you might include on your Web site. Ensure that the elements are free and have no copyright or other restrictions. If you are using your own computer, follow the Web site's instructions for downloading. Be sure to scan the files for viruses before opening them. Identify the elements you downloaded and the URLs of the Web sites from which you downloaded.

SECTION 2 CASE STUDY

The Case Study is an ongoing development process in Web design using the concepts, techniques, and Web Design Tips presented in each section. In Section 1, you selected the type of Web site (personal, organization/topical, or commercial), a topic of interest and title, goals, elements, and design tools.

With these components in place and your understanding of the connection between a detailed design plan and a successful Web site, complete the assignment to implement the six steps for developing the solid design plan presented in Chapters 3 and 4 for your Web site. The time you spend developing your plan is a wise investment, which will yield high dividends.

Assignment

Instructions: Expand your outline to the next level in Web design using the concepts and techniques presented in Section 2. Review the specifications of the investment Web site and any other chapter materials to complete this assignment.

1. Open the one-page document in which you created the outline using a text editor or your word processing program. Name the document Design Plan.

2. Use the six steps presented in Section 2 to define the purpose, identify the audience, plan the content, plan the structure, plan the Web pages, and plan the navigation to develop the design plan for your Web site.

3. Include all of the components presented in the Design Plan Checklist to make your design plan detailed and specific.

4. Hand in the design plan to your instructor.

CHAPTER 5

Typography and Graphics on the Web

OBJECTIVES

After completing this chapter you will be able to:

- Differentiate among the features that define type

- Explain and apply the basic principles of good typography on the Web

- Understand the Web variables that limit typographic control

- Employ strategies to overcome Web variables that limit typographical control

- Identify the Web-useable graphics file formats and explain the circumstances under which each should be utilized

- Identify sources of Web graphics

- Understand methods of obtaining and/or creating Web graphics

- Explain and apply the procedures to prepare graphics for the Web

- Understand and apply strategies for optimizing the size of Web graphics files

- Explain and apply strategies for optimizing the appearance of Web graphics

- Understand various types of graphics file compression

- Utilize typography and graphics tips and techniques

INTRODUCTION

With your research complete and a solid design plan developed, you are prepared to create a successful Web site. The two primary components that Web site's utilize to attract viewers are text and graphics. Chapter 5 introduces you to the use of typography and graphics on the Web. The chapter presents the standards for applying good typography, which include visual contrast of font and graphics elements on your Web pages, methods to help you prepare and optimize graphics for use on the Web, and useful tips and techniques to make your Web site visually exciting and interesting.

TYPOGRAPHY

WEB INFO

For more information about the rules of good typography, visit the Web Design Chapter 5 Web Info page (scsite.com/web/ch5/webinfo.htm) and then click Typography.

Chapter 2 stressed the importance of writing text specifically for the Web environment and audience so that it is accurate, easy to read, understandable, comprehensive, and concise. Once written, text can be made even more effective if you follow the rules of good **typography**, which is the appearance and arrangement of the characters that make up your text. These characters commonly are referred to as **type**. The following features, illustrated in Figure 5-1, define type:

- **Typeface:** The actual design of the type regarding the slant and thickness of the lines. Examples of common typefaces include Times New Roman, Arial, and Garamond.
- **Type style:** Variations in style such as roman (regular), bold, or italic.
- **Type size:** The size of the type on the page, measured in points, where 72 points = 1 inch.
- **Font:** The combined features of the typeface and type style.

Type can be categorized as display type or body type. **Display type** is a larger type that is used for elements such as headings and subheads. **Body type** is the type used for the main content, and typically is smaller than display type.

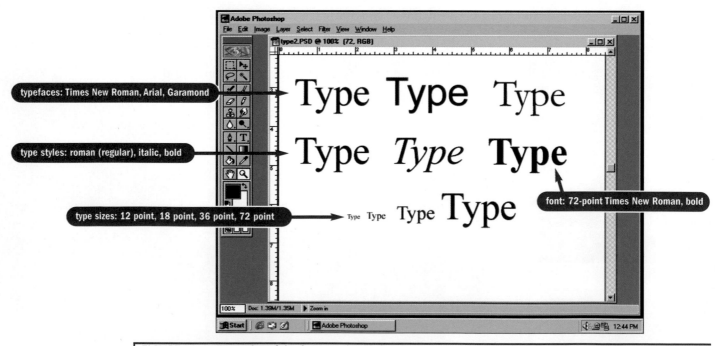

FIGURE 5-1   Examples of the features that define type.

Typography is a powerful design tool. Applied effectively, typography can communicate visually both the literal and implied meaning of words. Figure 5-2 illustrates how applying specific typefaces visually conveys meaning. Variables on the Web significantly limit typographic control. Guidelines for offsetting the limitations are discussed shortly. Despite the limitations, as a designer, you should abide by basic typographic principles. To maximize the legibility and readability of type on your Web pages, follow these guidelines:

• For short paragraphs, headings, lists, and type on buttons, use a sans serif typeface. **Serifs,** are short lines or ornaments on each character. Sans serif type does not include these ornaments. Sans serif type, especially at smaller sizes, is more legible on the screen. Use **serif type** for large blocks of text and pages that are intended to be printed and then read. Figure 5-3 demonstrates the difference between serif and sans serif type.

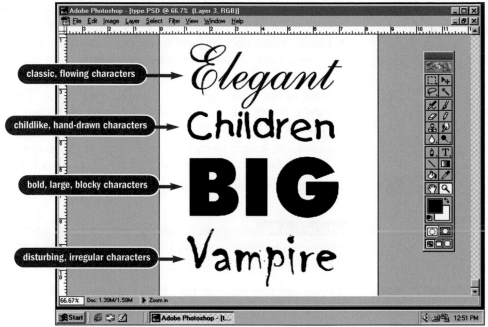

FIGURE 5-2   The proper typeface visually conveys the meaning of a word.

FIGURE 5-3   Serif and sans serif type. The serifs lead the eye from one letter to the next.

- Choose a body type size that is neither too small nor too big. A standard recommendation is 10 to 14 points.
- Avoid setting large amounts of type in all caps, bold, or italic. Type set this way is difficult to read. Instead, use all caps, bold, or italic type sparingly for emphasis.
- Create a high level of contrast between type and page background. For example, use dark-colored type on a light-colored background. Ensure that backgrounds with textures or images do not interfere with the readability and legibility of the type.
- Create a high level of contrast between display type and body type through font choice, size, and color. Such contrast will organize information on pages and lead the reader's eye.
- Limit the number of fonts to two to three fonts per page. Excessive font changes create a ransom note effect, and can be distracting.
- Do not create large text blocks that stretch completely across the screen and continue downward in one seemingly never ending mass of gray. Even the most enthusiastic reader would view type set this way as uninviting. Instead, format text in easy-to-read columns. Provide visual relief between paragraphs with white space.
- Limit line length to eight to ten words. If you layout your pages with tables, a cell that is 365 pixels wide will limit the length of text placed inside to eight to ten words per line.

The benefit of abiding by the rules of good typography is stated in the following Web Design Tip:

Web Design Tip

Utilizing basic typographical principles can help maximize the legibility and the readability of your Web pages.

WEB INFO

For more information about how monitor resolution affects the way type displays on the Web, visit the Web Design Chapter 5 Web Info page (scsite.com/web/ch5/webinfo.htm) and then click Monitor Resolution.

As you just learned, you have little control over the way type displays on the Web. Two variables that lessen your control include operating systems and monitor resolution settings. For example, the same typeface will appear two to three points larger on a computer running on a Windows platform versus a computer running on a Macintosh platform, which can significantly affect your page layout. View your pages on different platforms to determine if the layout is acceptable, or if you need to make adjustments.

Monitor resolutions similarly can impact layout. A monitor resolution setting of 640 x 480 pixels, for instance, will display text larger than higher resolution settings of 800 x 600 and 1280 x 1024. If your audience is not in a controlled environment, such as an intranet with a static monitor resolution setting, view how the text on your pages displays at different settings. Keep in the mind the following Web Design Tip to view how type displays:

Web Design Tip

Before publishing your Web pages, view how they display on different platforms and at different monitor resolution settings.

Browser settings are a third variable limiting typographic control. The default browser font setting is the Times New Roman typeface, in a 12-point type size. This default setting displays text on Web pages as 12-point Times New Roman, or at any other font setting specified by the user in the browser preferences. Suggestions for countering these variables follow in the next section.

Typography Tips

A realistic approach to typography on the Web includes applying the basic principles of good typography, accepting the control limitations, and utilizing, as appropriate, the following methods for overriding font settings, antialiasing type, and selecting styles and type.

OVERRIDE DEFAULT FONT SETTINGS   To override the default font settings in browser preferences, specify the desired typeface in your Web document. The specified typeface, however, must reside in your viewer's computer. If the specified typeface is not resident, the default typeface will display. Therefore, choose fonts that are common to the operating system. The table in Figure 5-4 includes some of the more common fonts for the Windows and Macintosh operating systems.

WEB INFO

For more information about how fonts are used on Web pages, visit the Web Design Chapter 5 Web Info page (scsite.com/web/ch5/webinfo.htm) and then click Fonts.

Common Fonts

Operating System	Font	Operating System	Font
Windows	Arial	**MacOS**	Helvetica
	Courier		Courier
	Times New Roman		Geneva
	Verdana		Palatino
			Times

FIGURE 5-4   Common fonts used with the Windows and Macintosh operating systems.

To decrease the possibility of the default font setting appearing, specify multiple resident font possibilities, as in the sample HTML code below:

<FONT FACE="Arial, Helvetica, Verdana, Geneva">Typography</FONT>

The browser looks for the typeface in the order listed. If none of the typefaces is resident, the browser displays the word, Typography, in the default font setting. When determining fonts, keep in mind the following Web Design Tip:

> **Web Design Tip**
> Specify commonly used fonts in your Web documents to increase your chances of overriding default font settings.

To avoid the font residency issue, designers sometimes convert text to graphics. Using illustration and image editing software such as Illustrator, Photoshop, or Freehand, you can create the text in the desired typeface and style, then save it in a graphics file format that can be inserted in your Web document as an image (Figure 5-5a on the next page).

Text as graphics is for specialized, occasional use; for example, as a dramatic element on a home page (Figure 5-5b on the next page). Text converted to graphics, called **graphic typography**, will display as intended even if the typeface is not resident in the viewer's computer. The drawbacks of graphic typography are that load time of the page will increase; it will not be visible if the viewer has turned off graphics in the browser; and it cannot be searched or indexed by search engines if saved in the current more commonly used graphics file formats.

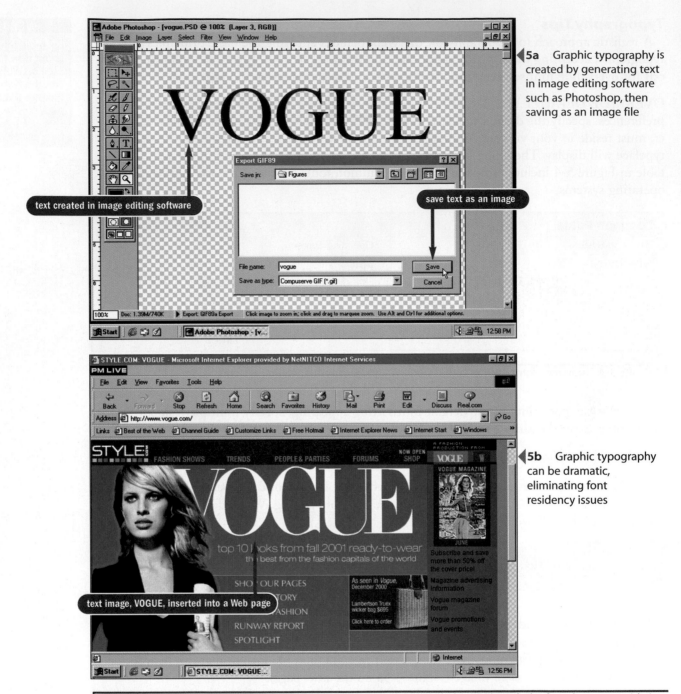

5a   Graphic typography is created by generating text in image editing software such as Photoshop, then saving as an image file

text created in image editing software

save text as an image

5b   Graphic typography can be dramatic, eliminating font residency issues

text image, VOGUE, inserted into a Web page

FIGURE 5-5   A viewer will see graphics typography as it was intended even though the font does not reside in the viewer's computer.

ANTIALIASING TYPE   **Antialiasing** is a technique frequently used to smooth the appearance of graphics or type. This technique eliminates jagged edges on type by inserting extra pixels. Figure 5-6 illustrates the technique applied to type. You can use Photoshop, Illustrator, or Freehand to generate antialiased type. Follow the Web Design Tip for this technique:

Web Design Tip

Utilize the antialiasing technique only for large type. Type that is 10 points or smaller becomes soft and fuzzy if antialiased.

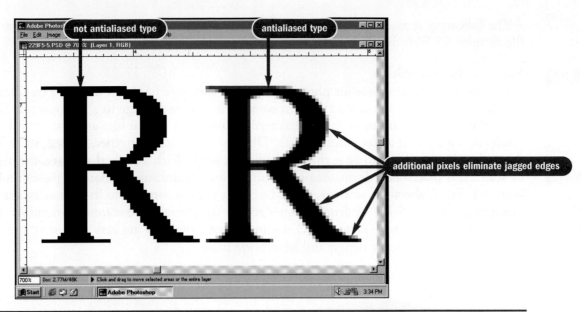

FIGURE 5-6   When type is antialiased, additional pixels smooth the edges of the type, eliminating the jagged edges.

SELECTING STYLES AND TYPE   Chapter 4 introduced styles as a layout method for Web pages. Styles also can be used to format text and offer more typographical possibilities than HTML tags. Chapter 4 indicated that style sheets are considered an up-and-coming technology, because no current browser supports all style specifications. If you choose to use style sheets for typographical purposes, test how your specifications display in different browsers before publishing your Web pages.

By applying styles to elements sharing the same HTML tag, you can exercise the following typographical controls:

- Embed fonts in a page by specifying the URL of a font.
- Specify paragraph **leading** (pronounced LED-ing), which is the space between lines. Leading creates white space that increases legibility. In general, set leading at two to four points higher than type size.
- Control **tracking**, which is the space between words, and **kerning**, which is the space between letters.

Concerns about selecting styles and type have led to developments that affect typography on the Web. For example, in a joint effort, Netscape and Bitstream have developed **Dynamic Fonts** created in HTML that allow designers to create their Web sites and Web pages using default fonts that display in the browser with the correct formatting. Collaboration between Microsoft and Adobe has resulted in a file format for fonts called **OpenType** that incorporates embedding fonts within Web pages, unifying competing fonts.

GRAPHICS

In Chapters 3 and 4 you learned how photographs on the Web could personalize and familiarize the unknown, deliver a message, and prompt action. When you choose photographs, be sure you select:

- Quality, relevant photographs to add value to your Web site.
- Photographs and illustrations to match or complement the Web site's color scheme.
- Photographs and illustrations for image mapping that accurately represent the content they link to and enhance the Web site's mood.

WEB INFO

For more information about the use of graphics on the Web, visit the Web Design Chapter 5 Web Info page (scsite.com/web/ch5/webinfo.htm) and then click Graphics.

The following sections discuss sources, techniques for preparing and optimizing graphics, and file formats for Web display.

WEB INFO

For a listing of sources for graphics, visit the Web Design Chapter 5 Web Info page (scsite.com/web/ch5 webinfo.htm) and then click Graphics Sources.

Sources for Graphics

The most common source for photographs for a Web page has been to scan a traditionally processed photo with a scanner and then convert the scanned image to a Web-useable file format. A **scanner** is an input device that reads printed text or graphics and then translates the results into a file that a computer can use. Three common scanner types, flatbed, sheet-fed, and drum, handle the object to be scanned in different ways. With a **flatbed scanner**, the object to be scanned is placed face down on a glass surface, and a scanning mechanism passes under it (Figure 5-7a). A **sheet-fed scanner**, pulls the object to be scanned into its stationary scanning mechanism (Figure 5-7b). A **drum scanner** rotates the object to be scanned around its stationary scanning mechanism (Figure 5-7c). Drum scanners typically are very expensive and are used primarily by large graphic design and advertising firms.

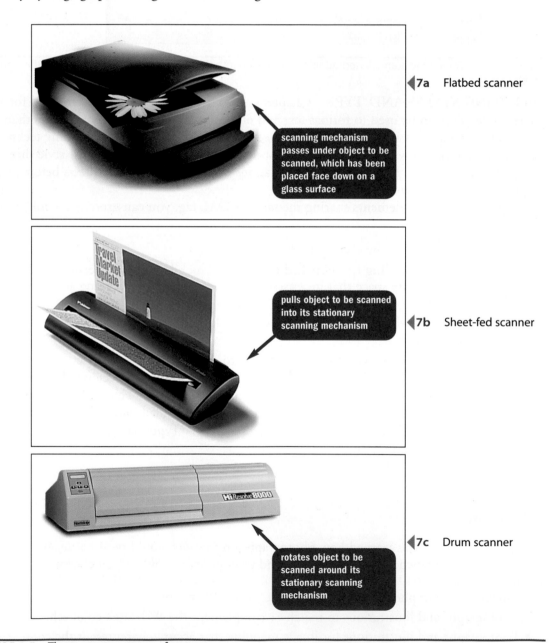

7a   Flatbed scanner

scanning mechanism passes under object to be scanned, which has been placed face down on a glass surface

pulls object to be scanned into its stationary scanning mechanism

7b   Sheet-fed scanner

7c   Drum scanner

rotates object to be scanned around its stationary scanning mechanism

FIGURE 5-7   Three common types of scanners.

To prepare graphics for the Web using a scanner, follow these guidelines for scanning photographs and illustrations.

- Scan photos and illustrations at approximately the size at which they will be displayed on your Web pages unless you plan to manipulate them with image editing software. If so, scan the image a little larger to make it easier to manipulate, and then scale it down to the approximate display size.

- Scan images at 72 dots per inch. **Dots per inch** (**dpi**) specifies the number of dots per inch a monitor can display or a printer can print. If manipulating the image with image editing software, scan it at a higher resolution, such as 150 dpi, to generate a larger image that is easier to manipulate, and then reduce it to 72 dpi with image editing software.

- Scan illustrations at 256 colors. Scan photos at higher color settings such as thousands or millions of colors. Keep in mind, however, that only those visitors with monitors capable of displaying thousands or millions of color will be able to view these photos at the higher settings.

- Save images in **Tagged Image File Format** (**TIFF**), which is a standard file format for scanning and storage. When saved in this format, the images are your source files that later must be converted into one of three graphics file formats for use on the Web. These formats are discussed later in this chapter.

A **digital camera** takes a digital image and stores it electronically, instead of on film that requires processing. A digital camera provides a useful alternative to scanning traditionally processed photos. Transferring images from early digital cameras to a computer frequently required downloading the images utilizing proprietary software and a cable connected from the camera to a computer. Some digital cameras, which store the images on CD-ROMs or floppy disks, greatly simplify the transfer process (Figure 5-8). One-megapixel digital cameras produce excellent quality photos for Web pages. Digital cameras can be invaluable if you need to publish time-dependent photos on your Web pages.

FIGURE 5-8   A digital camera takes a digital image and stores it electronically. Some cameras store the image on CD-ROMs or floppy disks.

If you do not have access to a scanner or a digital camera, have your film processed as both regular printouts and digital files. Typically, the film processor will return the digital files to you on a CD-ROM. If necessary, the digital files can be imported into image editing software and converted to a Web-useable format. You also can purchase quality photos for Web pages on CD-ROMs or download them from the Web.

Clip art, drawings, and diagrams can be categorized as illustrations. **Clip art** is a collection of art frequently organized by theme or subject matter. It may be in a printed format, which you can scan, or it may be in electronic format. Digitized clip art can be purchased on CD-ROM, downloaded from the Web, and often is included in word processing or Web authoring packages. Follow the advice regarding downloading photos or illustrations in this Web Design Tip:

Web Design Tip

Before downloading photos or illustrations from the Web, ensure that there are no copyright restrictions or royalty charges, which are fees to be paid to the creator/owner of the art for its use.

Diagrams and drawings for Web pages can be generated by hand and then scanned into electronic format, or they can be computer-generated. **Adobe Illustrator** and **Macromedia Freehand** are examples of illustration software that you can utilize to create diagrams and drawings. Illustrator and Freehand generate **vector graphics**, which are images defined by mathematical statements regarding the drawing and positioning of lines. Vector graphics can be resized without degrading the quality, unlike **raster graphics** or **bitmaps**, which are images defined by rows and columns of different colored pixels. Frequently, an illustration will be created and manipulated as a vector graphic, and then converted to a raster graphic.

Preparing and Optimizing Graphics

A primary reason visitors turn away from a Web site is pages that take an excessive amount of time to load. To provide an acceptable loading time for visitors utilizing 28 Kbps to 56 Kbps modems, limit the file size of pages to 35 kilobytes each. Diagnostic Web sites, such as Web Site Garage will check the loading time of your pages using modems to T1 connections. Graphics that have not been prepared or optimized properly can contribute to excessive file size of your Web pages. A discussion of Web-useable graphics file formats follows, as well as methods to prepare and optimize them.

To display on the Web, images must be in one of three graphic file formats:

- Graphics Interchange Format (GIF)
- Joint Photographic Experts Group (JPEG)
- Portable Network Graphics (PNG)

If your images are not in a Web-useable format, you can convert them in image editing software. Photoshop and Paint Shop Pro are popular image editing packages that require a significant expense. For an introduction to image editing software without making a large investment, investigate the shareware at the Tucows Web site.

Most Web authoring packages will convert graphics to a Web-useable format automatically. This capability eliminates the need to use image editing software for conversion purposes. Such software, however, can be utilized for additional purposes.

If your photo contains more subject matter than you want to include, utilize image editing software to crop the image. For example, you may want only a head and shoulders shot instead of a full body shot. When you **crop**, you select the part of the image you want to keep and remove the unwanted portion. Figure 5-9 illustrates using the crop tool. The benefits of cropping an image are stated in the following Web Design Tip:

Web Design Tip

Cropping an image can eliminate distracting background elements and establish the focal point. Discarding unwanted portions also results in a smaller file size.

An image may be in need of image correction because it is too dark, blurry, or has unwanted spots or markings. Image editing software has image correction capabilities ranging from predetermined, automatic settings to very precise, sophisticated controls.

Paint Shop Pro includes automatic photo enhancement features that retouch, repair, and edit photos. From the Effects menu, you can remove small scratches from a photo automatically using Automatic Small Scratch Removal on the Enhance Photo submenu (Figure 5-10a). **Photoshop**, considered the premiere photo editing package, can be used across all media to enhance photos utilizing its sophisticated capabilities. With its Adjust Levels feature, for example, you can manipulate the levels of shadows, mid-tones, and highlights (Figure 5-10b).

You also may want to resize your image, especially if you scanned it a little larger because you planned to manipulate it. Typically, the resizing you will be doing is making the image smaller. Remember that bitmap images, unlike vector images, degrade if you enlarge them beyond their original size. In Photoshop and Paintshop Pro, you can resize an image by percentages or pixels (Figure 5-11 on the next page).

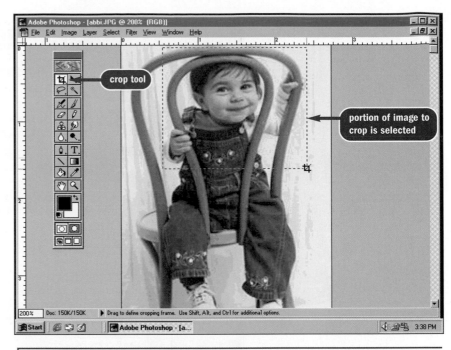

FIGURE 5-9   Crop an image to create a focal point and reduce file size.

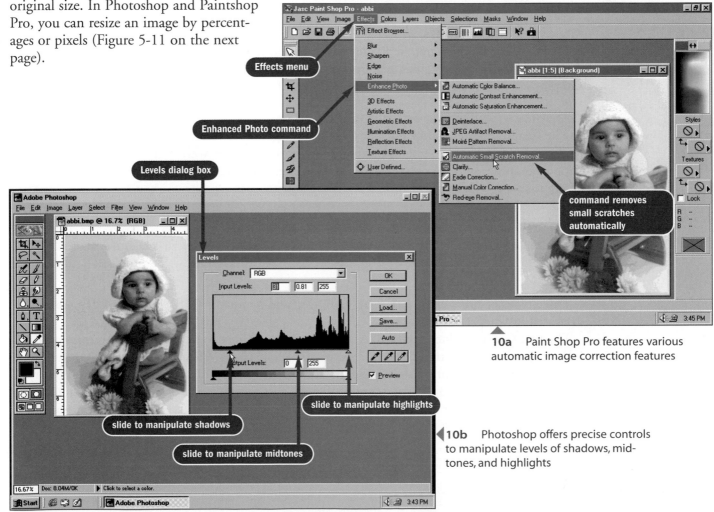

10a   Paint Shop Pro features various automatic image correction features

10b   Photoshop offers precise controls to manipulate levels of shadows, mid-tones, and highlights

FIGURE 5-10   Image editing software offers a range of image correcting capabilities.

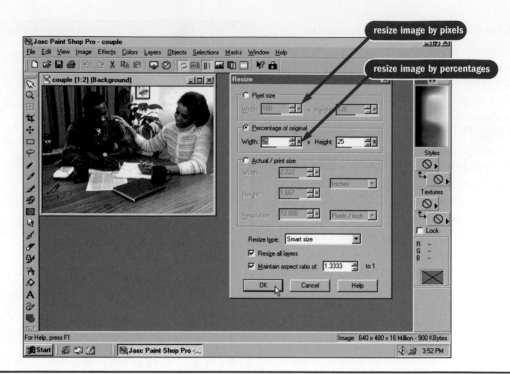

FIGURE 5-11   With image editing software, images can be resized using pixels or percentages.

WEB INFO

For more information about the graphics file formats used on the Web, visit the Web Design Chapter 5 Web Info page (scsite.com/web/ch5/webinfo.htm) and then click Graphics File Formats.

Graphics File Formats

On the Web, the two graphic file formats most utilized are Graphics Interchange Format (GIF), and Joint Photographic Experts Group (JPEG). A third format, Portable Networks Graphic (PNG), is predicted in time to replace GIFs.

Graphics Interchange Format (GIF)

The **Graphics Interchange Format** (**GIF** pronounced giff with a hard g) file format, created by CompuServe, was the original graphics format used on the Web. Almost all browsers that support graphics support cross-platform GIFs. The following Web Design Tip identifies appropriate usages of GIFs on the Web:

> **Web Design Tip**
>
> GIFs are most suitable for solid color images such as logos, illustrations, and graphic typography. GIF images are 8-bit indexed color, meaning they can display only up to 256 colors. This color limitation makes GIFs inappropriate for displaying photographs.

Three types of GIFs exist: GIF 87A, GIF 89A, and Animated GIF. Animated GIFs are discussed in Chapter 6.

The first GIF introduced, **GIF 87A**, featured the capability to be interlaced. An **interlaced GIF** image displays on the screen in a sequence of four passes. Each pass displays the whole image at a higher resolution than the previous pass. Gradually, the image changes from blurry to distinct (Figure 5-12). An interlaced GIF gives a preview of the image to come without extensively affecting file size. Interlacing, which produces insignificant results when applied to small images, should be reserved only for large images.

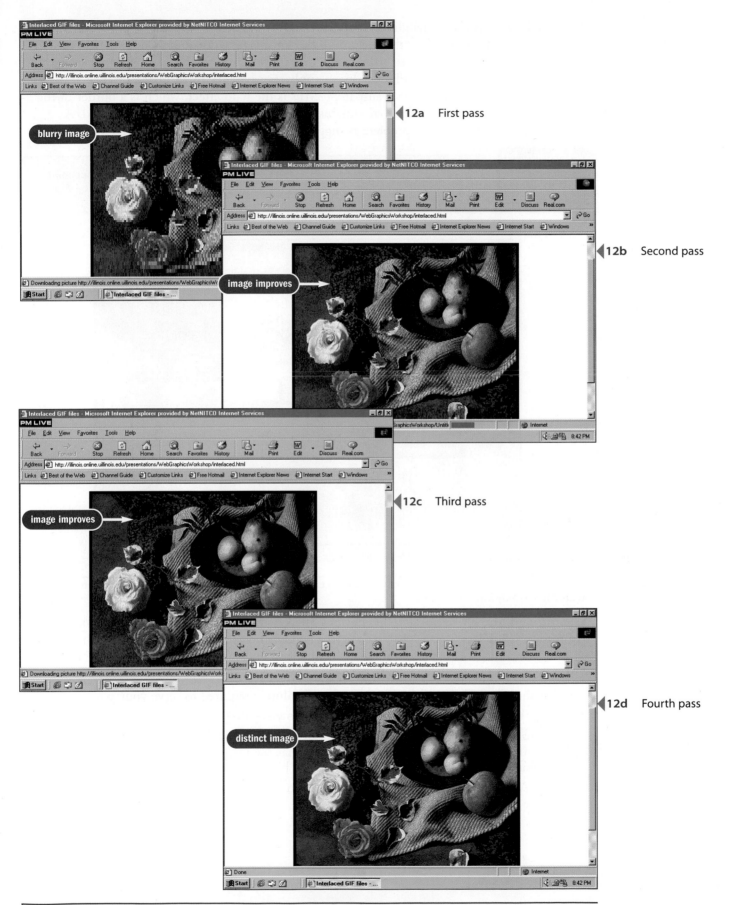

FIGURE 5-12   This interlaced GIF image gradually changes from blurry to distinct.

A GIF 89A features the capabilities to be interlaced, transparent, and animated. The transparency capability removes the background of an image, consequently eliminating the rectangular shape and incorporating the image more subtly into a Web page. You can utilize image editing software, such as Photoshop, to apply transparency to an image (Figure 5-13). A common problem associated with transparent GIFs is the **halo effect**, which is a border of the image's original background color that remains after the transparency has been applied. A method to avoid this common problem is suggested in the following Web Design Tip:

> **Web Design Tip**
>
> The halo effect occurs typically because the image is antialiased. Recall that an antialiased image's appearance is made sharper by inserting extra pixels. By changing the image to aliased before applying transparency, you usually can avoid the halo effect.

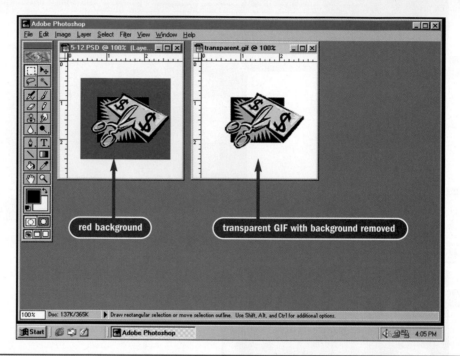

FIGURE 5-13   By making a transparent GIF, you can eliminate a rectangular background and incorporate the image more subtly into a Web page.

Compressing the file size of graphics ensures quicker transfer and loading time of images. GIF compression is **lossless**, meaning all data is retained when the image is compressed. The retention of data means the quality of the image is maintained. To keep the file size of GIF images as small as possible, follow these guidelines:

- Limit the physical size of the image to that absolutely required to serve your purpose.
- Create the image with solid colors using the browser-safe palette.
- Minimize the image's bit depth or number of colors. Simply because a GIF can be a maximum of 8 bit/256 colors does not mean that the image has to created at those settings. Experiment to see whether 6 bit/64 colors or 4 bit/16 colors yields a satisfactory image.
- Utilize Adobe ImageReady, which is included in the latest versions of Photoshop or similar software to optimize the image (Figure 5-14).

FIGURE 5-14   With ImageReady and similar software, images can be optimized to speed up load time.

WEB INFO

For more information about the JPEG file format, visit the Web Design Chapter 5 Web Info page (scsite.com/web/ch5/webinfo.htm) and then click JPEG.

Joint Photographic Experts Group (JPEG) Format

The **Joint Photographic Experts Group (JPEG** pronounced JAY-peg) file format is acknowledged as being best suited for photographs on the Web. The following Web Design Tip identifies additional appropriate usages for JPEGs on the Web:

Web Design Tip

In addition to photographs, cross-platform JPEGs also are recommended for photo-like paintings, watercolors, and complex illustrations. They are not suggested for solid color images.

JPEG files are 24-bit RGB color, which means they can be displayed as millions of colors when viewed with a 24-bit capable monitor. If they are viewed on an 8-bit monitor, the colors in the photograph will be dithered.

Two types of JPEGs exist: standard and progressive JPEGs. A **progressive JPEG**, similar to an interlaced GIF, displays on the screen in a sequence of passes, giving the viewer a preview of the image to come. You can specify the number of passes in a progressive JPEG (Figure 5-15). This format creates a file size slightly smaller than a standard JPEG. Unlike an GIF 89A, a progressive JPEG cannot be made transparent.

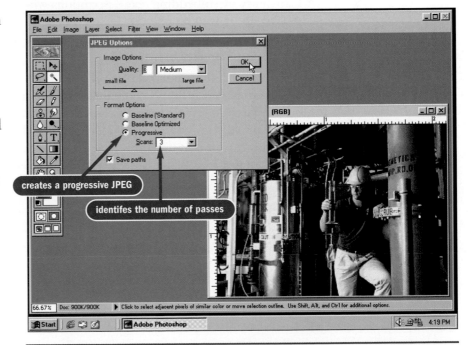

FIGURE 5-15   The number of passes can be specified for progressive JPEGs.

JPEG compression is **lossy**, meaning that data, especially redundant data, is lost during compression. You can control the level of compression of JPEGs, unlike GIFs. Different software gauges the range of compression numerically and/or from quality levels of low to high. Regardless of how the range is expressed, the results are the same. Greater compression equals lower image quality. Try different compression levels to determine the acceptable balance between file size and image quality. An important Web Design Tip regarding JPEGs follows:

> **Web Design Tip**
> Each time a JPEG is edited and saved, the image is compressed and decompressed, which degrades its quality. Consequently, you should make a copy of your original source file and never alter the original image.

The JPEG file format enjoys a wide level of browser support. Versions 3.0 and higher of both Netscape Navigator and Internet Explorer support standard and progressive JPEGs. To create and optimize JPEGs for your Web pages, use Adobe Photoshop (with ImageReady built in), Macromedia Fireworks, or PaintShop Pro.

Portable Network Graphics (PNG) Format

In 1995, an announcement was made that any developer who created software that allows files to be saved as a GIF would have to pay a royalty to both CompuServe, that created the format, and Unisys, that developed the LZW compression utilized by GIFs. The **Portable Network Graphics** (**PNG** pronounced ping) format was developed as a direct result of these legal issues surrounding GIFs.

PNGs are expected to replace GIFs eventually on the Web, for the following reasons:

- Superior transparency capabilities. PNGs are able to make up to 256 colors in one image transparent. GIFs allow only one transparent color per image.
- Better-quality interlacing capabilities. The lowest resolution interlaced PNG image is superior to the lowest resolution interlaced GIF image.
- Greater range of color depths. PNGs can be 16-bit grayscale, 256 color indexed, and 16.7 million true colors.
- Capability of embedding text descriptions within images. The text descriptions can be picked up by search engines.
- Lossless compression. Cross-platform PNG files use the same lossless compression as GIFs, but result in smaller files.

PNGs will not immediately replace JPEGs, due in part to the larger files generated by the lossless compression of PNGs compared with the smaller files generated by JPEGs lossy compression. A larger question concerns how soon PNGs will replace GIFs. The answer is entirely dependent on when browsers will widely support the PNG format. Browser compatibility has been a major reason that designers have chosen not to include PNGs on their Web pages. Presently, support is available only by means of browser plug-ins.

GRAPHICS TIPS AND TECHNIQUES

In addition to utilizing the previously discussed techniques for preparing and optimizing images, always include the ALT attribute, and consider using thumbnails and the LOWSRC attribute as appropriate. Creating a drop shadow, a tiling background color bar, or an image map for graphics, also can be effective techniques, and are discussed below.

ALT Attribute

The ALT attribute was introduced and illustrated in Chapter 4. The importance of the ALT attribute is summarized in the following two Web Design Tips:

Web Design Tip

If viewers have graphics turned off, they will not see the images on your Web pages. By utilizing the ALT attribute, they will see a description of the images that are not being displayed.

Web Design Tip

Utilizing the ALT attribute is especially important if an image is serving as an image map. If the image is not visible and no description is provided, viewers will not realize a hyperlink is present.

Web authoring packages typically allow you to add a description when you insert an image. If you are working in a text editor, the HTML code to include a description would resemble the following:

<IMG SRC= "inflation.gif" ALT= "Inflation figures for 2000-2005">

Thumbnails

A **thumbnail** is a version of an original image that has been greatly reduced in size. Besides being physically smaller, a thumbnail's file size is much smaller than the original. As a result, a thumbnail allows a quick preview of an image without waiting for a full-size image to load. Typically, the thumbnail is image-mapped, or a text hyperlink is provided to link to another page with the full-sized image (Figures 5-16 on the next page). The following Web Design Tip offers guidelines for thumbnails:

Web Design Tip

Provide information on the thumbnail page specifying the file size of the original image so viewers can decide if they want to click the link and wait for the image to load. On the full-size image page, include additional, pertinent information and a link back to the previous page.

WEB INFO

For more information about using thumbnails on Web pages, visit the Web Design Chapter 5 Web Info page (scsite.com/web/ch5/webinfo.htm) and then click Thumbnails.

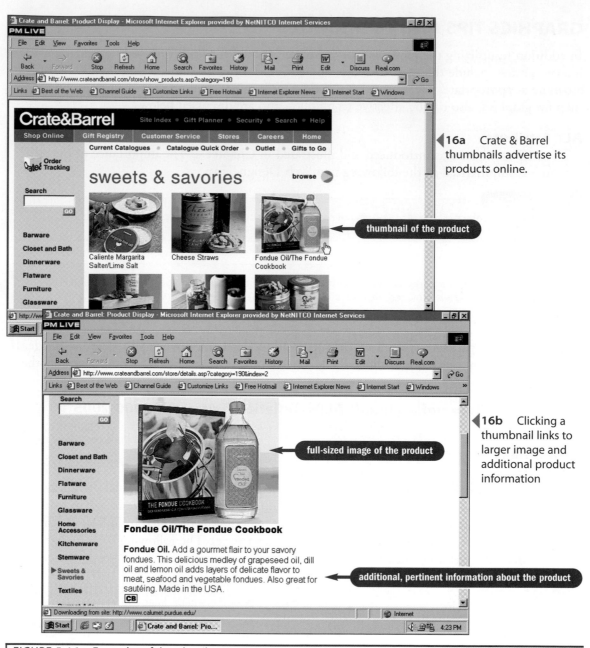

16a Crate & Barrel thumbnails advertise its products online.

16b Clicking a thumbnail links to larger image and additional product information

FIGURE 5-16 Examples of thumbnails.

Large and small commercial Web sites use thumbnails extensively. Large retailers, such as Crate & Barrel, provide online catalogs of their merchandise. If you click a thumbnail, typically you will see a close-up version of the merchandise, along with available colors and styles, prices, and instructions for ordering. A small business can advertise its products just as effectively with thumbnails, whether selling wedding cakes or custom-made jigs for fly-fishing.

The LOWSRC Attribute

The <IMG> image tag's **LOWSRC attribute** is another method to give a quick preview of an original image. The preview is especially advantageous for visitors with slow connection speeds. With this method, the browser initially loads a lower-quality version of an image, and then loads a higher-quality version on top of it. The lower-quality image could be a black and white version of a high-quality color image, or it could contain fewer colors, for example 256 colors, instead of thousands of colors. Because the lower-quality image requires less information to describe it, the file is much smaller and loads more quickly than the high-quality image.

The lower-quality image will load only when the page initially is opened, not when reloaded. All versions of Netscape support the <LOWSRC> attribute; Internet Explorer initiated support for the attribute with Version 4.0.

Drop Shadow

Although not a new technique, **drop shadows** frequently are utilized to create a 3-D effect for both text and images on the Web. A drop shadow differentiates text or images from a Web page's background.

Image editing software such as PaintShop Pro or Photoshop can be utilized to create drop shadows. The following Web Design Tip offers guidelines for the placement of the shadow:

Various shades of black are the frequent color choice for drop shadows. When making your choice, consider other colors based on the shadow color that would be most effective against the page background color. To soften a shadow's hard edge, a blur could be applied using image editing software. Figure 5-17 illustrates a text drop shadow appropriate for the investment Web site.

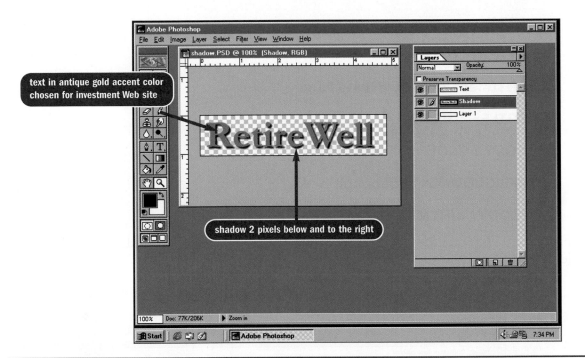

FIGURE 5-17   A text drop shadow for the investment Web site.

Sidebar

A colored **sidebar** that tiles, or repeats, down the length of a page is a popular feature for Web pages. Navigation links frequently are located in such a bar via a table. A sidebar utilized this way positions navigation links in a prominent, consistent location, distinctly separate from the main content.

To create a sidebar, a background image must first be created utilizing image editing software (Figure 5-18 on the next page). The image can be filled with color or graphics. Using special image editing tools, a sidebar can be softened or the color manipulated so it gradually blends into the color of the main background.

WEB INFO

For more information about the drop shadow technique, visit the Web Design Chapter 5 Web Info page (scsite.com/web/ch5/webinfo.htm) and then click Drop Shadow.

WEB INFO

For more information about the sidebar technique, visit the Web Design Chapter 5 Web Info page (scsite.com/web/ch5/webinfo.htm) and then click Sidebar.

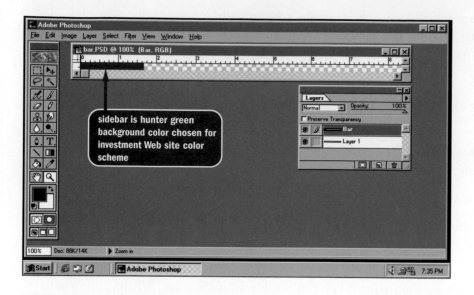

FIGURE 5-18   Photoshop is used to generate a tiling sidebar for the investment Web site.

After the background image is completed, it can be incorporated into a Web page. The following is the HTML code to accomplish this:

<HTML>

<HEAD> <TITLE>

Investment Web Site Home Page

</TITLE> </HEAD>

<BODY BGCOLOR="#FFFFFF"

BACKGROUND="sidebar.gif">

</BODY> </HTML>

Figure 5-19 illustrates the investment Web site, Retire Well, text drop shadow and the tiling sidebar incorporated into a Web page.

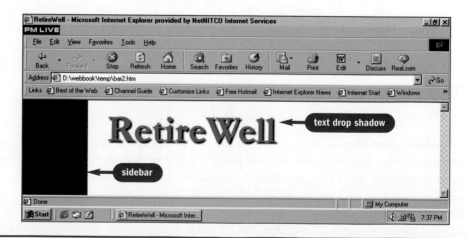

FIGURE 5-19   A Web page with the text drop shadow and tiling color sidebar incorporated.

Image Map

An **image map** provides an attractive alternative to hyperlinked text. Image maps, which can be photographs or illustrations, contain designated **hot spots** that link to a specific URL when clicked by a Web site visitor. Recall that Chapter 4 discusses the difference between client-side and server-side image maps. You can create image maps manually; however, utilizing a Web authoring package that features image mapping capability such as FrontPage is much simpler (Figure 5-20).

WEB INFO

For more information about using image maps to link Web pages, visit the Web Design Chapter 5 Web Info page (scsite.com/web/ch5/webinfo.htm) and then click Image Maps.

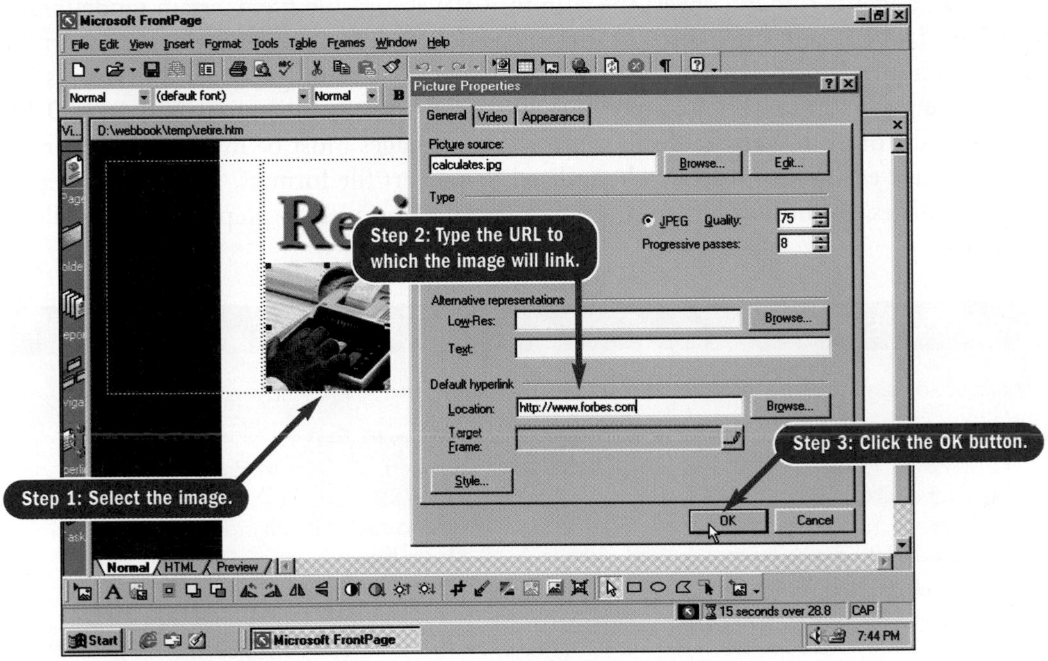

FIGURE 5-20 Creating an image map with FrontPage is a simple task.

You also can utilize shareware such as MapEdit to image map photographs or illustrations. The mapping process initially involves opening the Web page containing the image to be mapped and identifying that image. Hot spots are designated utilizing a tool shape best suited for the image: rectangular, circular, or polygonal. After designating the hot spots, the URL for each spot is specified. Depending on whether the image map is server-side or client-side, the information is either exported as a separate file or saved within the Web page.

Utilizing the ALT attribute, thumbnails, and the LOWRC attribute on a Web site gives visitors a text description of an image if they have turned images off and quick previews of images. Adding a drop shadow, tiling sidebar, or an image map creates visually appealing Web pages. By applying these graphics tips and techniques to your Web site, you will offer visitors a very positive, memorable experience that will encourage return visits.

CHAPTER SUMMARY

Text for Web pages can be made more effective by following the rules of good typography — the appearance and arrangement of the characters that make up text. The characters commonly are referred to as type. The features that define type include typeface, type style, and type size. A font is comprised of the combined features of typeface and type style. Despite the Web variables limiting typographic control, designers should abide by basic typographic principles.

To prepare a photograph for a Web page, the traditional method has been to scan a photograph with a scanner, then convert the scan into a Web-useable file. Certain guidelines should be followed when scanning photos or illustrations. A digital camera provides an alternative to scanning photos. Illustrations for Web pages include clip art, diagrams, and drawings in digital or scanable print format. Photographs and illustrations also can be purchased on CD-ROM or downloaded from the Web. To display on the Web, images must be in GIF, JPEG, or PNG file format. Image editing software can be utilized to convert file formats, and also to crop, correct, or resize images. Additional tips and techniques can be applied to prepare graphics file formats optimally.

KEY TERMS

Instructions: Use the following terms from this chapter as a study review.

Adobe Illustrator (5.10)
antialiasing (5.6)
bitmaps (5.10)
body type (5.2)
clip art (5.10)
crop (5.10)
digital camera (5.9)
display type (5.2)
dots per inch (dpi) (5.9)
drop shadows (5.19)
drum scanner (5.8)
Dynamic Fonts (5.7)
flatbed scanner (5.8)
font (5.2)
GIF 87A (5.12)
GIF 89A (5.14)
graphic typography (5.5)
Graphics Interchange Format (GIF) (5.12)
halo effect (5.14)
hot spots (5.21)
image map (5.21)
interlaced GIF (5.12)
Joint Photographic Experts Group
    (JPEG) (5.15)
kerning (5.7)
leading (5.7)

lossless (5.14)
lossy (5.16)
LOWSRC attribute (5.18)
Macromedia Freehand (5.10)
OpenType (5.7)
Paint Shop Pro (5.11)
Photoshop (5.11)
Portable Network Graphics (PNG) (5.16)
progressive JPEG (5.15)
raster graphics (5.10)
sans serif type (5.3)
scanner (5.8)
serif type (5.3)
serifs (5.3)
sheet-fed scanner (5.8)
sidebar (5.19)
Tagged Image File Format (TIFF) (5.9)
thumbnail (5.17)
tracking (5.7)
type (5.2)
type size (5.2)
type style (5.2)
typeface (5.2)
typography (5.2)
vector graphics (5.10)

CHECKPOINT   Matching

Instructions: Match each term with the best description.

_____ 1. vector graphics

_____ 2. thumbnail

_____ 3. typography

_____ 4. GIF

_____ 5. body type

_____ 6. PNG

_____ 7. raster graphics/bitmaps

_____ 8. JPEG

_____ 9. graphic typography

_____ 10. display type

_____ 11. antialiasing

_____ 12. typeface

_____ 13. type style

_____ 14. type size

_____ 15. font

a. The combined features of the typeface and the type style.

b. The actual design of the type regarding the slant and thickness of lines.

c. A version of an original image that has been greatly reduced in size.

d. The appearance and arrangement of type.

e. Text converted to graphics.

f. The main type comprising the content.

g. Images defined by rows and columns of different colored pixels.

h. The graphics file format most suited for solid color images.

i. Measured in points, where 72 points = 1 inch.

j. Images defined by mathematical statements regarding the drawing and positioning of lines.

k. Larger type such as that used for headings and subheads.

l. The graphics file format most suited for photographs.

m. A graphics file format predicted to replace GIFs on the Web.

n. Variations in style of type, such as roman, bold, or italic.

o. A technique used to smooth the appearance of graphics or type.

CHECKPOINT   Fill in the Blanks

Instructions: Fill in the blank(s) with the appropriate answer

1. The same typeface will display two to three pixels _____ on a computer with a Windows versus a Macintosh platform.

2. Basic guidelines for typography should be followed to increase the _____ and _____ of type on Web pages.

3. Create a high level of _____ between display and body type, and between type and page background.

4. For short paragraphs, headings, lists, and text on buttons, use _____ type. For large blocks of text and pages intended to be printed and then read, use _____ type.

5. Instead of large, gray text blocks, format text into _____ with line lengths of _____ to _____ words.

6. Three types of scanners include _____, _____, and _____.

7. As they display, interlaced GIFs and progressive JPEGs change from _____ to _____.

8. A halo effect occurs around a transparent GIF because the image is _____.

9. A(n) _____ is a version of an original image that has been greatly reduced in _____.

10. The LOWSCR attribute initially loads a(n) _____ version of an image and then loads a _____ version on top of it.

CHECKPOINT   Multiple Choice

Instructions: Select the letter of the correct answer for each question.

1. Font refers to _____.

    a. typeface
    b. type size
    c. typeface and type style
    d. typeface and type size

2. By applying styles to elements sharing the same HTML tag, you can _____.

    a. embed fonts in a page
    b. specify paragraph leading
    c. control tracking and kerning
    d. all of the above

3. PNGs are predicted to replace GIFs on the Web when a greater level of _____ exists.

    a. monitor resolution settings
    b. browser support
    c. compression/decompression rates
    d. browser plug-ins

4. Unlike GIFs, with JPEGs, you can control the levels of _____.

    a. compression

    b. colors

    c. gamma

    d. LZW

5. The drawback(s) of graphic typography include(s) _____.

    a. increased load time of pages

    b. no visibility if graphics are turned off

    c. fonts required to be resident

    d. both a and b

6. Compared with HTML tags, styles offer _____.

    a. equal typographic possibilities

    b. no typographic possibilities

    c. more typographic possibilities

    d. less typographic possibilities

7. Antialiasing should be utilized only for _____.

    a. type larger than 10 points

    b. type 10 points or smaller

    c. sans serif type larger than 10 points

    d. serif type 10 points or smaller

8. If you plan to manipulate an image with image editing software, you should scan it at _____.

    a. the size it will be displayed on the Web

    b. a larger size

    c. a higher resolution

    d. both b and c

9. A vector graphic is an image defined by _____.

    a. rows and columns of different colored pixels

    b. bitmaps

    c. mathematical statements regarding the drawing and positioning of lines

    d. color depth

10. GIF images can display up to _____.

    a. thousands of colors

    b. 16 colors

    c. millions of colors

    d. 256 colors

CHECKPOINT Short Answer

Instructions: Write a brief answer to each question.

1. Briefly describe the features that define type.

2. Explain seven basic guidelines for applying good typography on the Web.

3. Discuss briefly the variables that limit typographic control on the Web.

4. Explain the purposes of the following: overriding a default font setting, antialiasing type, and utilizing styles.

5. Identify the file formats for displaying graphics on the Web. Explain the circumstances in which each should be utilized.

6. Describe briefly three additional purposes for which you can use image editing software other than converting images into a Web-useable format.

7. Differentiate between lossy and lossless compression.

8. Identify the guidelines for scanning photos and illustrations.

9. Identify the guidelines for limiting the file size of images.

10. Discuss briefly five reasons why PNGs are predicted to replace GIFs on the Web.

AT ISSUE

Instructions: Write a brief essay in response to the following issues. Be prepared to discuss your findings in class. Use the Web as your research tool. For each issue, identify one URL utilized as a research source.

1. Image editing software constantly is evolving, thereby increasing designers' capabilities to apply highly sophisticated techniques. Cloning, editing, blending, and image correction tools can reconfigure an image so even experts cannot perceive that the image was altered. The negative to these evolving capabilities is the potential to misrepresent reality; for example, placing an individual in a photo to suggest he or she was present when the photo actually was taken. This capability of inaccurately depicting reality raises the question of intellectual honesty. Describe a specific instance that exemplifies this growing problem. Identify legal and moral issues, and designers' and software developers' responsibilities.

2. Branding is a popular marketing buzzword frequently associated with commercial and large organization Web sites. The goal of branding is to create instant recognition for the Web site owner and its products and/or services. Define and exemplify branding on the Web. Describe how typography and graphics can contribute to the branding process. Identify a Web site that demonstrates successful branding and list the components contributing to its success.

HANDS ON

Instructions: Complete the following exercises.

1. Start your browser and locate a Web site that has applied good graphic typography, and then locate a Web site that has not applied good graphic typography.

    a. Identify the basic graphic typography principles that have and have not been applied to each Web site.

    b. Explain what you think might be the impression on a visitor viewing each Web site for the first time.

    c. Print the Web pages you review and identity each URL.

2. Identify a software package that offers image mapping capabilities. Utilize a package that you own, or, if you are using your own computer, download a free or demo version from a Web site such as Mapedit or Tucows.

    a. Using the Help link, find and print the instructions to image map a graphic.

    b. Identify a graphic that you will utilize as an image map on your Web site.

CHAPTER 6

Multimedia and Interactivity on the Web

OBJECTIVES

After completing this chapter you will be able to:

- Identify the guidelines for utilizing multimedia on a Web site

- Identify sources of multimedia for the Web

- Explain the purposes for which animation can be used

- Identify and explain the basic process for creating animations with the most widely used animation format for the Web

- Employ methods of optimizing animations for downloading

- Discuss the formats associated with downloadable and streaming audio and video

- Identify the advantages and disadvantages of downloadable media

- Describe the advantages and disadvantages of streaming media

- Identify sources of audio files for the Web

- Identify sources of video files for the Web

- Identify methods of file compression for Web-based multimedia

- Explain methods to optimize downloadable audio and video

- Describe elements that can add interactivity to Web pages

- Discuss the benefits of interactive Web pages

INTRODUCTION

With an understanding of the rules of good typography and the methods to prepare and optimize graphics for your Web site learned in Chapter 5, you created a site utilizing these tools. Chapter 6 presents the use of multimedia and interactivity to enhance your Web pages, including basic concepts and guidelines that will allow you to take your Web site to the next level of development. While neither multimedia nor interactivity are required elements for a successful Web site, using them adds a dimension of excitement and entertainment on your Web pages in which users can participate actively. This type of user involvement is successful at bringing in visitors and influencing return visits. If you choose to include multimedia and/or interactivity, it is likely that you will draw from the myriad ready-made elements available for purchase or by downloading from the Web. Development tools and techniques also are introduced in this chapter for those who desire to create original multimedia content or interactive Web page elements.

WEB INFO

For more information about multimedia on the Web, visit the Web Design Chapter 6 Web Info page (scsite.com/web/ch6/webinfo.htm) and then click Multimedia.

WHAT IS MULTIMEDIA?

Multimedia is some combination of text, graphics, animation, audio, and video. A combination of these elements can produce stimulating, engaging Web pages. Creating splash pages is one common application of multimedia on the Web, but separate multimedia elements also can be utilized effectively. For example, a video clip can demonstrate how to use a product correctly, such as a fly fishing rod, or audio can be utilized to extend a personal greeting or teach the proper pronunciation of a foreign language. Most current Web authoring packages, such as FrontPage and Dreamweaver, include tools for incorporating multimedia with ease. The Motion Over Time Web site shown in Figure 6-1 effectively utilizes animation and sound elements.

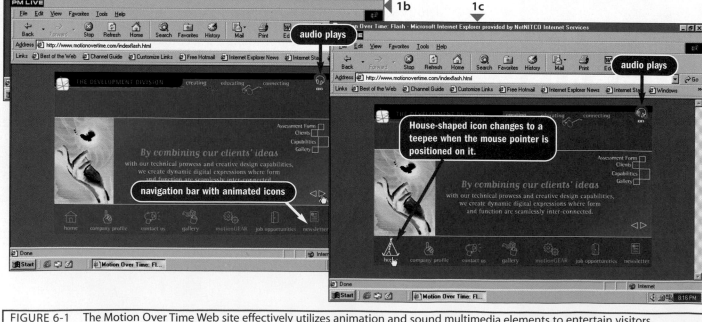

FIGURE 6-1   The Motion Over Time Web site effectively utilizes animation and sound multimedia elements to entertain visitors.

In Figure 6-1a, for example, a gyroscope twirls as elements fly around it. The intention of this animation is to show in very general terms the purpose of the Web site without requiring the visitor to read a lot of words. In Figures 6-1b and 6-1c, the animated icons on the navigation bar draw viewers' attention so they can check their choices. The audio buttons in all three figures offer visitors the opportunity to listen to an audio presentation, which describes motion over time.

Although multimedia is widely used in Web design, it is not essential, and many well-designed Web sites achieve their objectives without it. Certain drawbacks associated with using multimedia include considerable download time, requirements for plug-ins or players, and the utilization of substantial bandwidth. In addition, not all multimedia elements are accessible for everyone, causing a disadvantage for people with disabilities, such as individuals who are hearing or visually impaired. Creating the professional quality multimedia seen on such Web sites as Disney or IBM, often exceeds the expertise and budget of many designers. When incorporating multimedia, adhere to the following Web Design Tip:

Web Design Tip
Utilize multimedia sparingly for distinct purposes, ensuring that it adds value and furthers Web site objectives.

In addition to optimizing your multimedia for Web delivery as discussed later in this chapter, follow these general guidelines for multimedia to meet the usability needs of your audience.

- Identify high-bandwidth areas. Let your visitors know file sizes, format, and estimated time required to download. Do not risk annoying visitors or making them feel their time is being wasted.
- Create home pages that give visitors a choice of high- or low-bandwidth content.
- List any necessary plug-ins or players and provide links to locations where they can be acquired. You also can use JavaScript to detect the need for plug-ins within a browser and initiate a download automatically.
- Provide brief explanations of what visitors will see or hear to help them determine if they really do want to access the multimedia.
- Offer low-bandwidth alternatives such as audio or a slide show instead of video. Do not, for instance, waste bandwidth on a uninteresting video clip with little action, when an audio clip alone will convey the real content of value.
- When developing original multimedia, break audio or video files into short segments to create smaller files. Visitors also will be able to choose the segments they want to listen to, rather than having to listen to one long file.

USING SLIDE SHOWS

A **slide show**, which is a series of slides incorporating value-added text and graphics with interesting transitions, can be an effective low-bandwidth addition to a Web site. A more sophisticated presentation can be achieved via the addition of audio and/or video. A discussion of two popular software packages for creating slide shows for the Web follows in this section.

WEB INFO

For more information about incorporating slide shows in a Web site, visit the Web Design Chapter 6 Web Info page (scsite.com/web/ch6/webinfo.htm) and then click Slide Shows.

WEB INFO

For more information about Web-ready Microsoft PowerPoint presentations, visit the Web Design Chapter 6 Web Info page (scsite.com/web/ch6/ webinfo.htm) and then click PowerPoint.

Microsoft PowerPoint

Microsoft PowerPoint offers designers a quick and easy process for making a slide show Web-ready. After completing the slide show, you simply click the Save as Web Page command on the File menu. Before publishing the presentation on the Web, preview it for acceptability in a browser. Figure 6-2 illustrates a simple slide show created with PowerPoint for the investment Web site. Real Network **RealPresenter Plus** can be utilized to convert a PowerPoint presentation effortlessly to streaming format. RealPresenter Plus also facilitates the addition of audio and video to a presentation. The program additionally offers an extensive image library and navigation options for viewers.

FIGURE 6-2   A slide show can be an effective alternative to video on the Web. This example is appropriate for the investment Web site.

RealSlideshow Plus

Real Network **RealSlideshow Plus** is a powerful tool for creating dynamic streaming slide shows for the Web. A special feature of the program is the capability of deviating from the standard rectangular slide show orientation and creating a custom layout suited for your specific elements. The program allows an image such as a logo to display repeatedly throughout the presentation. RealSlideshow Plus also includes expansive image and sound collections, as well as features to facilitate navigation.

ANIMATION

Animation on the Web can be utilized effectively to catch a visitor's attention, demonstrate a simple process, or illustrate change over time, such as the metamorphosis of a butterfly. Ready-to-use animations can be purchased on CD-ROM or downloaded free from countless Web sites. Custom animations can be created using specific development tools. A discussion of the two more widely used animations, animated GIFs and Flash animation, follows.

Animated GIFs

Animated GIFs are both popular and prevalent on the Web. They are not a separate file format but rather a variation of the GIF 89A format. This type of animation consists of a sequence of frames containing graphic images in GIF format that simulate movement, for example, a spinning globe or a flashing advertising banner (Figure 6-3). Animated GIFs, like standard GIFs, include up to 256 colors. Nearly all browsers support animated GIFs, which do not require plug-ins to function. They do not, however, include sound or interactivity. To be effective, not more than one animated GIF per Web page should be included so a visitor can concentrate on the content. Multiple animations on one Web page can distract and annoy.

WEB INFO

For more information about the use of animation on the Web, visit the Web Design Chapter 6 Web Info page (scsite.com/web/ch6/webinfo.htm) and then click Animation.

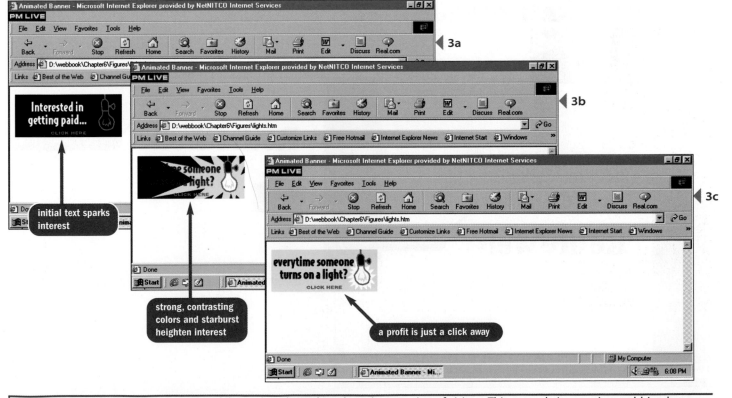

FIGURE 6-3   Animated banners are widely used on the Web to draw the attention of visitors. This example is attention grabbing because of the colors, the starburst effect, and the lure that making a profit is just a click away.

Several freeware and shareware tools specifically designed to create animated GIFs can be downloaded from the Web, for example, **Microangelo GIFted** and **GIF Construction Set Professional**™. These tools make creating animated GIFs a quick and simple process, and include many wizards to guide you through the process. In general, when using tools to create animated GIFs, follow this process:

1. Identify in sequential order the GIF images you want to animate. You can create the images using illustration or image editing software.

2. Specify the time, typically in seconds or fractions of a second, between each frame that holds the images.

3. Specify whether the background should be transparent and if the animation should **loop**, which means the image continues to repeat itself as long as the Web page is being viewed. Most tools will allow you to choose how many times the animation should repeat.

Figure 6-4 illustrates a simple animated GIF appropriate for the investment Web site. The following Web Design Tip suggests important guidelines for animated GIFs:

Web Design Tip

Like multiple animated GIFs, endlessly looping animated GIFs on a Web page can distract and annoy. Follow good design practice and include no more than one animated GIF per Web page, and limit the number of repetitions.

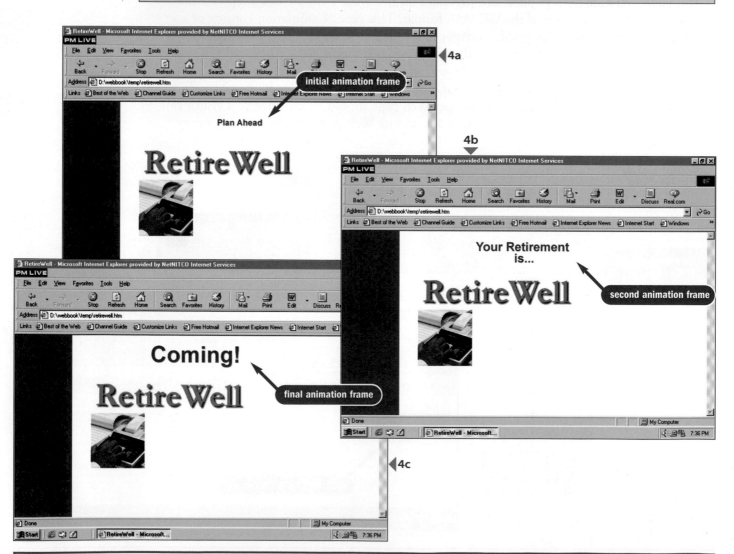

FIGURE 6-4 An animation consisting of text appropriate for the investment Web site announces to Plan Ahead. Your Retirement is Coming!

Software specially designed for creating Web graphics to generate an animated GIF also is an option. Packages such as Macromedia Fireworks, Adobe ImageReady, and PaintShop Pro Animation Shop contain illustration, image editing, and animation tools.

Software that creates animated GIFs compresses the files utilizing different methods. Smaller file sizes means a shorter loading time. To generate animated GIFs that are optimized for Web delivery, follow these guidelines:

- Limit the physical size of the images exactly to the size required to serve your purpose.
- Create the images with solid colors using the browser-safe palette.
- When possible, decrease the bit depth or number of colors of images. Instead of 8-bit/256 colors, experiment to see if 6-bit/64 colors or 4-bit/16 colors yields satisfactory images.
- Limit the number of frames in animations to only those necessary.

Flash Animation

Macromedia Flash is a powerful, flexible, efficient tool for creating simple to sophisticated streaming animation. The program can be utilized to generate small, scaleable vector graphics, which adjust to different browser sizes without degrading quality. You also can import into Flash bitmap images and vector graphics created in other programs such as Adobe Illustrator or Macromedia Freehand.

Flash simulates motion via fast-paced presentation of changing static images. The changing images are recorded in frames in the timeline (Figure 6-5). The animation process is accomplished in Flash by means of either frame-by-frame animation or animation with tweening.

WEB INFO

For more information about using Flash animation to generate graphics, visit the Web Design Chapter 6 Web Info page (scsite.com/web/ch6/webinfo.htm) and then click Flash Animation.

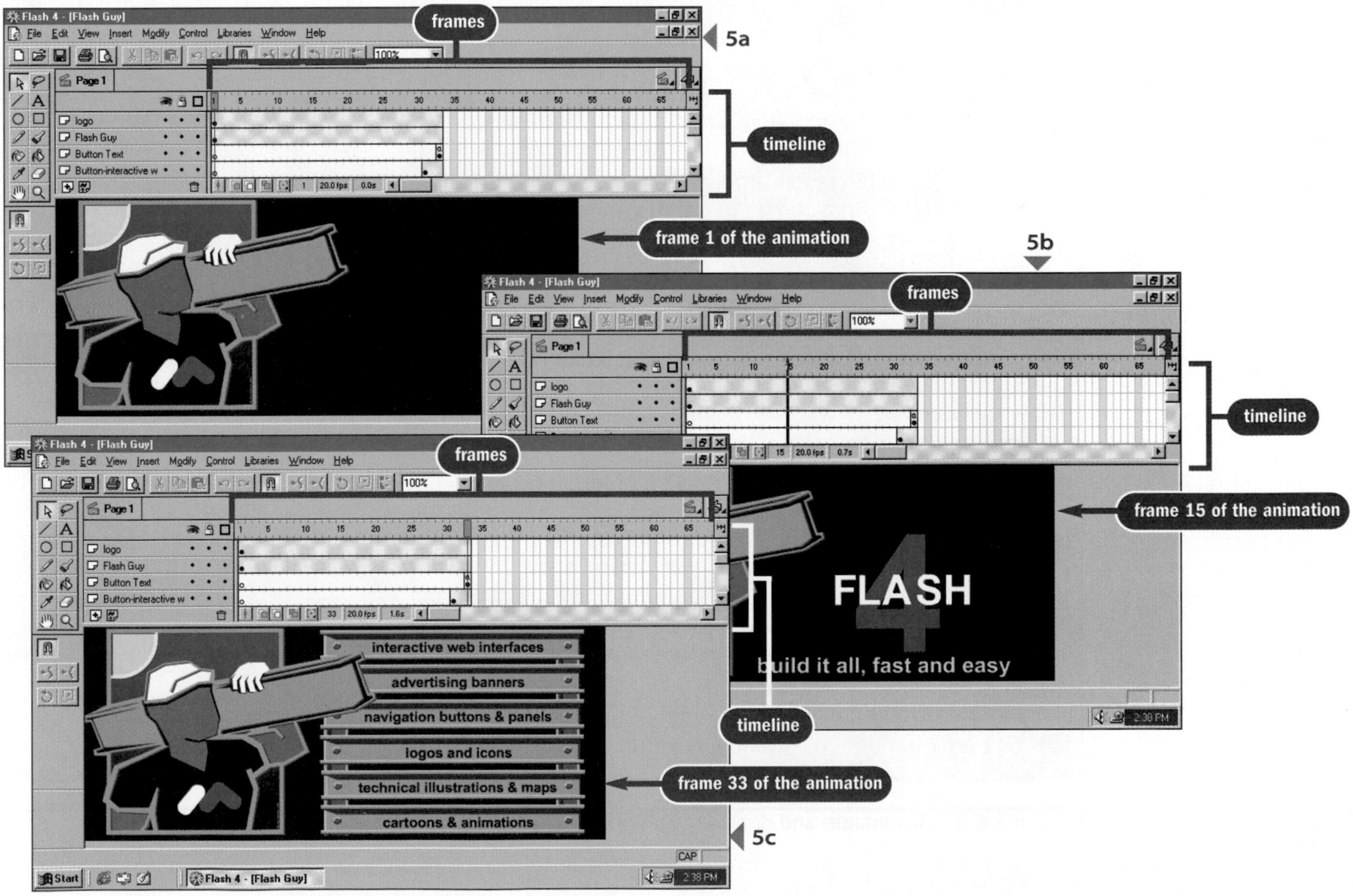

FIGURE 6-5   A Flash animation and its timeline.

With **frame-by-frame animation**, the image is changed manually, for example, erasing a portion or increasing the size of the image. A frame that holds an image that has changed is called a **key-frame**. With **animation with tweening**, the image is not changed manually. Instead, a beginning and ending key-frame identifies the original and final location and/or appearance of an image. Then, Flash automatically creates the necessary frames within the changing image in between the beginning and ending key-frames. Animation with tweening is a more expedient, less intensive method than frame-by-frame animation.

A completed Flash file is called a movie and can be viewed with a Flash player. Flash has wide browser support, and players are included in current Macintosh and Windows operating systems. Flash movies also play on WebTV and via ActiveX controls. Movies additionally can be converted to animated GIFs or QuickTime movies.

Downloadable and Streaming Media

Web audio and video can be either downloadable or streaming. As discussed in previous chapters, **downloadable media** must be downloaded in its entirety to the user's computer before it can be heard or seen. In contrast, **streaming media** begins to play as soon as the data begins to stream, or transfer in. In addition to this distinction, each media type has specific advantages and disadvantages, which are illustrated in Figure 6-6.

ADVANTAGES OF DOWNLOADABLE MEDIA
- The quality of downloadable media typically is superior to streaming media.
- Once the file has been downloaded, it can be accessed again and again.
- Downloadable media utilizes HTTP protocol to transfer the data, and therefore does not require a specific media server.

DISADVANTAGES OF DOWNLOADABLE MEDIA
- Downloading media can take anywhere from a few minutes to hours, depending on the speed of the Internet connection and the size of the file.
- Typically, the file is extremely large, resulting in both a long download time and considerable storage space being consumed on the user's computer.
- Copyright and/or distribution rights might be ignored by unscrupulous users.

ADVANTAGES OF STREAMING MEDIA
- Users have **random access** to the data, meaning they can choose which portion of the file they want to play via the player's control buttons.
- Streaming media consumes RAM only while being played and is purged after viewing.
- In the past, streaming media files could not be downloaded to a user's computer, thereby protecting any copyright and/or distribution rights. Today, with certain streaming media encoding software, the creator of the streaming media file has the option of allowing a file to be downloaded. The capability of downloading the file should be offered only if doing so does not infringe on copyright and/or distribution rights.

DISADVANTAGES OF STREAMING MEDIA
- Streaming media has very high bandwidth requirements.
- Generally, the quality of streaming media is not as high as downloadable media.
- Streaming media frequently requires a specific media server to transfer the data.

FIGURE 6-6   Advantages and disadvantages of downloadable and streaming media.

AUDIO

Including **audio files** on a Web site can add sound effects, entertain visitors with background music, deliver a personal message, or sell a product or service with testimonials. Sources of Web-deliverable audio include royalty-free audio files that can be downloaded from the Web or purchased on CD-ROM, or creating your own files. Adhere to the following Web Design Tip regarding copyright:

WEB INFO

For more information about including audio files in a Web site, visit the Web Design Chapter 6 Web Info page (scsite.com/web/ch6/webinfo.htm) and then click Audio.

> **Web Design Tip**
>
> Be careful to avoid copyright infringement when incorporating music into your Web site. For example, including music from a CD on your Web site without permission violates the artist's copyright.

With a personal computer, you can create a personal audio message, such as a welcome message to visitors, inexpensively and easily. Locate the Sound Recorder accessory by clicking the Start button on the taskbar, point to Programs, point to Accessories, and then click Multimedia. Utilize this accessory and a microphone connected to your computer to record your message. The results might be adequate for your needs, but if you want professional quality, customized audio, you may choose to outsource the project to a qualified service.

Audio must be in digital format to be used on the Web. Analog audio files can be digitized, or **encoded**, using specialized hardware and software. In addition to being in digital format, Web audio can be either downloadable or streaming. The more extensively used downloadable audio file formats on the Web include Waveform Audio (WAV) format, Audio Interchange File Format (AIFF), Moving Pictures Experts Group (MPEG), and Musical Instrument Digital Interface (MIDI) (Figure 6-7). The popularity of these formats can be attributed to their cross-platform and browser support.

WAV	Microsoft file format used for sounds ranging from those for games, to audio equivalent to CD-quality. The WAV file extension is .wav. Macintosh also supports this file format.
AIFF	AIFF is the sound format used originally on Apple computers. Windows also supports this format. The AIFF PC file extension is .aiff. An extension is not required on a Macintosh.
MPEG	MPEG is a set of standards. The .mp3 file format compresses sound at about a 12:1 ratio of the original file size. To listen to the files, an mp3 player is required. Creating an mp3 file is relatively simple. You can use a special program called a **ripper** to extract an audio segment from a CD and store it as a WAV file on your hard drive. You then can convert the WAV file to mp3 format with another program called an **encoder**. Remember that you are violating copyright if you extract and redistribute audio from a CD without the artist's permission. The MPEG file extension is .mpeg.
MIDI	An advantage of using a MIDI file format is its generally small size. This file format replicates only instrumental music, not voice. The MIDI file extension is .mid.

FIGURE 6-7 Commonly used downloadable Web audio formats.

Optimizing Downloadable Audio

The primary disadvantage associated with downloadable audio is the extremely large file size, which significantly impacts the transfer time to a user's computer. To decrease download time, you must reduce the file size of your audio. Reducing the file size results in more acceptable download times, but may deteriorate the quality of the audio. Therefore, you need to create balance between satisfactory download time and sound quality. You can accomplish this goal by manipulating certain audio aspects, including size and channels, and more complex hardware and software related characteristics.

LIMITING FILE SIZE VIA DURATION AND CHANNELS By manipulating various audio characteristics, you can create smaller files if you follow these guidelines:

- Simply stated, shorter audio clips equal smaller files. A generally reliable practice is to utilize audio clips no longer than one minute.
- Mono (one-channel) and stereo (two-channel) are the two more well-known audio channels. A stereo audio file will be double the size of a mono file. For Web usage, choose mono.

LIMITING FILE SIZE VIA HARDWARE AND SOFTWARE Manipulating the following aspects of audio will require specific hardware, software, and expertise. Although you may never manipulate audio yourself, understanding these aspects will make you more knowledgeable about Web audio.

- During the conversion of analog to digital audio, samples of the audio wave are obtained. **Sampling rate**, measured in kilohertz (kHz), refers to the amount of samples obtained per second. A sampling rate of 48 kHz will yield higher quality audio and also a much bigger file than a sampling rate of 11.127 kHz. The 8 kHz voice-only and 22 kHz music files will yield satisfactory Web audio.
- When applied to digital audio, **bit depth** is another measure of quality. The greater the number of bits means a higher quality level. An 8-bit audio file, although lower in quality than a 16-bit audio file, generally is recommended for Web usage.
- **Codecs** are special computer programs that greatly reduce audio file size. The codecs (compressors/decompressors) utilize lossy compression to remove redundant and less-significant data. Each time you apply compression, however, the quality level of the file will diminish.

The reason for optimizing downloadable audio and video files is stated in the following Web Design Tip:

> **Web Design Tip**
>
> Optimize downloadable audio and video files to prevent long download times, which may deter visitors from your Web site.

Streaming Audio

In contrast to downloadable audio, file size and quality issues are not significant to streaming audio. The following technologies are widely utilized for creating both a mixture of streaming audio and video, and for generating streaming audio only. Among their differences is the need for additional components to deliver and play the audio.

REALAUDIO RealNetworks streaming audio technology, **RealAudio**, introduced in 1995, is the most widely used format on the Web. Its popularity stems in part from a reputation for stereo FM quality and the availability of its player. Current Netscape Navigator and Internet Explorer browsers feature the RealAudio player. Delivery of RealAudio requires it to be served up by a RealAudio server, which has been set up with specific software. Consider the advice in the following Web Design Tip if you are thinking about adding RealAudio to your Web site:

> **Web Design Tip**
>
> If you are considering including RealAudio in your Web site, check first with your Internet service provider or online service provider to ensure that it has a server configured to deliver RealAudio.

You can encode audio in the RealAudio format utilizing Real Networks **RealProducer Plus**. The software features a recording wizard that allows you to record from an existing file such as a WAV or MPEG file, or record from a media device such as a VCR, CD player, or microphone. After encoding the file, you can utilize the wizard to create a Web page that includes the RealAudio file, and publish the Web page to a RealAudio server (Figure 6-8).

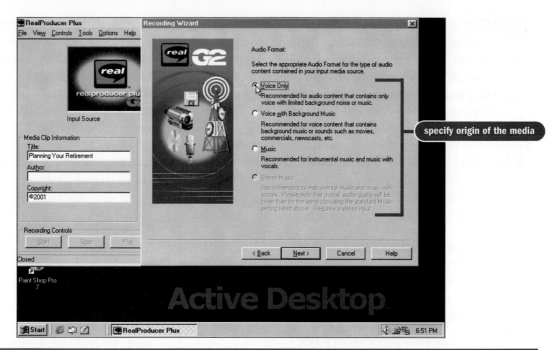

FIGURE 6-8   The RealProducer Plus Recording Wizard simplifies the process of recording in streaming media format.

SHOCKWAVE AUDIO   Macromedia developed Shockwave for Web-based multimedia. **Macromedia Shockwave** has gained great popularity for generating quality streaming audio, playable on both the Windows and Macintosh platforms. Many Web sites use Shockwave files to promote their products and services. To listen to Shockwave audio, a Shockwave player must be downloaded. Unlike RealAudio, Shockwave does not require specific server software to be set up to deliver the audio. Macromedia products Director, Freehand, or Authorware can be used to create Shockwave files. These products, however, are complex and costly.

QUICKTIME   Apple created **QuickTime** for Web-based multimedia. Apple's QuickTime movies (.mov) also can be utilized to create cross-platform streaming audio. Premier Web sites such as HBO, CNN, and Disney feature QuickTime media. Current versions of Netscape Navigator and Internet Explorer include the QuickTime plug-in. QuickTime 3.0 for Macintosh and Windows included new codecs for compressing audio and the capability of creating small, high-quality instrumental files.

Keep in mind the following Web Design Tip when considering streaming audio software:

> **Web Design Tip**
> Some streaming audio software packages require additional components to deliver and play audio files.

VIDEO

As with audio, you can download royalty-free video files from the Web, purchase them on CD-ROM, or create your own files. File size is a much greater issue with downloadable video than with downloadable audio because of the enormous amount of data necessary to describe the dual components of video and audio.

The efficient delivery of video via the Web is a challenging issue. A lack of bandwidth can cause transmission delays that affect the reproduction of the video, and you may run the risk of alienating visitors by offering unpredictable, out-of-sync video or video files that require intolerable download times. Video can have a powerful impact on furthering your Web site's objectives, but the majority of users will not fully embrace streaming video until bandwidth issues are alleviated and data can be transferred efficiently, with little or no interference. As bandwidth limitations are reduced and streaming technology becomes more advanced, the use of streaming video will become increasingly common.

Before making a decision to include video on your Web site, consider simpler alternatives such as animation, audio, or a slide show that could circumvent issues related to delivering video on the Web. If you decide that only video will best further your Web site's objectives, review the specific issues related to downloadable and streaming video.

Downloadable Video File Formats

The more common downloadable video file formats on the Web include Microsoft AVI (.avi), Moving Pictures Experts Group MPEG (.mpeg), and QuickTime Movie (.mov). The MPEG and QuickTime file formats can be transformed into streaming formats. An overview of the common downloadable file formats follows.

AUDIO VIDEO INTERLEAVED AVI (.avi) Microsoft developed the AVI standard to be used with Windows 95 Video for Windows, a format for video and audio data storage. The concept behind interleaving the audio and video was that a video file would play very smoothly. AVI files are not suitable for **full-screen video** (640 pixels x 480 pixels) and **full-motion video** (30 frames per second). For PCs, AVI is the most prevalent video file format. A special utility is required to view AVI files on the Macintosh platform.

MOVING PICTURES EXPERTS GROUP MPEG (.mpeg) MPEG video files are superior in quality to AVI or QuickTime files, due to their excellent compression capabilities, which result in a barely noticeable degrading of quality. The quality level of an MPEG video is a little less than VCR-level video. MPEG-1 and MPEG-2 are the primary MPEG standards. A computer with considerable processing power is required to encode an MPEG.

QUICKTIME MOVIE (.mov) Apple originally developed QuickTime for the Macintosh, but Windows users can view QuickTime movies if they install a specific driver. Generating movies on a Windows platform is possible with QuickTime 3.0. Recent versions of Internet Explorer and Netscape Navigator have built-in QuickTime plug-ins that allow movies to be viewed directly in the browser. Because of their high compression capabilities and resulting small file sizes, QuickTime movies are especially well-suited for downloading.

Optimizing Downloadable Video

WEB INFO

For more information about how you can optimize downloadable video on Web pages, visit the Web Design Chapter 6 Web Info page (scsite.com/web/ch6/webinfo.htm) and then click Downloadable Video.

With the enormous amounts of data involved, file size is a much greater issue with downloadable video than with downloadable audio. Reducing the file size of video is imperative to improve download times, but may deteriorate the quality of the video. Certain aspects of video can be manipulated to create a balance between satisfactory download times and quality. Manipulating these aspects of video requires specific hardware, software, and expertise. You may never manipulate video yourself, but understanding these aspects will make you more knowledgeable about Web video.

- Use video clips one to two minutes in length.
- The dimensions of full-screen video are 640 pixels x 480 pixels. Use a smaller frame size for Web video. The standard frame size for displaying video on the Web is 160 pixels x 120 pixels (Figure 6-9).

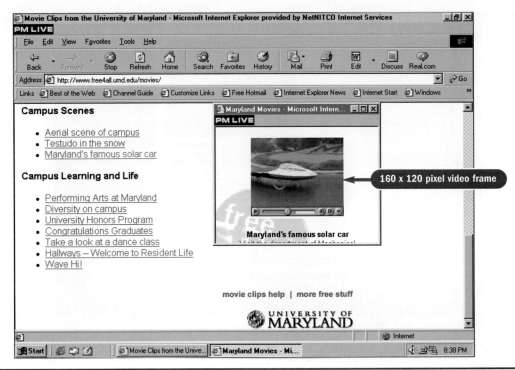

FIGURE 6-9   A video clip of the University of Maryland's famous solar car displays in a 160 x 120 pixel frame.

- To achieve smooth motion, the frame rate for television is 30 frames per second (fps). To avoid jerky video on the Web, the recommended rate is 10 to 15 fps.
- You can define the general quality level of your video, which automatically adjusts the compression. If you define the quality between low and medium, you will achieve a good balance between sufficient compression and video quality that is suitable for the Web.
- As with audio, the greater the number of bits means the bigger the file size. If you decrease a video segment from 16-bit to 8-bit, the file size will decrease significantly, as will the quality. Experiment with different settings to find a balance that is acceptable to you.
- Intel Indeo and Radius Cinepak are two well-known video codecs that utilize lossy compression. The preferred codec for Web video is Cinepak, due in part to its QuickTime and AVI compatibility.

The following Web Design Tip offers a guideline to optimizing downloadable video:

Web Design Tip

When optimizing downloadable video, you must find a balance between the size of the file and the quality of the video that will yield satisfactory results for both criteria.

Streaming Video

Recall that streaming video begins to play as soon as the data begins to stream, or transfer in. Several companies have developed products that make streaming video possible. MPEG and QuickTime file formats can be transformed into streaming video files. RealNetworks' and Microsoft's streaming video formats are discussed next.

REALNETWORKS REALVIDEO   RealNetworks has led the way in the streaming video arena with its product, **RealVideo**. Like RealAudio, delivery of RealVideo requires a server configured with the RealServer software to serve it up. You can create one RealVideo file for various audience connection capabilities, such as 28 Kbps or 56 Kbps, ISDN, or cable (Figure 6-10 on the next page). After the request for the video is received, the connection rate is determined, and the video of the appropriate speed is transferred. RealVideo also can be used to deliver live Web video.

WEB INFO

For more information about using streaming video, visit the Web Design Chapter 6 Web Info page (scsite.com/web/ch6/webinfo.htm) and then click Streaming Video.

FIGURE 6-10   With RealVideo, you can create one video file targeted for various audience connection capabilities.

You can use **RealProducer Plus** to encode video into the RealVideo format. This software includes a recording wizard that allows you to record from an existing file such as an AVI file, or record from a media device such as a VCR, CD player, or digital video camera. After encoding the file, you can utilize the wizard to create a Web page that includes the RealVideo file, and publish the Web page to a specially configured server.

MICROSOFT WINDOWS MEDIA   Microsoft introduced its Windows Media technology for creating and delivering high-quality streaming media via broadband Internet and corporate intranets. Current predictions are that Windows Media significantly will impact the following areas:

- **Consumer Electronics**. Small digital audio players support this technology, as do car stereos and TV set-top boxes.
- **Film/Music.** The quality levels for media created with this technology are CD-level quality for audio and almost DVD-level quality for video. Additionally, the technology is designed to safeguard artists' rights while helping customers legitimately obtain content.
- **Business**. Corporations are utilizing Windows Media to deliver streaming media for virtual meetings and training, and to facilitate e-commerce. Aetna, Charles Schwab, and Hewlett-Packard are some of the companies using this technology.

Windows Media currently requires the Windows Media Technologies 7 encoder and player to create and play streaming media. Distribution of this media requires a server configured with special Windows Media software.

On the user-end, both Windows 2000 and Windows Me come with **Windows Media Player**, which can be used by visitors to your Web site to play video, audio, and mixed-media files. Windows Media Player also can perform tasks such as viewing live news updates on the Internet, playing clips from a movie, or viewing a music video on a Web site.

Broadband Internet services include cable modem, DSL, ISDN, and satellite connections. These connections are much faster than dial-up services and do not require you to dial your Internet service provider and wait for a connection. The benefits of broadband services are high-speed, always-on connections. The drawback of broadband service is that most homes and businesses do not yet have access to it. Those that do, find that broadband makes streaming video very practical.

The following Web Design Tip suggests important factors to consider regarding choosing between downloadable or streaming media:

Web Design Tip

To determine whether downloadable or streaming media is best for your Web site, consider such factors as Web site objectives, audience needs, budget, available expertise and resources, and the need to protect copyright and distribution rights.

In general, if you want media exceeding one minute in length delivered relatively quickly, think about streaming media. Remember this format most likely will require encoding and a specially configured server. If your media is less than one minute in length and delivery time is not a significant issue, consider downloadable media.

INTERACTIVITY

Interactivity requires user participation with one or more elements on a Web page. For interactivity to occur, a user must perform an action such as typing text or moving and clicking the mouse. An interactive Web page allows a user to participate rather than passively observer. Possibilities for interactive content range from the use of simple forms to more sophisticated Web page elements. The following sections detail design principles to incorporate when creating online forms and a discussion of current software and technologies that can be used to generate other interactive Web page elements. The benefit of including interactivity is stated in the following Web Design Tip:

Web Design Tip

Use interactive elements on your Web site to keep the user interested and involved with your content.

Online Forms

Chapter 2 introduced **forms**, which are structured Web documents in which information can be entered or options selected. Common form elements include text boxes, check boxes, option buttons, and drop-down list boxes. Forms frequently are used to obtain comments and feedback or order products or services. Follow these design guidelines to create attractive online forms with a high degree of usability:

- Require that fields containing essential information are completed before the form can be submitted. Some form-generation software allows you to prompt the user to provide the missing information. Required information might include name, address, telephone number, and e-mail address. Optional information might consist of position title, income, or marital status, for example.
- One browser may display a form differently than another. To counteract this effect and create a professional looking form, use a table to align elements.
- Make text boxes large enough to hold the approximate number of characters for a typical response.
- Restrict responses to contain characters or numbers only when appropriate.
- Use check boxes to allow users to submit more than one response to a query.
- Provide space for additional comments or requests for further information.
- Use color to highlight and segment information.
- Include a reset button so that the user can clear the form quickly and re-enter the information if necessary.
- Build in the capability of confirming information.
- Send a confirmation notice assuring the user that the form has been submitted.

An attractive, highly useable online form is illustrated in Figure 6-11 on the next page.

WEB INFO

For more information about the benefits of using interactivity for user participation, visit the Web Design Chapter 6 Web Info page (scsite.com/web/ch6/webinfo.htm) and then click Interactivity.

WEB INFO

For more information about using interactive forms on Web pages, visit the Web Design Chapter 6 Web Info page (scsite.com/web/ch6/webinfo.htm) and then click Online Forms.

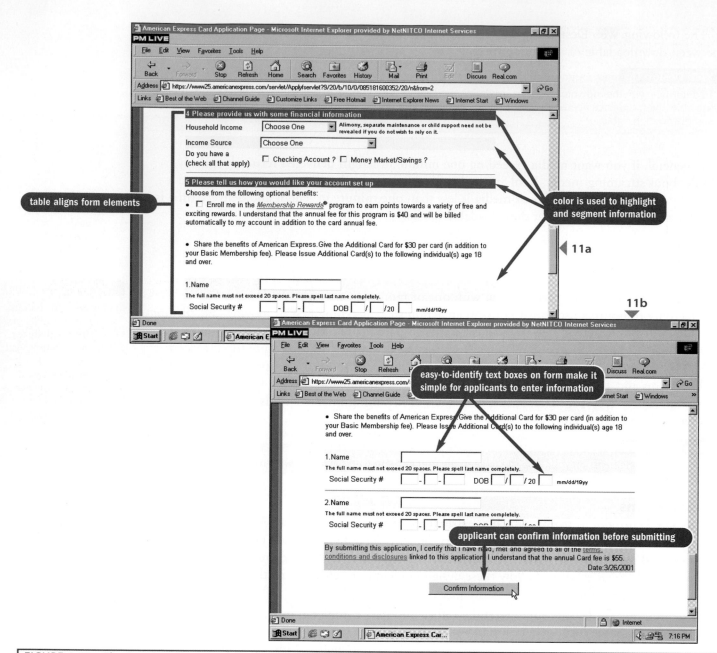

FIGURE 6-11 The American Express application form embodies the design guidelines for attractive and usable online forms.

Additional Interactive Page Elements

Including other **interactive Web page elements** on your Web pages can offer your Web site visitors a more involved, exciting experience. An overview of the software and other technologies that can be used to generate the elements and examples of the Web page elements follow.

MACROMEDIA FLASH In addition to its benchmarking animation capabilities, **Macromedia Flash** is a leading tool for developing simple to advanced levels of interactivity for Web pages. Flash, for example, can be utilized to create a basic interactive element, a rollover button. A **rollover button** changes its appearance in reaction to certain movements of the mouse. for example, if the mouse pointer is positioned on the button, it could change color or shape. The color or shape also might change once the button is clicked (Figure 6-12). With Flash, you also can create animated buttons with video and audio or buttons with attached actions such as, *go to* or, *load movie*. Advanced capabilities for adding interactivity to Web pages include navigation, menus, and games.

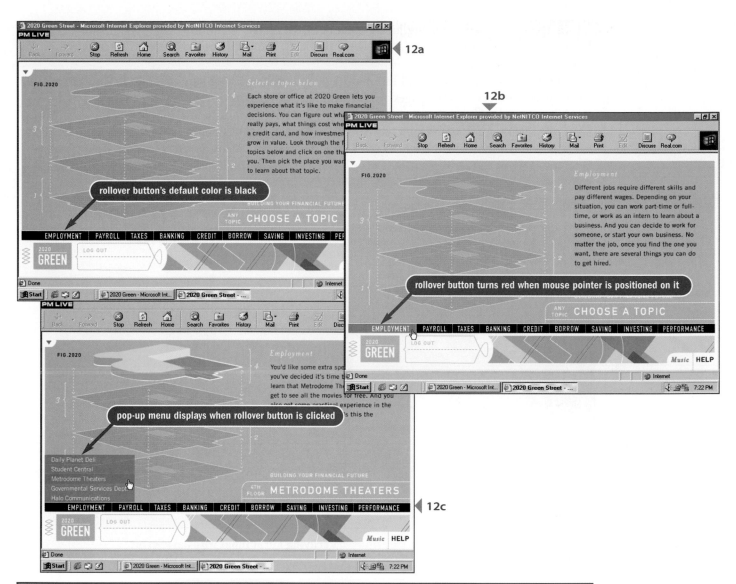

FIGURE 6-12   A rollover button on the 2020 Green Street Web site created with Flash.

MACROMEDIA SHOCKWAVE   Macromedia originally developed Shockwave to create multimedia games and movies for CDs and kiosks. **Macromedia Shockwave** also can produce high-quality interactive Web experiences, such as user-controlled training and multiuser, real-time sophisticated games. Shockwave can be streamed without the need of special server software, and its plug-in is widely available. **Director**, a powerful, expensive multimedia authoring tool, is used to create Shockwave files and utilizes a complex programming language called Lingo. Large corporations and organizations often employ designers who are Director and Shockwave experts to generate multimedia and interactive multimedia segments for their Web sites. The use of this technology might be cost-prohibitive for smaller companies

Java Applets and JavaScript

Chapter 1 introduced Java applets as short programs that make Web pages more dynamic and interactive. **Java applets** do not require plug-ins and are used widely in games, flight simulations, specialized audio effects, and calculators (Figure 6-13a on the next page). You can find free applets or purchase them on the Web. Browsers sometimes react negatively to applets, either by crashing or requiring unacceptable load times. Java applets are sent to the browser as a separate file alongside the HTML document.

WEB INFO

For more information about the use of Java applets in games and specialized audio effects, visit the Web Design Chapter 6 Web Info page (scsite.com/web/ch6/webinfo.htm) and then click Java Applets.

Java applets are written using Java Developer's Kit (JDK) from Sun Microsystems or Microsoft's Visual J++. For applets to work properly, browsers should be configured with applets enabled.

JavaScript also was introduced in Chapter 1 as a scripting language that can be used to create customized interactive Web pages. Unlike applets, **JavaScript scripts** are inserted directly into the HTML code. JavaScript frequently is used to verify form information and to create rollover buttons, advertising banners, pop-up windows, and content-changing Web pages (Figure 6-13b). You can download ready-made scripts from many Web sites.

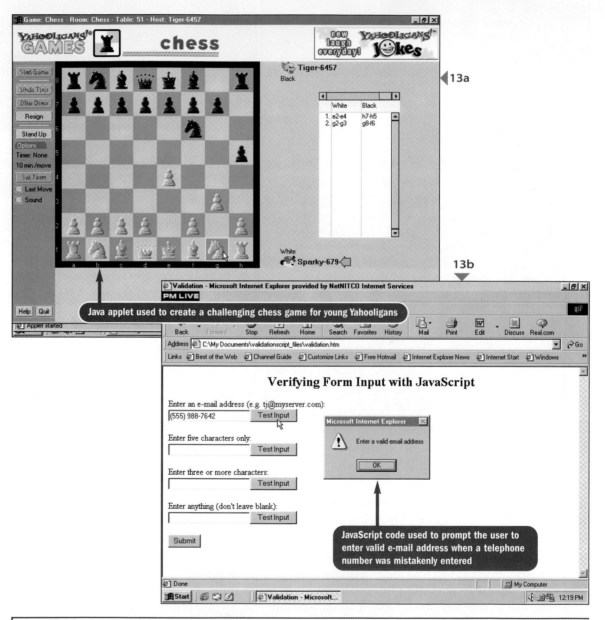

FIGURE 6-13 Java and JavaScript create dynamic, interactive Web pages.

CHAPTER SUMMARY

Multimedia generally is defined as some combination of text, graphics, animation, audio, and video. A combination of these elements can generate exciting, entertaining Web pages. Individual multimedia elements also can be utilized effectively on their own. Multimedia is not essential for the success of a Web site. Drawbacks associated with multimedia include considerable download time, need for players or plug-ins, substantial bandwidth requirements, and limited access for people with special needs. Multimedia should be included in a Web site if it is utilized sparingly for distinct purposes, adds value, furthers Web site objectives, and meets the usability needs of the audience.

Animation can be employed to catch a visitor's attention, demonstrate a simple process, or illustrate change over time, such as the metamorphosis of a butterfly. Animated GIFs are the most popular and widely used form of animation on the Web. Free and shareware tools and software specially designed for creating Web graphics can create animated GIFs. Macromedia Flash is a powerful, flexible, efficient tool for creating simple to sophisticated streaming Web animation.

Web audio and video can be in either downloadable or streaming format. Both formats have distinct advantages and disadvantages. Efficiently delivering quality video via the Web is very challenging due to bandwidth limitations. Designers should consider alternatives to video that would circumvent issues related to delivering video on the Web.

Interactivity means user involvement with one or more elements on a Web page. The user participates rather than passively observes. For the interactivity to occur, user input such as typing text or moving and clicking the mouse is required. Interactive possibilities range from a simple form to sophisticated Web page elements.

KEY TERMS

Instructions: Use the following terms from this chapter as a study review.

animated GIFs (6.5)
animation (6.5)
animation with tweening (6.8)
audio files (6.9)
bit depth (6.10)
broadband (6.14)
codecs (6.10)
Director (6.17)
downloadable media (6.8)
encoded (6.9)
encoder (6.9)
forms (6.15)
frame-by-frame animation (6.8)
full-motion video (6.12)
full-screen video (6.12)
GIF Construction Set Professional™ (6.6)
interactive Web page elements (6.16)
interactivity (6.15)
Java applets (6.17)
JavaScript scripts (6.18)

key-frame (6.8)
loop (6.6)
Macromedia Flash (6.7, 6.16)
Macromedia Shockwave (6.11, 6.17)
Microangelo GIFted (6.6)
Microsoft PowerPoint (6.4)
multimedia (6.2)
QuickTime (6.11)
random access (6.8)
RealAudio (6.10)
RealPresenter Plus (6.4)
RealProducer Plus (6.10, 6.14)
RealSlideshow Plus (6.5)
RealVideo (6.13)
ripper (6.9)
rollover button (6.16)
sampling rate (6.10)
slide show (6.3)
streaming media (6.8)
Windows Media Player (6.14)

CHECKPOINT Matching

Instructions: Match each term with the best description.

_____ 1. encoded audio files

_____ 2. random access

_____ 3. full-motion video

_____ 4. broadband

_____ 5. codecs

_____ 6. ripper

_____ 7. loop

_____ 8. full-screen video

_____ 9. rollover button

_____ 10. animation with tweening

_____ 11. frame-by-frame animation

_____ 12. key-frame

_____ 13. slide show

a. Video that is 640 pixels x 480 pixels.

b. Causes an animation to continue repeating itself as long as the Web page is being viewed.

c. Analog audio that has been digitized for the Web using specialized hardware and software.

d. Animation in which the image is changed manually.

e. Video with a frame rate of 30 frames per second.

f. High-speed, always-on Internet connections.

g. An advantage of streaming media giving users the choice as to which portion of the file they want to play via the player's control buttons.

h. Animation in which the image is changed automatically between beginning and ending key-frames.

i. A frame that holds an image that has been changed.

j. An interactive element that changes its appearance based on certain movements of the mouse.

k. A special program to extract an audio segment from a CD and store it as a WAV file.

l. Compressors/decompressors utilized to reduce file size.

m. A series of slides that may incorporate text, graphics, audio, video, and transitions between slides.

CHECKPOINT Fill in the Blanks

Instructions: Fill in the blank(s) with the appropriate answer.

1. A common application of multimedia on the Web is on _____ pages.

2. The combination of multimedia elements can produce _____ and _____ Web pages.

3. Generally, include no more than _____ animation(s) per page.

4. Animated GIFs can include up to _____ colors.

5. Animated GIFs do not include _____ or _____.

6. Incorporating music in your Web site from a CD without permission _____ the artist's copyright.

7. Audio must be in _____ format to be used on the Web.

8. Certain aspects of video and audio can be manipulated to create a _____ between satisfactory download times and quality.

9. File size is a much greater issue with downloadable _____ than with downloadable _____.

10. Interactivity on a Web page allows a visitor to _____ rather than _____.

CHECKPOINT Multiple Choice

Instructions: Select the letter of the correct answer for each question.

1. Animated GIFs are a _____.
   a. variation of the GIF 87A format
   b. variation of the GIF 89A format
   c. combination of the GIF 87A and the GIF 89A formats
   d. separate file format

2. To optimize downloadable audio for Web delivery, audio should be _____.
   a. one minute or less in length
   b. stereo
   c. mono
   d. both a and c

3. To generate animated GIFs that are optimized for Web delivery, you should _____.
   a. limit the number of frames in animations to only those required
   b. create the images with millions of colors
   c. increase when possible the bit depth or number of colors of images
   d. all of the above

4. The most widely used streaming audio format on the Web is _____.
   a. Shockwave
   b. RealAudio
   c. QuickTime
   d. AVI

5. For PCs, the most prevalent downloadable video file format is _____.

    a.   MPEG

    b.   QuickTime

    c.   AVI

    d.   RealVideo

6. For optimum delivery of downloadable video, a clip should be no longer than _____.

    a.   one to two minutes

    b.   three to five minutes

    c.   six to eight minutes

    d.   ten minutes

7. To avoid jerky video on the Web, the recommended frame rate is _____.

    a.   30 frames per second

    b.   10 to 15 frames per second

    c.   5 frames per second

    d.   none of the above

8. The format designed to deliver high-quality streaming media via broadband Internet and corporate intranets is _____.

    a.   RealVideo

    b.   MPEG

    c.   Windows Media

    d.   AIFF

9. To create an attractive online form with a high degree of usability, you should _____.

    a.   utilize a table to align elements

    b.   never require specific information to be completed before a form can be submitted

    c.   exclude any type of confirmation notice

    d.   all of the above

10. _____ is (are) utilized to create interactive page elements.

    a.   Flash

    b.   Shockwave

    c.   Java applets and JavaScript

    d.   all of the above

CHECKPOINT   Short Answer

Instructions: Write a brief answer to each question.

1. Identify the general guidelines for utilizing multimedia on a Web site, including those that address meeting the usability needs of your audience.

2. Identify the most widely used animation format found on the Web and explain the basic process for creating this format.

3. Differentiate between frame-by-frame animation and animation with tweening. Identify which type of animation is more expedient.

4. Identify the advantages and disadvantages of downloadable and streaming media.

5. Discuss the formats associated with downloadable and streaming audio.

6. Discuss the formats associated with downloadable and streaming video.

7. Identify methods to optimize downloadable audio.

8. Identify methods to optimize downloadable video.

9. List elements that can facilitate interactivity on Web pages.

10. Explain the design guidelines for creating attractive online forms with a high degree of usability.

AT ISSUE

Instructions: Write a brief essay in response to the following issues. Be prepared to discuss your findings in class. Use the Web as your research tool. For each issue, identify one URL utilized as a research source.

1. In this chapter, you learned that Java applets are used in creating interactive online games. Games of seemingly endless varieties abound on the Web. Many offer players fun, excitement, and a welcome break from reality. Others present adult entertainment and opportunities to gamble. Discuss the pros and cons of online games, including any legal or ethical issues. Identify the roles and responsibilities that game developers and game site hosts should assume.

2. Broadband Internet services were introduced in this chapter. Recall that high-speed, always-on broadband connections include cable modem, DSL, ISDN, and satellite. Businesses and homes with broadband services find streaming media to be very practical via a broadband connection. Research and discuss the availability of broadband services in the area where you work or live. Explain the obstacles the broadband services suppliers are encountering as they try to provide more widespread access. Discuss the impact of the availability of broadband service will have/has had on your place of work or home.

HANDS ON

Instructions: Complete the following exercises.

1. Search for two Web sites in this exercise to reinforce concepts presented in the chapter about utilizing animation and multimedia elements.

   Part A: Locate a Web site the effectively utilizes animation for one of the three following purposes:

       (1)   Attention getting

       (2)   Demonstrating a simple process

       (3)   Illustrating change over time

   Print the Web page and identify its URL. Describe the steps of the animation and explain how the animation achieves its purpose.

   Part B: Locate a Web site that contains multimedia elements such as video or sound and follows the guidelines for multimedia to meet the usability needs of its audience. Print the Web page and identify its URL. Indicate specifically how the designer has incorporated the guidelines.

2. Surf the Web to find an online form that is both attractive and highly useable. Print the form and identify its URL. Indicate what guidelines the designer followed to create the form. Suggest one way the form could be improved.

SECTION 3 CASE STUDY

The Case Study is an ongoing development process in Web design using the concepts, techniques, and Web Design Tips presented in each section. In Section 1, you selected the type of Web site (personal, organization/topical, or commercial), a topic of interest and title, goals, elements and design tools. With these components in place, in Section 2, you utilized the six steps for developing a solid design plan in preparation for the next activity. In the Section 3 Case Study, you are to create your Web site.

Assignment

Instructions: Create your Web site. Using the procedures presented in Chapters 1 through 5, implement the design plan for your personal, organizational/topical, or commercial Web site. Use the fundamental design principles of balance and proximity, contrast and focus, and unity, and the functions commonly associated with home and secondary pages. Design the Web pages for audience usability needs. Include the appropriate use of multimedia and interactivity, considering budget and expertise.

Follow the steps below in creating your Web site related to this Case Study. Review the specifications of the investment Web site and other chapter materials to complete this assignment.

1. Choose whether you will generate your pages with HTML code and a text editor such as Notepad or with a Web authoring package such as FrontPage, DreamWeaver or GoLive.

2. Develop your home page first and the subsequent secondary pages according to the Web site structure you defined. Remember that your home page and secondary pages should have a visual connection.

3. To achieve unity, establish a consistent page layout throughout your site when using a text editor by creating a page template with a table(s). To establish consistency when using a Web authoring package, you also can create a page template by means of a table(s), or choose a ready-made template that these packages typically offer.

4. Apply a consistent color scheme to maintain unity in your Web pages. Limit the color scheme to no more than three complementary colors. To ensure a uniform color scheme, you may use a Web authoring package that has predefined themes for this purpose or you can modify them while staying within the confines of three colors.

5. Add original or repurposed text content to your Web pages first, and apply the rules of good typography.

6. If you are using traditional photos and illustrations instead of images taken with a digital camera, scan, edit, and optimize them for Web delivery. Place the images on your Web pages in positions where they will be relative and effective. Remember to include alternate text descriptions for images, and to consider using thumbnails and the LOWSRC attribute when appropriate. Test the load time of pages once images have been added. Consider using fewer or smaller images if the load time is excessive.

7. Download from the Web, purchase, or create any multimedia you want to include on your Web pages. Insert the elements into your pages following the guidelines for multimedia to meet the usability needs of your audience.

8. Develop any online forms you want to include on your Web pages. Utilize a table to align form elements, and follow the guidelines for creating highly useable forms. For forms that you want to use for confirmation or feedback, you may use a Web authoring package that features predefined templates for this purpose.

9. Download from the Web, purchase, or create the components to make other elements on the page interactive. The components may include Java applets or JavaScript scripts.

10. Download from the Web, purchase, or create navigation elements to link your pages. Place the elements in consistent logical places throughout your Web site.

CHAPTER 7

Testing, Publishing, Marketing, and Maintaining a Web Site

OBJECTIVES

After completing this chapter you will be able to:

- Explain the steps necessary to test a Web site before publishing

- Identify the important questions to ask when group testing a Web site

- Understand the steps associated with acquiring server space

- Know the important questions to ask service providers

- Understand and apply the process involved to obtain a domain name

- Explain the function of the domain name system (DNS)

- Understand and apply the steps to upload a Web site

- Identify sources to acquire an FTP application

- Utilize several different methods of uploading a Web site

- Explain the steps necessary to test a Web site after publishing

- Understand the relationship between marketing and high traffic volume

- Describe and apply Web-based marketing methods

- Describe and apply traditional marketing methods and advertising

- Understand the importance of regularly maintaining and updating a Web site

- Identify the specific aspects to address to maintain and update a Web site effectively

INTRODUCTION

Thus far, you have learned the Web design basics you need to accomplish the various facets of preparing, planning, and creating successful Web pages. Before you could begin this process, you needed to be aware of technical issues involved in Web publishing and understand how to define a Web site's purpose and identify its audience. To recognize the specific functions of Web pages, you have sought examples of the various types of content on the Web. In Chapter 3 and Chapter 4, you developed a solid design plan, a prerequisite to publishing on the Web, including an understanding of the tools of layout and color. Finally, identifying Web-useable graphics and applying the principles of good typography, you started to create a Web site. To ensure a successful Web site, one that involves your visitors and offers them a reason to return, the previous chapter discussed the fundamental concepts and guidelines for including multimedia and interactivity on Web pages. With these elements in place, you are ready to test the Web site. Chapter 7 explains the necessary steps for testing and publishing your completed Web site on the Web. Effective methods for marketing, maintaining, and updating your Web site also are presented.

WEB INFO

For more information about conducting thorough Web site testing, visit the Web Design Chapter 7 Web Info page (scsite.com/web/ch7/ webinfo.htm) and then click Testing.

TESTING A WEB SITE BEFORE PUBLISHING

After considerable planning and effort, you have utilized design effectively to create a Web site that is dedicated to a specific purpose and objectives, targeted to a particular audience, designed to meet the usability needs of the audience, based on a detailed design plan, built according to a specific Web site structure, comprised of timely, valuable content, and designed to be easily navigated. With your Web site finished, you can make it available to its intended audience. Before doing so, however, you must test crucial aspects of your Web site. It is important to identify and fix any problems before publishing to avoid any embarrassment or credibility loss with your potential users. Without testing, you run the risk of appearing unprofessional, and you may even alienate potential users if problems are not discovered until the site is live on the Web. Conducting a thorough Web site inspection, utilizes self-testing and group testing.

Self-Testing

If you have been performing various tests while creating your Web site, few, if any, problems should exist. In preparing to publish your Web site, the first phase of testing is the **self-test** to ensure the functionality of the following features and elements:

1. **Page display** – test the page display using different browsers and on various platforms. Expect the page display to vary. Have reasonable expectations as to what you will consider acceptable.

2. **Image display** – ensure that images display when images are turned on in the browser. If the images do not display, verify that the file names are spelled correctly and that the image files are in the locations specified by the links.

3. **Alternate text descriptions** – be sure that alternate text descriptions for images display when images are turned off in the browser. Make certain that all images have alternate text descriptions.

4. **Internal links** – test internal links for functionality before your site is uploaded to a Web server.

5. **External links** – use a Web authoring package that offers the capability of checking the functionality of external links before a site is uploaded to a Web server. If your software does not offer this capability, or if you have used a text editor to develop your Web site, access the Web and verify the accuracy of the URLs.

After conducting the self-testing, correct any identified problems.

Group Testing

The second phase of testing, called **group testing**, involves recruiting a small group of people representative of your audience to test your Web site. Having this group test your Web site will help give you a better idea of how your audience will respond to your Web site. If possible, be present when they test, but do not instruct or explain. You may want to have others help you observe the group. Observe their experience as they explore your Web site. Use their responses on the following aspects of your Web site to evaluate the group test:

1. Which pages appear to appeal to them?

2. Which pages appear to disinterest them?

3. How much time do they spend on various pages?

4. Which links do they visit or ignore?

5. How easily do they navigate the Web site?

6. Do they at any time demonstrate any confusion or annoyance?

After observing the testing, ask the individuals to express their candid opinions about their experience on your Web site. Ask questions such as the following:

1. Did they find the Web site interesting and the content valuable?

2. What could improve the Web site?

3. What should be added or deleted?

4. What helped or hampered navigation?

5. And most importantly, would they return to the Web site?

The actions to be taken once the group testing concludes is summarized in the following Web Design Tip:

> **Web Design Tip**
> After group testing your Web site, seriously consider all comments and suggestions, both negative and positive. Recall the original purpose and objectives you established for the Web site and the needs and goals identified for the audience. Implement those comments and suggestions that will further the original purpose and objectives, meet the audience's needs and goals, and generally improve the Web site's value, functionality, and usability.

As will be discussed later in the chapter, it also is important to test your Web site after it has been published to its real environment, the World Wide Web.

PUBLISHING THE WEB SITE

With the Web site thoroughly tested and any problems corrected, you can proceed to make it available to your audience. Before making your site live on the Web, you must prepare by:

1. Acquiring server space.

2. Obtaining a domain name.

3. Uploading your Web site.

WEB INFO

For more information about making a site available on the Web, visit the Web Design Chapter 7 Web Info page (scsite.com/web/ch7/webinfo.htm) and then click Publishing.

WEB INFO

For more information about acquiring server space to upload files, visit the Web Design Chapter 7 Web Info page (scsite.com/web/ch7/webinfo.htm) and then click Server Space.

Acquiring Server Space

The initial step in making your site live on the Web is to acquire server space. So visitors can view your site on the Web, all the files that comprise it must be uploaded to a Web server. You learned that a Web server is a computer that constantly is connected to the Internet with special software that allows it to serve up documents and data requested through a user's browser. Functions taking place on a user's computer, such as browser requests, are termed **client-side functions**. **Server-side functions** refer to those functions happening on the remote server, such as serving up Web pages or executing scripts. It provides content that must be identified in such a way that a Web browser can download and display that content correctly.

Server space in available in one of two ways: either you pay for it or obtain it free. Typically, Internet service providers (ISPs) or online service providers (OSPs) host a Web site on their Web servers for a monthly fee. Some providers offer free server space if you are a customer already paying a monthly fee for an Internet connection (Figure 7-1). Free hosting services such as NetZero.com offer free server space to everyone. The drawback to utilizing free server space, however, is that Web site visitors are subject to constant advertisements while online. If you are a student, or staff or faculty member, a second possible source of free server space could be available on a university's or college's Web server.

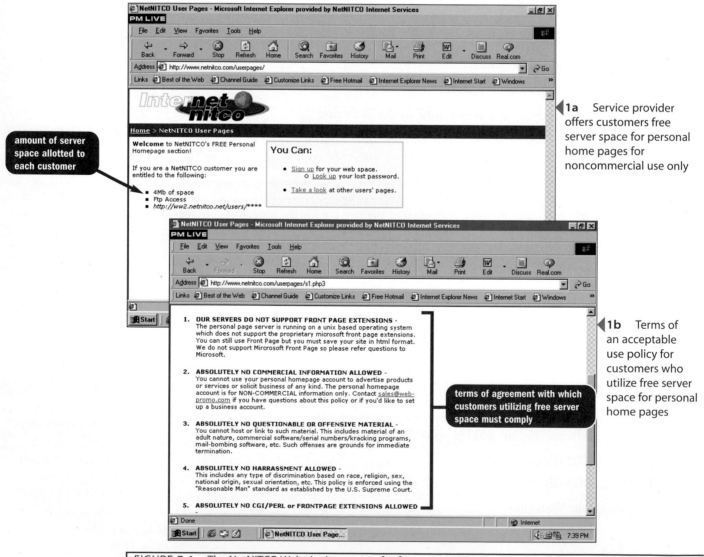

1a Service provider offers customers free server space for personal home pages for noncommercial use only

1b Terms of an acceptable use policy for customers who utilize free server space for personal home pages

amount of server space allotted to each customer

terms of agreement with which customers utilizing free server space must comply

FIGURE 7-1   The NetNITCO Web site is a source for free server space.

Online communities are a third source for free server space. **Online communities** are Web sites where visitors with common interests can communicate. Two widely used online communities include MSN Web Communities (communities.msn.com) and Yahoo! GeoCities (geocities.yahoo.com) (Figure 7-2). The following Web Design Tip suggests issues to consider regarding online communities and Web site hosting:

Web Design Tip

Although online communities offer free server space, it is restricted. Another disadvantage is limited page design options.

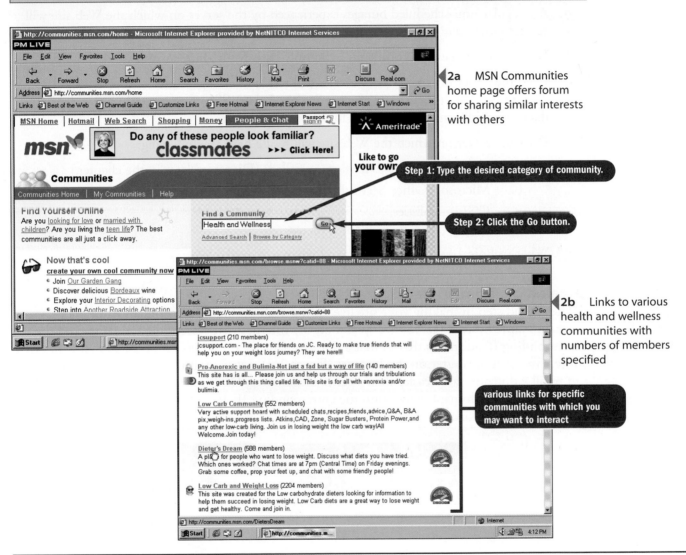

2a MSN Communities home page offers forum for sharing similar interests with others

2b Links to various health and wellness communities with numbers of members specified

FIGURE 7-2   Online communities offer free server space and opportunities to interact with others.

Large academic institutions, corporations, and organizations often build and maintain their own Web servers with fast, high-capacity Internet connections. Most individuals and small businesses and organizations, however, utilize service providers to host their Web sites. A variety of sources are available to help choose a service provider. You can ask friends and/or business associates for recommendations. Ask them which provider they use; how long they have utilized the provider; and how they would rate the quality of the service and the support. Web sites devoted to providing information about service providers, for example, HostGlobal.com and Hosting Repository, also are good sources to help you choose a provider. Such Web sites offer service provider directories, reviews, and ratings.

The following list of questions can help you make an educated decision when you are evaluating service providers to see which one best fits your Web site needs. Some questions may not be relevant if your Web site does not incorporate certain features or capabilities.

1. What is the monthly fee to host a personal or commercial Web site?

2. How much server space is allotted for the monthly fee? What would additional space cost?

3. What are the naming conventions for files on the provider's server(s)? For example, should file extensions be .htm or .html? Should the home page be named index or default?

4. Are regular non-scheduled outages experienced by the server on which the Web site will reside? How long?

5. What is the longest downtime on a monthly basis for maintenance and backing up?

6. Does the server on which the Web site will reside offer capabilities of supporting e-commerce, multimedia, and **Secure Sockets Layer (SSL)** for encrypting confidential data? Are additional fees required for these capabilities?

7. Does the server on which the Web site will reside have the following:

    a. FrontPage Server Extensions installed? (Discussed later in the chapter.)

    b. Microsoft Office Server Extensions installed?

    c. CGI capabilities?

    d. Active Server Page (ASP) support?

8. What technical support is offered, and when is it available?

Obtaining a Domain Name

WEB INFO

For more information about obtaining a domain name for a Web site, visit the Web Design Chapter 7 Web Info page (scsite.com/web/ch7/webinfo.htm) and then click Domain Name.

The second step in making your site live on the Web is obtaining a domain name. The **Domain Name System (DNS)** is a system on the Internet that stores domain names and their corresponding IP addresses. Recall that a domain name is a text version of the numeric, or IP, address for each computer on the Internet (Figure 7-3). DNS originated because most people can recall a domain name easier than a series of numbers. **DNS servers** are Internet servers that translate specified domain names into the corresponding IP addresses so data is correctly routed.

```
199.95.72.10  ◄——— ( IP address )
www.scsite.com  ◄——— ( domain name )
```

FIGURE 7-3   An IP address versus a domain name.

An Internet service provider or online service provider that will host your Web site often will obtain a domain name for you, usually for an additional fee. First, they verify that the desired domain name is available. If it is, then they will register your domain name. Typically, a provider pays less than $100.00 for a domain name for the first two years and then, after the second year, the cost is less than $50.00 a year. The rate the provider charges might include an additional fee for registration.

If you want to obtain a domain name yourself, **accredited registration sites** are available on the Web for this purpose. The **Internet Corporation for Assigned Names and Numbers (ICANN)** Web site can provide you with a list of accredited registration sites. ICANN is a non-profit organization responsible for the accreditation of registration sites. Figure 7-4 depicts an accredited registration Web site. The accredited registration sites vary. Different registration sites offer different means of submitting the information. Most offer online registration services, but you can register by telephone or mail. Many will work with your provider to obtain the required information.

When you register a domain name, it will be associated with the computer on the Internet you authorize during the registration period. To register a domain name, you will be asked to provide various contact and technical information that makes up the registration. You also will be required to enter a registration contract with the registrar, which specifies the terms under which your registration is accepted and will be maintained. After you decide on a domain name, you will be informed if the name is available. If the name is available, you then pay the registration fee, usually by credit card. If the name is not available, you must choose another one.

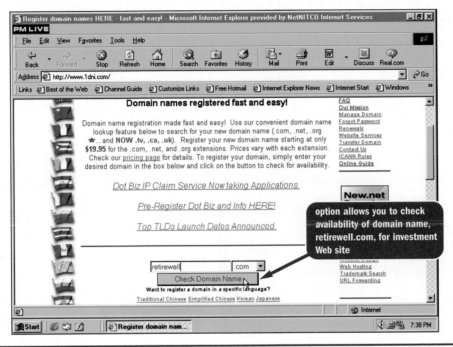

FIGURE 7-4   A domain registration Web site accredited by the Internet Corporation for Assigned Names and Numbers (ICANN).

Uploading Your Web Site

The third step to making your site live on the Web is **uploading**, or transmitting, all the files that comprise your Web site including Web pages, images, audio, video, and animation to the Internet. The following section discusses four methods for uploading a Web site: FTP applications, Web authoring packages, Web Wizard, and Web Folders.

FTP APPLICATIONS   FTP applications provide one option for uploading a Web site. In Chapter 1, you learned that File Transfer Protocol (FTP) is the most common method for transferring files on the Internet. Internet service providers overwhelmingly support using an FTP application to upload files to a Web server. Possible sources for acquiring an FTP application are suggested in the following Web Design Tip:

Web Design Tip

A freeware or shareware FTP application, frequently called an FTP client, can be downloaded from such Web sites as CNET Share.com or Tucows. Your service provider might suggest and even provide you with a specific FTP application.

WEB INFO

For more information about using FTP applications for uploading a Web site, visit the Web Design Chapter 7 Web Info page (scsite.com/web/ch7/webinfo.htm) and then click FTP.

To establish your initial FTP connection, you need to supply specific information, some of which you will need to obtain from your service provider. The following information typically is required:

1. **Profile name.** A profile name specifies a particular connection. You create your own profile name.

2. **Host name/address.** The host name/address is the space on the Web server where your Web site will reside physically.

3. **Host type.** The host type identifies the server configuration.

4. **User ID and password.** Your service provider will create your user ID and password, which uniquely identifies your connection each time you log on. If you save your password during the initial connection, you will not have to re-enter it for future connections.

Figure 7-5 illustrates a popular FTP application, called WS_FTP95 LE, for uploading files to the Web.

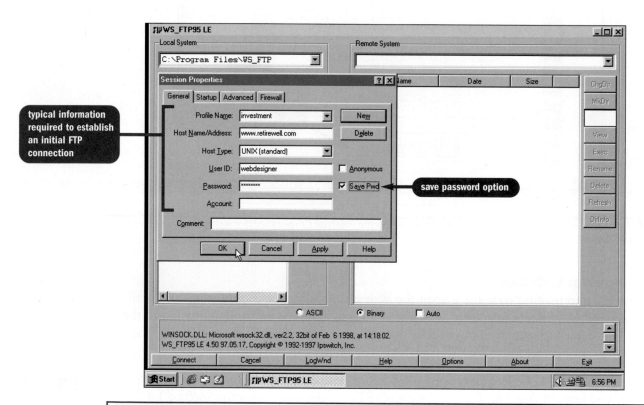

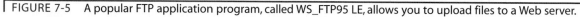

FIGURE 7-5   A popular FTP application program, called WS_FTP95 LE, allows you to upload files to a Web server.

After establishing your initial connection, the next step is to replicate the file system on your computer on the Web server that hosts your site to minimize the occurrence of broken links. As the designer of the investment Web site, for example, if you created one folder named invest-ment, which contains all your Web pages, graphics, and other Web site elements, you would create an investment folder on the server. Then, upload all your Web pages, graphics, and other Web site elements to this folder.

If you created a file system consisting of different folders for the investment Web site for Web pages, images, and audio files, in this case, you would create three folders with the identical names on the server. Then upload the Web pages, images, and audio files in the folders on your computer to the respective folders on the server. Do not upload any source files such as image or word processing files to the Web server. When naming folders on the Web server, ensure that the names are exact. Naming a folder *photograph* instead of *photographs* will result in broken links.

WEB AUTHORING PACKAGES   **Web authoring packages** provide a second option for uploading a Web site. Several current Web authoring packages allow you to upload a Web site directly from within the program. Uploading capability at this level eliminates the need for a designer to utilize a separate FTP application or interface. As with other uploading methods, you need to obtain server space and provide certain information, which includes the following:

1. Host name/address

2. Host type

3. User ID and password

4. Directory path

If your Web site was created with Microsoft FrontPage, you will need a Web server with the FrontPage Server Extensions installed if the circumstances described in the following Web Design Tip apply:

WEB INFO

For more information about using Web authoring packages for uploading a Web site, visit the Web Design Chapter 7 Web Info page (scsite.com/web/ch7/webinfo.htm) and then click Web Authoring Packages.

> **Web Design Tip**
>
> If you designed your Web site with FrontPage and it includes a form, Search feature, or hit counter, verify that the correct version of the FrontPage Server Extensions is installed on the server on which your Web site will reside so these elements will function.

To upload a site to a Web server with FrontPage, you use the **Publish Web feature**. You can identify specific files to publish or not publish. FrontPage offers effective file management features, including the capability of identifying and publishing only those files located on your local computer that have changed. Figure 7-6 illustrates options available when using the FrontPage Publish Web feature.

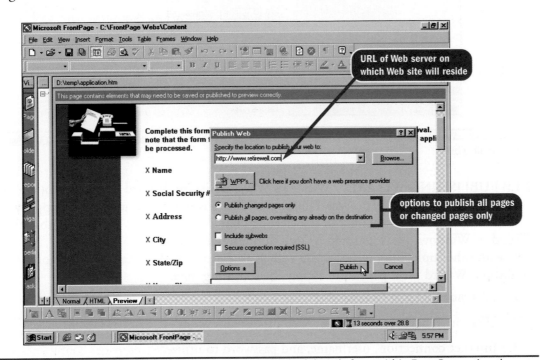

FIGURE 7-6   A form for the investment Web site can be published directly from within FrontPage using the Publish Web feature.

WEB INFO

For more information about using Microsoft Web Folders for uploading a Web site, visit the Web Design Chapter 7 Web Info page (scsite.com/web/ch7/webinfo.htm) and then click Web Folders.

WEB FOLDERS   **Microsoft Web Folders** offers a third option for uploading and administering a Web site (Figure 7-7). The Web server on which your Web site will reside, however, must be configured to support Web Folders. Before seriously considering Web Folders as an upload option, check with your service provider to determine if such support exists. A Web Folder can be created utilizing one of the following:

- Microsoft Office 2000 or Microsoft Office XP
- My Computer (Microsoft Windows 98)
- My Network Places (Microsoft Windows Me, Microsoft Windows 2000, or Microsoft Windows XP)

After you have created a Web Folder, you can move and manage your Web site's files on the Web server.

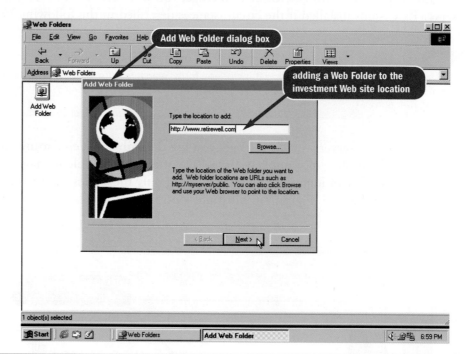

FIGURE 7-7   Web Folders in the My Computer window allows the creation of Web folders using the Add Web Folder dialog box.

WEB INFO

For more information about using Windows Web Publishing Wizard for uploading a Web site, visit the Web Design Chapter 7 Web Info page (scsite.com/web/ch7/webinfo.htm) and then click Web Publishing Wizard.

WEB PUBLISHING WIZARD   **Windows Web Publishing Wizard** provides a fourth option for uploading a Web site. The Web Publishing Wizard is not as versatile as FTP applications, but is a simple, practical method of transferring your Web site's files. The Web Publishing Wizard in Windows leads you step by step through the process.

As with other uploading options, you will be asked to provide certain information; the Web Publishing Wizard prompts you to supply the following data:

1. File(s) or folder(s) to upload (Figure 7-8)
2. URL or IP address where your Web pages will reside
3. Internet connection, user name, and password to utilize

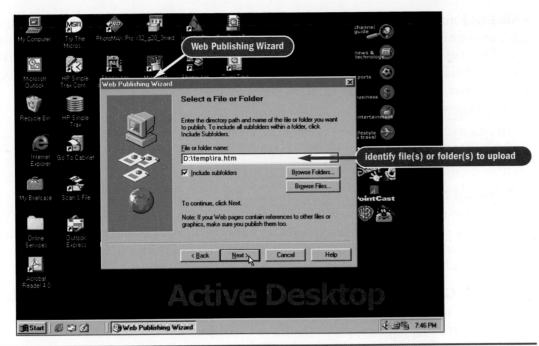

FIGURE 7-8   Windows Web Publishing Wizard provides an easy way to transfer personal Web pages to an ISP's Web server.

Testing a Web Site After Publishing

Whatever method you utilized to publish your Web site, after your files have been uploaded to the Web you should test all the Web pages in the site immediately according to the following Web Design Tip:

> **Web Design Tip**
>
> After you have published your Web site and before you market it, re-test every aspect of its appearance and functionality.

Similarly to the criteria for testing a Web site before you publish it, you should check the following components after it has gone live:

- Determine that all images display properly.
- Make certain that no broken links exist.
- Ensure all interactive elements such as forms are functioning properly.
- If any changes are necessary, correct the source file(s) on your local computer and then upload them again to the server. The corrected file will overwrite the older file as long as the file name is identical.

MARKETING THE WEB SITE

With a great looking Web site that follows all of the proper design conventions and meets the needs of your audience, the time arrives to announce your Web site's presence on the World Wide Web. Whether you have designed a personal, organization/topical, or commercial Web site, you want to encourage visits from members of the audience you have identified for your Web site.

Attracting numerous visitors may or may not be a top-level concern for a personal Web site. A high volume of traffic is essential, however, for organization/topical and commercial Web sites. The volume of traffic on these Web sites can determine success or failure, usually in terms of profit or loss. The following Web Design Tip includes advice for favorably impacting a Web site's traffic volume:

Web Design Tip

To generate a high volume of traffic on your Web site, launch a full-scale campaign utilizing both Web-based marketing and traditional marketing methods and advertising.

Web-Based Marketing

This section discusses types of Web-based marketing that you can utilize to announce your site's presence on the Web and encourage a high volume of traffic. Specifically, these include search engines, submission services, reciprocal links, banner advertising, awards, and e-mail newsletters and mailing lists.

WEB INFO

For more information about marketing a Web site using search engines, visit the Web Design Chapter 7 Web Info page (scsite.com/web/ch7/webinfo.htm) and then click Search Engines.

SEARCH ENGINES   One form of marketing your Web site is to have it included in the databases of search engines. Inclusion in the databases of search engines has the obvious advantage of making more people aware of your Web site's existence. To draw a parallel to the non-technical world, not being listed in Web directories is like owning a business and not having your telephone number or address listed in the Yellow Pages. Many search engines find new Web sites and add them to their databases manually or by means of spiders and robots.

You can increase the possibility of your Web pages displaying in search results by including meta tags, which are special description and keyword tags, in the HTML code of your Web documents. Keywords in the title section of a Web page, and an impressive number of links to your Web site, also influence the appearance and placement of your Web pages in search results. Many widely used search engines will find your Web site, although it may take anywhere from a few days to several weeks to be added to their databases.

Instead of waiting for the search engines to find your Web site, you can take the initiative and register your site with several search engines without having to pay a fee. Some popular search engines such as MSN, Yahoo!, and AOLNetfind require that you submit a form. Being listed in many search engines, perhaps more than any other Web-based marketing method, will make Web users aware of your presence online.

WEB INFO

For more information about the benefits of using a submission service, visit the Web Design Chapter 7 Web Info page (scsite.com/web/ch7/webinfo.htm) and then click Submission Service.

SUBMISSION SERVICES   A submission service is a viable alternative to waiting for search engines to find you, or to spending considerable time registering your Web site with search engines. A **submission service** is a business that for a fee will register your Web site with hundreds of search engines. Figure 7-9 illustrates the fee range of one submission service.

The submission service needs your Web site's URL and title, and a brief description of your site. The service also may ask for additional site characteristics and suggested site keywords. Following is an important Web Design Tip regarding search engines and submission services:

Web Design Tip

If you redesign your Web site or add substantial new content, you or your submission service should re-register your site with search engines.

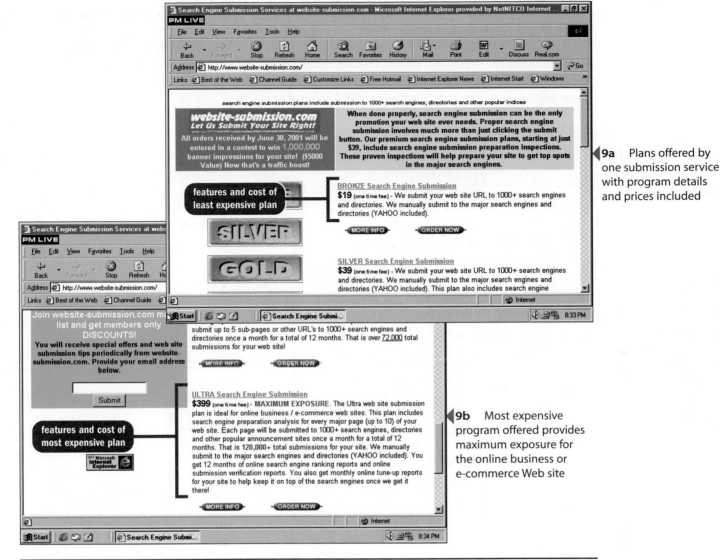

9a   Plans offered by one submission service with program details and prices included

9b   Most expensive program offered provides maximum exposure for the online business or e-commerce Web site

FIGURE 7-9   A submission service will register a Web site with search engines.

RECIPROCAL LINKS   Believing the arrangement to be mutually beneficial, two Web site owners might agree informally to put a respective link to the other's site on their Web pages. Links such as these are termed **reciprocal links**. The investment Web site, for example, might provide a link to a tax attorney's Web site; the tax attorney's Web site would in return provide a link to the investment Web site.

Link exchange sites on the Web utilize reciprocal links in a more formal manner and on a much larger scale. By becoming a member of a link exchange, for no fee, you can choose other member Web sites with which you want to exchange reciprocal links. The benefits of membership according to link exchange sites are as follows:

- Increased targeted traffic on your Web site.
- Higher ranking of your Web site by those search engines that rate a Web site based on the amount of reciprocal links to a site.

WEB INFO

For more information about the beneficial arrangement of using reciprocal links, visit the Web Design Chapter 7 Web Info page (scsite.com/web/ch7/webinfo.htm) and then click Reciprocal Links.

Figures 7-10a and 7-10b illustrate utilizing a link exchange site to identify reciprocal link possibilities for the investment Web site.

Exchanging reciprocal links via link exchanges generally is free. Web site owners willingly place the links on their Web pages. To have a link placed on premiere Web sites, in contrast, usually involves substantial fees. Large corporations and organizations more often than not are quite willing to pay for such prominent link placement.

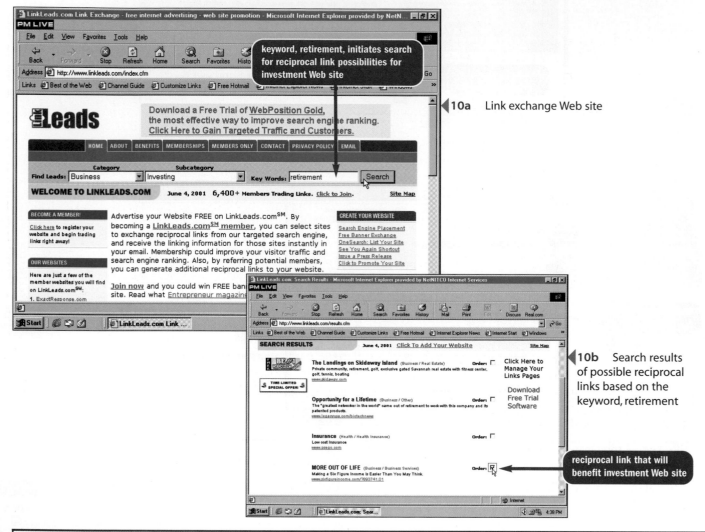

FIGURE 7-10 One Web site on which reciprocal link possibilities can be identified for the investment Web site.

WEB INFO

For more information about the use of banner advertising on the Web, visit the Web Design Chapter 7 Web Info page (scsite.com/web/ch7/webinfo.htm) and then click Banner Ads.

BANNER ADVERTISING Banner ads currently are a widely used advertising method, although some estimate their popularity is on the decline. The intent of a **banner ad** is to motivate viewers to click the ad, which then will take them to the advertiser's Web site. If a banner ad accomplishes this, the action is called a **click-through**. Click-throughs are one basis for determining fees for banner advertising. Figures 7-11a and 7-11b illustrate examples of banner ads and a click-through. Impressions are a second basis for fee determination. An **impression** refers to a viewing of the Web page on which a banner ad is placed.

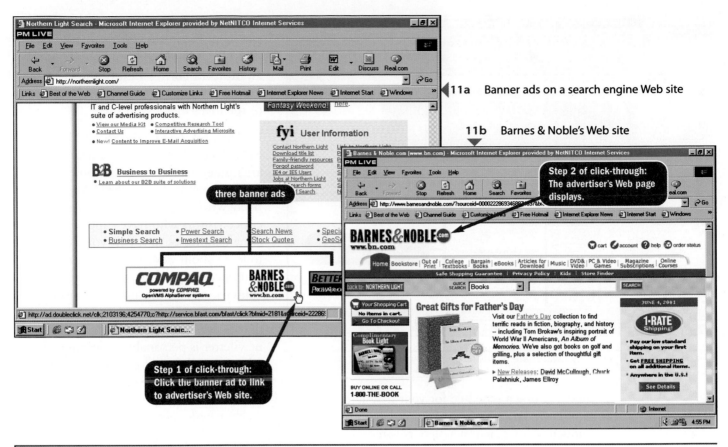

11a Banner ads on a search engine Web site

11b Barnes & Noble's Web site

FIGURE 7-11 Banner advertising on the Web.

Banner exchange sites are similar to link exchange sites, in that they facilitate an exchange of banner ads among members. As a member of a banner exchange site, you agree to display other members' banners on your Web site at no charge; in return, they display your banner on their Web sites at no charge. A major drawback of this arrangement is that you may not be getting a fair trade if your Web site has a higher traffic volume than that of the member with which you traded banner ads.

Banner exchange sites usually provide their services free. To have a banner placed on premiere Web sites, in contrast, usually involves substantial fees. Large corporations and organizations often are quite willing to pay for such prominent banner advertising.

AWARDS Receiving an award for your Web site can help market your site, but be selective of the awards you pursue. The following Web Design Tip offers valuable advice about Web awards:

Web Design Tip

An award will benefit your Web site only if it comes from a respected, credible source. Avoid the numerous trivial award sites that unfortunately populate the Web.

Figure 7-12 on the next page illustrates one of the more prestigious Web award sites. Popular search engines such as Yahoo! and Lycos acknowledge Web sites deserving of special recognition. Yahoo! showcases such Web sites as Picks of the Week. Search engines also may provide links to award winning Web sites categorized alphabetically or as currently popular Web sites. Professional, respected Web sites such as CNET and PCMagazine also recognize exemplary Web sites with awards.

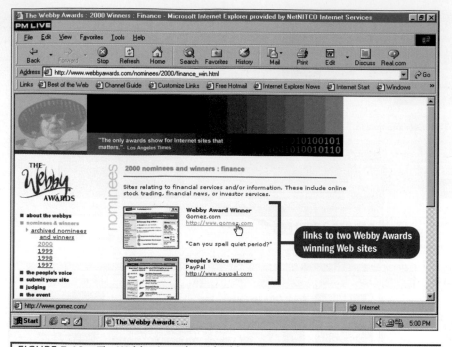

FIGURE 7-12   The Webby Awards are highly respected by the Internet community.

If you decide to compete for an award, ensure that the award is relative to your Web site's content and objectives. An award from Forbe's Best of the Web, for example, would enhance the credibility of the investment Web site.

E-MAIL NEWSLETTERS AND MAILING LISTS   E-mail newsletters are influential and have the potential to market your Web site easily. An effectively written, free e-mail newsletter can entice visitors who have supplied their e-mail addresses to revisit your Web site to learn about new products or services and upcoming events, participate in contests, or take advantage of special promotions. When creating a newsletter, devote the time to ensure that your newsletter is personable, engaging, relevant, and free of grammatical and spelling errors. Be realistic when determining a schedule for your newsletter. One well-written, motivating monthly newsletter will have more impact than four hastily written, dull, weekly newsletters. A fundamental guideline for e-mail newsletters is represented in the following Web Design Tip:

Web Design Tip

Be considerate and always provide a means to unsubscribe from an e-mail newsletter.

WEB INFO

For more information about e-mail newsletters and mailing lists for Web site marketing, visit the Web Design Chapter 7 Web Info page (scsite.com/web/ch7/webinfo.htm) and then click Newsletters and Mailing Lists.

Mailing lists are another online source for recruiting new visitors. A **mailing list** is a group of e-mail names and addresses given a single name. When a message is sent to a mailing list, every person on the list receives a copy of the message in his or her mailbox. Some mailing lists are called **LISTSERVs**, named after a popular mailing list software product.

Thousands of mailing lists exist on a variety of topics such as entertainment, business, education, and health. To locate a mailing list dealing with a specific topic, you can search for the keyword(s), mailing lists or LISTSERVs, using your Web browser's Search feature.

You also can recruit new visitors by purchasing e-mail lists from such Web sites as Links Are Us. Ensure that any e-mail list that you acquire matches the profile of the intended audience for which you have geared your Web site.

Traditional Marketing Methods and Advertising

Traditional marketing methods and advertising can be utilized successfully to market Web sites. This section discusses various traditional marketing methods and advertising that you can use in combination with Web-based marketing to announce your Web site's presence on the Web and encourage a high volume of traffic. These approaches include word of mouth, print, promotional items, and advertising on radio and television.

WORD OF MOUTH **Word of mouth** simply is telling people about your Web site. It is an easy, free way to market your Web site. To get the word out, announce the creation of your Web site to family, friends, colleagues, and business associates. Inform them of your Web site's URL through face-to-face or telephone conversations, voice mail recordings, e-mail, newsgroups, and LISTSERVs. When you update your Web site, notify them again. If you belong to an organization or company, encourage other members or coworkers to utilize their personal networks to publicize the news of your Web site.

PRINT If your Web site is organization/topical or commercial, it is likely that you publish and utilize various print materials. Your Web site's URL should appear on every print publication you use including stationery, business cards, brochures, reports, ads, signage, and magazines. The company or organization URL should be as recognizable as the company or organization logo. **Print materials** that display URLs can serve as a bridge to the more dynamic content on your Web site.

PROMOTIONAL ITEMS **Promotional items** are interactive and add an element of fun to your Web site. Easy marketing strategies, promotional materials market your Web site with little effort, but do require an expenditure. You can give promotional items to new customers or distribute them at events. Any items that you hand out should be boldly inscribed with your Web site's URL. Examples of promotional objects are magnets, coffee mugs, coasters, T-shirts, caps, pens, memo pads, calendars, and Frisbees. Contests and memberships also promote your Web site.

RADIO AND TELEVISION Radio and television advertising is far reaching, but requires the financial resources to advertise effectively in this media. If you have the budget to advertise on radio or television, ensure that your Web site's URL always is announced, and if possible, displays on the television screen. If your funds are fixed, advertising on local radio spots or PBS television stations may be feasible.

WEB INFO

For more information about traditional marketing and advertising methods that can be utilized on the Web, visit the Web Design Chapter 7 Web Info page (scsite.com/web/ch7/webinfo.htm) and then click Traditional Marketing and Advertising.

MAINTAINING AND UPDATING THE WEB SITE

A Web site should never be considered completely designed. A savvy Web designer knows that Web design is a continuing process. Develop and follow a regular schedule to ensure that you practice ongoing Web maintenance and keep your site up to date, such as the following:

1. **Add changing, timely content.** For example change photographs, add to/substitute text, publicize upcoming events, and offer timely tips. Fresh, appealing content will encourage visitors to return to your Web site.

2. **Check for broken links, and add new links.** Avoid navigational frustration for your visitors, and provide updated and additional information.

3. **Document the last reviewed date on Web pages.** Even if you have not revised any Web pages, including the date you last reviewed your Web site will indicate to visitors that the site is being examined on a timely basis. This practice will increase the Web site's credibility.

4. **Include a mechanism for gathering user feedback, and act on that feedback.** Audience suggestions and criticisms can help you improve your Web site to meet their goals and needs consistently.

5. **Identify benchmark and resource Web sites.** Evaluate and implement new technologies that will further site objectives and increase usability. Apply innovative ideas and solutions.

Observe good design steps when updating your Web pages. Although some authoring packages include the capability of updating live pages, generally, it is recommended that you avoid this practice. Updating live pages carries the risk that your audience will see incomplete or undesired changes. Follow these steps for maintaining and updating the Web site:

1. Download the desired Web page from the server to your computer.

2. Update the downloaded Web page.

3. Load the Web page into a browser and check the changes and the page display.

4. If the changes and the page display are acceptable, then upload the updated page to the server.

CHAPTER SUMMARY

This chapter introduced you to testing, publishing, marketing, and maintaining a Web site. You learned the important steps required before you can publish a Web site. These measures include conducting a thorough site inspection that utilizes self-testing and group testing and making corrections and changes. Necessary changes include those that will further the original purpose and objectives, meet the audience's needs and goals, and generally improve the Web site's value, functionality, and usability.

To publish the Web site, you must make your site live on the Web by first acquiring server space. You either can pay for server space or identify a free source. Next, you need to obtain a domain name. The service provider that will host your Web site may obtain and register a domain name for your site for an additional fee. Verifying the availability and registering a domain name for your Web site utilizing an accredited registration Web site is a second option. The third step in making your site live on the Web is to upload all the files that comprise the site using such methods as FTP applications, Web authoring packages, Web Folders, or the Windows Web Publishing Wizard. After publishing your Web site, you need to test your live Web pages for appearance and functionality.

To announce your presence on the Web, you learned that you need to utilize a combination of Web-based and traditional marketing and advertising methods. The design of a Web site should never be considered finished; therefore, you should develop and follow a schedule to maintain and update your Web site regularly.

KEY TERMS

Instructions: Use the following terms from this chapter as a study review.

accredited registration site (7.6)
banner ad (7.14)
banner exchange sites (7.15)
click-through (7.14)
client-side functions (7.4)
DNS servers (7.6)
Domain Name System (DNS) (7.6)
e-mail newsletters (7.6)
FTP applications (7.7)
group testing (7.3)
host name/address (7.8)
host type (7.8)
impression (7.14)
Internet Corporation for Assigned Names and
    Numbers (ICANN) (7.6)
link exchange sites (7.13)
LISTSERVs (7.16)

mailing list (7.16)
Microsoft Web Folders (7.10)
online communities (7.5)
print materials (7.17)
profile name (7.8)
promotional items (7.17)
Publish Web feature (7.9)
reciprocal links (7.13)
Secure Sockets Layer (SSL) (7.6)
self-test (7.2)
server-side functions (7.4)
submission service (7.12)
uploading (7.7)
user ID and password (7.8)
Web authoring packages (7.9)
Windows Web Publishing Wizard (7.10)
word of mouth (7.17)

CHECKPOINT Matching

Instructions: Match each term with the best description.

_____ 1. link exchange sites

_____ 2. Domain Name System (DNS)

_____ 3. click-throughs

_____ 4. impression

_____ 5. banner exchange sites

_____ 6. LISTSERVs

_____ 7. online communities

_____ 8. ICANN

_____ 9. DNS servers

_____ 10. mailing list

_____ 11. reciprocal links

_____ 12. submission service

a. Stores domain names and their corresponding IP addresses on the Internet.

b. Web sites on which exchange members choose other member sites with which to exchange free reciprocal links.

c. The process of clicking a banner ad and linking to an advertiser's Web site.

d. A group of e-mail names and addresses given a single name.

e. Links placed on two or more site owners' respective Web pages for the mutual benefit of both Web sites

f. A business that for a fee will register a Web site with hundreds of search engines.

g. A viewing of a Web page on which a banner ad is placed.

h. Web sites on which exchange members agree to display each other's banner ads on their Web pages at no charge.

i. Mailing lists named after a popular mailing list software product.

j. Web sites where free server space can be acquired and visitors can share common interests and exchange information.

k. Translate specified domain names into the corresponding addresses so data is routed correctly.

l. Responsible for the accreditation of domain name registration sites.

CHECKPOINT Fill in the Blanks

Instructions: Fill in the blank(s) with the appropriate answer.

1. To conduct a thorough inspection of a Web site before publishing, utilize _____ and _____.

2. Although people prefer domain names, the Internet is built on _____.

3. Four possible methods to upload a Web site include _____, _____, _____, and _____.

4. After publishing a Web site, you immediately should _____ all Web pages.

5. To generate a high volume of traffic on a Web site, both _____ and _____ marketing and advertising should be utilized.

6. To have a banner ad or link placed on a premiere Web site, usually involves a _____.

7. _____ is one of the more prestigious Web award Web sites.

8. A fundamental guide for e-mail newsletters is always to provide a means to _____.

9. A Web site never should be considered completely _____.

10. When updating Web pages, generally avoid updating _____ pages.

CHECKPOINT Multiple Choice

Instructions: Select the letter of the correct answer for each question.

1. Replicating your local computer file system on the Web server _____.
   a. satisfies a service provider requirement
   b. simplifies domain name registration
   c. facilitates establishing an initial FTP connection
   d. minimizes the occurrence of broken links

2. Attracting a high volume of traffic is essential for _____.
   a. personal Web sites
   b. organization/topical Web sites
   c. commercial Web sites
   d. both b and c

3. Which of the following is not a traditional marketing method?
   a. word of mouth
   b. print
   c. banner ads
   d. promotional items

4. The appearance and placement of a Web page in search results can be influenced by _____.

    a. keywords and description meta tags

    b. keywords in the title section of Web pages

    c. a small number of links to a Web page

    d. both a and b

5. The basis for determining fees for banner ads is (are) _____ .

    a. impressions

    b. ICANN

    c. click-throughs

    d. both and c

6. Disadvantages associated with utilizing server space on online communities include _____.

    a. restricted page design options

    b. server space fees

    c. server space limitations

    d. both a and c

7. The domain name of a Web site can be registered through _____.

    a. a DNS server

    b. an Internet or online service provider

    c. an accredited registration site

    d. both b and c

8. Internet service providers overwhelmingly support utilizing _____ to upload Web pages.

    a. Windows Web Publishing Wizard

    b. Microsoft Web Folders

    c. Web authoring packages

    d. FTP client

9. A submission service would be utilized to _____.

    a. register a domain name

    b. establish an initial FTP connection

    c. register a Web site with search engines

    d. both a and b

10. A Web site is completely designed under the following condition(s): _____.

    a. after it has undergone self-testing and group testing

    b. after it is uploaded to the Web

    c. never

    d. both a and b

CHECKPOINT Short Answer

Instructions: Write a brief answer to each question.

1. List five features/elements that should be checked as part of self-testing.

2. Identify seven important questions to ask service providers when acquiring server space.

3. Briefly explain two options for obtaining a domain name.

4. Discuss the origin and function of the DNS.

5. Briefly discuss four methods to upload a site to the Web.

6. Identify possible sources to acquire an FTP application.

7. Name four key aspects of a Web site to test after it has been published.

8. Briefly explain six methods of Web-based marketing that can increase traffic volume on a Web site.

9. Briefly explain four methods of traditional marketing and advertising that can increase traffic volume on a Web site.

10. Identify five aspects that a schedule to maintain and update a Web site should address.

AT ISSUE

Instructions: Write a brief essay in response to the following issues. Be prepared to discuss your findings in class. Use the Web as your research tool. For each issue, identify one URL utilized as a research source.

1. Web sites such as The Internet JUNKBUSTER and TopClick are advocates of protecting personal privacy on the Internet. They consider unsolicited banner advertising invasive, irritating, and ineffective. Research this issue and determine what the consensus is on banner ads. Identify how the design and usage of banner ads contributes to this consensus. Predict what the future will be for banner advertising.

2. Providing timely, fresh, useful content on a Web site is critical to its success. Consistently maintaining and updating, however, is very time consuming. Describe how individuals, organizations, and companies can manage this task successfully. Identify any technologies, design tools, or techniques that can assist in maintaining and updating Web sites.

HANDS ON

Instructions: Complete the following exercises.

1. Access the Web and identify the URLs of three service providers and three free hosting services. Research and document the advantages and disadvantages of the service providers and the free hosting services. The research you collect will be utilized in the case study at the conclusion of this chapter.

2. Surf the Web and identify the URLs of three link exchange sites and three banner exchange sites. Compare the features of the three link exchange sites and the three banner exchange sites. Identify one link exchange site and one banner exchange site of which you feel it would be beneficial to become a member. Explain the reasons for your choices.

SECTION 4 CASE STUDY

The Case Study is an ongoing development process in Web design using the concepts, techniques, and Web Design Tips presented in each section. In Section 1, you selected the type of Web site (personal, organization/topical, or commercial), a topic of interest and title, goals, elements and design tools. With these components in place, in Section 2, you utilized the six steps for developing a solid design plan in preparation for the next activity. In Section 3, you implemented the design plan to create your Web site. In the Section 4 Case Study, you will use the steps for testing and publishing your completed site on the Web and apply the methods for marketing, maintaining, and updating your Web site presented in Chapter 7.

Assignment

Instructions: Publish your Web site and announce its presence by completing the steps related to the Case Study. Review the specifications of the investment Web site and any other chapter materials to complete this assignment.

1. Test your Web site. Before publishing to avoid embarrassment and credibility loss associated with problems being discovered after the site is live on the Web, test the site. Conduct both self-testing and group testing.

2. Acquire server space. Review the research you collected in the first Hands On activity regarding service providers and free hosting services. Identify the service provider or free hosting service that would best meet the needs and goals of your Web site and its intended audience.

3. Obtain a domain name. Determine if your service provider or free hosting service will obtain and register your Web site's domain name and the related cost. Also, investigate the feasibility of registering your domain name utilizing an accredited registration site.

4. Upload your Web site. Consider the methods for uploading a Web site discussed in this chapter. Before implementing a method, discuss the compatibility of the methods with your service provider.

5. Market your Web site. Review the Web-based and traditional marketing methods discussed in this chapter. Identify and implement a combination of methods that will announce your Web site's presence to the world and generate a high volume of traffic.

6. Maintain and update your Web site. Develop and follow a regular schedule to add changing, timely content, check for broken links and add new links, document the last reviewed date on your Web pages, respond to audience feedback, and identify benchmark and resource sites.

APPENDIX

Web Design Tips

This appendix lists in chapter sequence the Web Design Tips boxed throughout this book. The first column contains the page number on which the corresponding Web Design Tip in the second column is presented. Use this page number to focus on the circumstances surrounding the development of the Web Design Tip. Use the second column as a quick overview of the Web Design Tips and as preparation for examinations.

Chapter 1 Web Design Tips

Page 1.10	As you develop a Web site, make sure you test the Web pages using different browsers.
Page 1.13	Include meta tags in Web pages to increase the possibility that they will be added to some search services' databases.
Page 1.14	Design your Web site so it communicates trustworthiness, currency, and value.
Page 1.15	To develop a formal educational Web site, you must understand effective approaches to teaching and learning online and methods to overcome barriers to online learning, such as attention span and lack of discipline. You must include elements to successfully convey content, provide feedback, maintain records, and assess learning.
Page 1.16	To develop an entertainment element on a Web site, identify what would appeal to your audience and what type of multimedia should be included.
Page 1.17	To develop an e-commerce Web site, determine the features that would make the product or service desirable or necessary.
Page 1.17	Gain an understanding of the methods for building e-commerce capability into Web pages, such as forms for customers to fill out. You also need to understand the role and support your OSP must supply to make e-commerce function on your Web site.
Page 1.18	Do not create Web pages that include personal information that can be misused.
Page 1.18	Only use content that has been professionally verified to create a Web page.
Page 1.19	When designing a Web page to promote and sell products, make sure you include the benefit associated with each feature you list.
Page 1.22	Choose tools based on your skill and knowledge level, and the degree of sophistication and complexity desired for your Web site. Make sure you and your developers have a strong working knowledge of HTML.

Chapter 2 Web Design Tips

Page 2.3 Plan to provide changing, timely content once your Web site is up and running.

Page 2.4 Build into your Web pages simple and convenient ways for visitors to interact with you.

Page 2.5 When you design Web pages, do not limit your creativity to the print environment. Where appropriate, include color, photographs, animation, video, and sound clips in your Web design.

Page 2.5 Consider using the Web when the need exists for economical and rapid distribution of information.

Page 2.6 Utilize proximity and white space to create effective organized Web pages.

Page 2.8 Create Web pages with contrast to elicit awareness and establish a focal point, the center of interest or activity.

Page 2.11 Generate a sense of unity or oneness within your Web site by utilizing a grid, consistent alignment, a common graphic theme, and a common color theme.

Page 2.13 Establish credibility for your Web site by providing accurate and verifiable content. Include the last reviewed date to show timeliness.

Page 2.13 Spell check and grammar check the textual portion of your Web site. After completing Web pages, set them aside for a day before proofreading for accuracy and completeness. Always have another person proofread your Web pages.

Page 2.15 Encourage visitors to spend time on your Web site by providing Web pages that are easy to scan and easy to read.

Page 2.15 Include only necessary links within the body of your content, and place supplementary, non-navigational links such as copyright, disclaimer, or privacy statements at the bottom of the Web page.

Page 2.16 Do not overuse transitional words or phrases, such as similarly, as a result, or as stated previously. These transitions will have no significance to a visitor who is skimming the Web page's content or who has arrived at your Web page via clicking a link at another Web site.

Page 2.16 In general, use language that is straightforward, contemporary, and geared toward an educated audience. Avoid overly promotional, full-of-fluff language that will divert visitors quickly.

Page 2.16 Use wording in headings that clearly communicates the content of a Web page or section. Avoid overly cute or clever headings. Such headings typically confuse or annoy visitors.

Page 2.16 Be cautious regarding the use of humor. Small doses of humor correctly interpreted can enliven content and entertain. Remember, though, that the Web audience frequently scans content, and that humor can be taken out of context and may be misunderstood or misinterpreted as sarcasm.

Page 2.16 Consider using the chunked format, rather than the paragraph format, to reduce long passages of text.

Page 2.17 Knowing how people perceive colors helps you emphasize parts of a Web page. Warmer colors (red and orange) tend to reach toward the reader. Cooler colors (blue, green, and violet) tend to pull away from the reader.

Page 2.19 Use a Web authoring package with a browser-safe palette to create your Web pages. If you use a text editor to create Web pages, make use of the color's hexadecimal code.

Page 2.19 Create fast-loading Web pages by restricting the number and file size of Web page elements.

Page 2.21 To avoid screen resolution issues with tables, use percentages instead of pixels to define width. A table, for example, defined at 90% instead of a fixed width of 600 pixels will display on 90 percent of the monitor's screen area at various resolution settings.

Page 2.22 Make sure that your Web site elements, such as photos, illustrations, animations, video, and sound files are free of copyright restrictions by creating or buying your own. If you want to use elements belonging to someone else, obtain written permission to do so. Always assume that an element is copyrighted, even if no such evidence appears.

Page 2.22   Protect your own works. If someone else is going to design and maintain your Web pages, obtain a written statement that you hold the copyright to the Web site's content. Put a copyright notice on your Web pages, which includes the word Copyright or the symbol ©, the publication year, and your name (for example, Copyright 2002 Trillium Consulting or © 2002 Trillium Consulting). You also may want to include an acceptable use policy, which tells visitors how they may or may not use your Web site's content. For example, you may permit visitors to print your text, but not allow them to download your graphics.

Page 2.23   If your Web site gathers information, include a privacy statement to ease visitors' concerns.

Page 2.23   To provide security, encrypt confidential information.

Page 2.23   Utilize resources and tools to make your Web pages more accessible to people with special needs.

Chapter 3 Web Design Tips

Page 3.3   Defining the purpose of a Web site requires a distinct site topic that is neither too broad nor too narrow, and a clear understanding of what the site should accomplish.

Page 3.4   To create a Web site with a high degree of usability, identify the goals and needs of its audience.

Page 3.5   Refer to your objectives constantly during the planning and creating phases. Include content that will contribute to the stated objectives. Test to see if you have met your objectives before making the Web site live.

Page 3.5   Develop relative, informative, and timely content. Include the latest research on investing in dot-com companies, tax tips, or advice on selecting a broker.

Page 3.5   Ensure that content is accurate and high quality. Keep current with the advice of respected financial journals and leaders, and include professional looking charts and graphs based on credible data.

Page 3.6   To advance the defined objectives of a Web site, choose content that adds value, that is, content that is relative, informative, and timely; accurate and high-quality; and useable.

Page 3.6   Do not duplicate content created for print on Web pages. Repurpose the content so it will add value.

Page 3.8   Photographs on Web pages can powerfully communicate and motivate. Select relatable, high-quality photographs that will further the Web site objectives.

Page 3.8   Utilizing development tools and techniques, designers can create original multimedia, or they can purchase ready-made elements on CD-ROM or download them from many Web sites.

Page 3.10   If plug-ins need to be downloaded to access multimedia on a Web site, provide a link on your Web pages to the download Web site.

Page 3.10   Limit the use of animation on Web pages so it is effective, yet allows visitors to focus on the content.

Page 3.10   Incorporate audio into a Web site to personalize a message, enhance recall, set a mood, or sell a product or service.

Page 3.13   Including cutting-edge technology on Web pages just because you can never is a valid reason to do so. Incorporate multimedia and/or dynamically generated content only for legitimate reasons.

Page 3.16   Structure the information in a Web site to accomplish the defined objectives, establish primary navigation paths, and maximize the Web site's usability.

Page 3.20   To fulfill a Web site's purpose and meet its audience's goals and needs, home, splash, and secondary Web pages should perform typical functions. Become familiar with these functions before beginning to plan Web pages.

Page 3.21   Give Web pages accurate and pertinent titles that will draw the attention of visitors.

Page 3.22   Organize the files of a Web site systematically to maximize productivity, reduce the possibility of lost content, and facilitate publishing the Web site.

Chapter 4 Web Design Tips

Page 4.2   A home page and a splash page must utilize the initial, visible screen area advantageously to achieve their objectives: to provide information about the Web site's purpose and to grab visitors' attention and draw them into the Web site.

Page 4.2   Secondary pages need not fit so rigidly within the initial, visible screen area. While organizing these pages, keep in mind the original screen dimensions so you do not force visitors to scroll horizontally to view them. If downward scrolling is necessary, ensure a smooth and logical flow of information.

Page 4.3   If information is designed to be read online, limit the pages to two screens, and provide any necessary links to additional information.

Page 4.3   The exception to the two screen length recommendation is for Web pages you intend to be printed and read offline. These Web pages should display in their entirety and contain no unnecessary links.

Page 4.4   Be careful not to over apply consistency to the extent that your pages become boring and uninteresting. The key is to balance harmony with elements that contrast, enliven, and intrigue.

Page 4.5   As a general rule, limit the number of colors in your scheme to three. Additional colors lessen the effectiveness of the color scheme.

Page 4.6   Test the results of different blends of background and superimposed text on onscreen legibility. Consider also the results when pages are printed. Imagine, for instance, the output of a Web page with white text on a yellow background using a monochrome printer.

Page 4.6   In addition to legibility and printout quality, choose a text color(s) for titles, headlines, subheads, and so on that enhances the Web site's mood, complements the background, and attracts the appropriate amount of attention.

Page 4.7   Developing and utilizing a basic layout grid will help unify your Web site by establishing a visual connection among your Web pages.

Page 4.10   Before you actually create any table, sketch it. Determine the number of rows and columns and the content you will place in the cells. Calculate the overall width of the table and the necessary width for each column. If you plan carefully, you will not find tables intimidating; rather, you will view them as manageable, powerful layout tools.

Page 4.11   Style sheets are considered an up-and-coming technology, because no current browser supports all style specifications. If you decide to use style sheets, test how your specifications display in different browsers before publishing your Web pages.

Page 4.12   If your Web site's navigation design is both user-based and user-controlled, your visitors will be able to move to different locations on a page or to other pages in your Web site to find useable information quickly and easily. A positive experience on your Web site equals satisfied customers who may return and express their approval to others.

Page 4.14   Use relative URLs for Web pages within your site, and absolute URLs for pages located on another server.

Page 4.16   If you utilize buttons as a navigation element, do not allow their size or appearance to detract from more important content. Their role is to serve as a link, not be a focus. Also, ensure that their look matches the mood of the Web site. For example for an antique dealer's Web site, you would choose a classic, conservative button style, not a neon, translucent style.

Page 4.17   Although all Web browsers can process server-side image maps, they are more complicated to create than client-side image maps, increase demands on a server, and typically have slower response times than client-side image maps.

Page 4.17   The main advantage of menus is that they allow you to offer many navigation options in a relatively small amount of space.

Page 4.19   A Search feature can give visitors the much desired flexibility and control to navigate a Web site in the manner they choose.

Page 4.23   At any time, visitors can click the Back or Forward button in the browser window that takes them to a Web site they previously have visited. Just as quickly, they can type another URL, jump to a search engine, or choose a bookmark. A well-designed navigation system that allows visitors to find usable information quickly and easily will encourage them to stay longer on your Web site and return in the future.

Chapter 5 Web Design Tips

Page 5.4   Utilizing basic typographical principles can help maximize the legibility and the readability of your Web pages.

Page 5.4   Before publishing your Web pages, view how they display on different platforms and at different monitor resolution settings.

Page 5.5   Specify commonly used fonts in your Web documents to increase your chances of overriding default font settings.

Page 5.6   Utilize the antialiasing technique only for large type. Type that is 10 points or smaller becomes soft and fuzzy if antialiased.

Page 5.10   Before downloading photos or illustrations from the Web, ensure that there are no copyright restrictions or royalty charges, which are fees to be paid to the creator/owner of the art for its use.

Page 5.10   Cropping an image can eliminate distracting background elements and establish the focal point. Discarding unwanted portions also results in a smaller file size.

Page 5.12   GIFs are most suitable for solid color images such as logos, illustrations, and graphic typography. GIF images are 8-bit indexed color, meaning they can display only up to 256 colors. This color limitation makes GIFs inappropriate for displaying photographs.

Page 5.14   The halo effect occurs typically because the image is antialiased. Recall that an antialiased image's appearance is made sharper by inserting extra pixels. By changing the image to aliased before applying transparency, you usually can avoid the halo effect.

Page 5.15   In addition to photographs, cross-platform JPEGs also are recommended for photo-like paintings, watercolors, and complex illustrations. They are not suggested for solid color images.

Page 5.16   Each time a JPEG is edited and saved, the image is compressed and decompressed, which degrades its quality. Consequently, you should make a copy of your original source file and never alter the original image.

Page 5.17   If viewers have graphics turned off, they will not see the images on your Web pages. By utilizing the ALT attribute, they will see a description of the images that are not being displayed.

Page 5.17   Utilizing the ALT attribute is especially important if an image is serving as an image map. If the image is not visible and no description is provided, viewers will not realize a hyperlink is present.

Page 5.17   Provide information on the thumbnail page specifying the file size of the original image so viewers can decide if they want to click the link and wait for the image to load. On the full-size image page, include additional, pertinent information and a link back to the previous page.

Page 5.19   Typically, a shadow is placed two pixels below and to the right of the original image. Some designers place the shadow below and to the left of the image. Whatever placement you choose, be consistent with all shadows throughout your Web site.

Chapter 6 Web Design Tips

Page 6.3   Utilize multimedia sparingly for distinct purposes, ensuring that it adds value and furthers Web site objectives.

Page 6.6   Like multiple animated GIFs, endlessly looping animated GIFs on a Web page can distract and annoy. Follow good design practice and include no more than one animated GIF per Web page, and limit the number of repetitions.

Page 6.9   Be careful to avoid copyright infringement when incorporating music into your Web site. For example, including music from a CD on your Web site without permission violates the artist's copyright.

Page 6.10   Optimize downloadable audio and video files to prevent long download times, which may deter visitors from your Web site.

Page 6.10   If you are considering including RealAudio in your Web site, check first with your Internet service provider or online service provider to ensure that it has a server configured to deliver RealAudio.

Page 6.11   Some streaming audio software packages require additional components to deliver and play audio files.

Page 6.13   When optimizing downloadable video, you must find a balance between the size of the file and the quality of the video that will yield satisfactory results for both criteria.

Page 6.15   To determine whether downloadable or streaming media is best for your Web site, consider such factors as Web site objectives, audience needs, budget, available expertise and resources, and the need to protect copyright and distribution rights.

Page 6.15   Use interactive elements on your Web site to keep the user interested and involved with your content.

Chapter 7 Web Design Tips

Page 7.3   After group testing your Web site, seriously consider all comments and suggestions, both negative and positive. Recall the original purpose and objectives you established for the Web site and the needs and goals identified for the audience. Implement those comments and suggestions that will further the original purpose and objectives, meet the audience's needs and goals, and generally improve the Web site's value, functionality, and usability.

Page 7.5   Although online communities offer free server space, it is restricted. Another disadvantage is limited page design options.

Page 7.7   A freeware or shareware FTP application, frequently called an FTP client, can be downloaded from such Web sites as CNET Share.com or Tucows. Your service provider might suggest and even provide you with a specific FTP application.

Page 7.9   If you designed your Web site with FrontPage and it includes a form, Search feature, or hit counter, verify that the correct version of the FrontPage Server Extensions is installed on the server on which your Web site will reside so these elements will function.

Page 7.11   After you have published your Web site and before you market it, re-test every aspect of its appearance and functionality.

Page 7.12   To generate a high volume of traffic on your Web site, launch a full-scale campaign utilizing both Web-based marketing and traditional marketing methods and advertising.

Page 7.12   If you redesign your Web site or add substantial new content, you or your submission service should re-register your site with search engines.

Page 7.15   An award will benefit your Web site only if it comes from a respected, credible source. Avoid the numerous trivial award sites that unfortunately populate the Web.

Page 7.16   Be considerate and always provide a means to unsubscribe from an e-mail newsletter.

Index